Poland's New Capitalism

Poland's New Capitalism

JANE HARDY

PLUTO PRESS
www.plutobooks.com

First published 2009 by Pluto Press
345 Archway Road, London N6 5AA and
175 Fifth Avenue, New York, NY 10010

www.plutobooks.com

Distributed in the United States of America exclusively by
Palgrave Macmillan, a division of St. Martin's Press LLC,
175 Fifth Avenue, New York, NY 10010

British Library Cataloguing in Publication Data
A catalogue record for this book is available from the British Library

ISBN   978 0 7453 2457 9   Hardback
ISBN   978 0 7453 2456 2   Paperback

Library of Congress Cataloging in Publication Data applied for

10   9   8   7   6   5   4   3   2   1

Designed and produced for Pluto Press by
Chase Publishing Services Ltd, Sidmouth, England
Typeset from disk by Stanford DTP Services, Northampton, England
Printed and bound by CPI Group (UK) Ltd, Croydon, CR0 4YY

For Kate and Shân

CONTENTS

LIST OF TABLES

ACKNOWLEDGEMENTS

In writing this book I owe many intellectual, political and practical debts. Andrzej Żebrowski and Ellisiv Rognlien deserve a special mention for the invaluable help that they have given me. Both through discussions of past and present Polish politics and through reading drafts of chapters they have enabled me to gain a much richer and nuanced understanding of the complexities of Poland's political scene. Joanna Puczwacka gave me enormous help in researching everyday life in Poland, and the nature of current labour disputes. In our many conversations Julia Kubisa has given me invaluable insights into the Polish feminist movement and women's activism. I would also like to acknowledge the information I have gained from discussions with Piotr Ostrowski and Filip Ilkowski. All of these people have made their own intellectual contributions, as well as being activists in the new political movements that are shaping the future of radical and left wing politics in Poland. They have organised resistance to war, neoliberalism and reactionary ideas and have reclaimed the language and ideas of liberation and socialism from the distortions of Stalinism. I feel humbled by their energy and persistence, in sometimes difficult circumstances.

I have benefitted enormously from the generosity of Polish academics, and Professors Wiesław Kozek, Bolesław Domanski and Maria Lissowska, in particular. I have learnt a lot from their seminal work on labour relations and the institutional and geographical restructuring of Polish capitalism, which has been a stimulating influence on my writing. I am also very grateful for their practical support and thoughtfulness during my sabbatical in 2004.

Some UK academics deserve a special mention. Mike Haynes has consistently been a constructive critic over the years and I have benefitted greatly from his work. I owe an intellectual debt to Al Rainnie. This book builds on our joint theoretical and empirical work from the early 1990s, which was both a steep learning curve and an exciting time. Alison Stenning has the well-deserved reputation of being a leading academic on Polish transformation and it has been a pleasure and a privilege to work with her on women's work and activism. Adrian Smith's support in reading articles and the book outline has been much appreciated, and I have benefitted from his thoughtful comments. In an era of publish and perish, which is undermining collegiality, Adrian and Alison have both been exceptionally generous with their time. I have enjoyed all of their work and found their focus on working-class lives refreshing and informative. Nick Clark, previously employed in the TUC's International Department, and now a researcher for the PCS trade union, has been extremely helpful, both in his critical gaze and constructive suggestions from a practitioner perspective.

I have drawn on the intellectual insights of many others, most notably: Stuart Shields, Martin Myant, Guglielmo Meardi, Jan Drahokoupil, Chris Harman, Colin Barker, Neil Davidson and Alex Callinicos. I would like to acknowledge the help that I received from the British Academy and the Business School at the University of Hertfordshire, which supported a sabbatical to Warsaw and Kraków in 2004, which enabled me to do extended research for this book. Mick Broadbent, in particular, has been supportive of my research.

I am fortunate to have close friends who have not only been encouraging, but also provided me with meals when I was trying to finish this book. Beyond this they have been extremely diligent in proofreading chapters. In no particular order these include: Keith Randle, Val Hamilton, Viv Bailey, Dave Barnes, Jon Berry, Barbara Thomas, Peter Segal, Angela Perry, Mark Smith, Graham Hollinshead, Dorothea Noble and Alexis Wearmouth.

Finally I would like to thank my editor, David Castle, who has been critical and supportive in the right proportions, in helping me complete the book.

ABBREVIATIONS AND GLOSSARY

AFL-CIO	American Federation of Labor and Congress of Industrial Organizations
AWS	Akcya Wyborcza Solidarność (Solidarity Electoral Action)
CBI	Central Bank Independence
CBOS	Centrum Badania Opinii Społecznej (Centre for the Research of Social Opinion)
CEE	Central and Eastern Europe
CMEA	Committee for Mutual Economic Assistance
EBRD	European Bank for Reconstruction and Development
eFKa	Fundacja Kobieca (Women's Foundation)
ERT	European Round Table of Industrialists
FDI	Foreign Direct Investment
FZZ	Forum Związków Zawodowych (Trade Union Forum)
GDP	Gross Domestic Product
gmina	The lowest territorial unit in Poland which could be a town or city, mixed urban and rural area or a rural area. In 2004 there were 2,478 gminas
GUS	Główny Urząd Statystyczny (Central Statistical Office)
IMF	International Monetary Fund
KOR	Komitet Obrony Robotników (Workers' Defence Committee)
LiD	Lewica i Demokraci (The Left and the Democrats)
LPR	Liga Polskich Rodzin (League of Polish Families)
NBP	National Bank of Poland

NFZ	Narodowy Fundusz Zdrowia (National Health Fund)
nomenklatura	An elite who held key administrative positions in all areas of the activities of post-communist countries, and who were analogous to the ruling class in Western capitalist economies
NSZZ	Niezależny Samorządny Związek Zawodowy: 'Solidarność' (Independent Self-governing Trade Union: Solidarity)
OECD	Organisation for Economic Cooperation and Development
OPZZ	Ogólnopolskie Porozumienie Związków Zawodowych (All-Poland Alliance of Trade Unions)
OSKa	Ośrodek Informacji Srodowisk Kobiecych (Women's Rights and Information Centre)
OZB	Ogólnopolski Związek Bezrobotnych (All-Poland Union of the Unemployed)
OZZPiP	Ogólnopolski Związek Zawodowy Pielęgniarek i Położnych (Polish Union of Nurses and Midwives)
PAEF	Polish American Enterprise Fund
PAIZ	Polska Agencja Informacji i Investycji Zagraniczych (Polish Agency for Foreign Investment)
PHARE	Poland and Hungary – Assistance for Economic Restructuring
PiS	Prawo i Sprawiedliwość (Law and Justice)
PO	Platforma Obywatelska (Civic Platform)
popiwek	Podatek of ponadnormatywnych wypłat wynagrodzeń. This refers to the state control over wages, lower than the rate of inflation
PPP	Polska Partia Pracy (Polish Labour Party)
PPR	Polska Partia Robotnicza (Polish Workers' Party)
PSL	Polskie Stronnictwo Ludowe (Polish Peasant Party)

PZPR	Polska Zjednoczona Partia Robotnicza (Polish United Workers' Party/Polish Communist Party)
Samoobrona	Self Defence
SdPl	Socjaldemokracja Polska (Social Democracy of Poland)
SdRP	Socjaldemokracja Rzeczypospolitej Polskiej (Social Democracy of the Republic of Poland)
Sejm	The most powerful lower chamber of the Polish parliament
SLD	Sojusz Lewicy Demokratycznej (Democratic Left Alliance)
SMEs	Small and Medium-sized Enterprises
SOEs	State Owned Enterprises
TNC	Transnational corporation
UP	Unia Pracy (Union of Labour)
UW	Unia Wolności (Freedom Party)
WTO	World Trade Organisation
WZZ	Wolny Związek Zawodowy 'Sierpień '80' (August '80 Free Trade Union)
ZNP	Związek Nauczycielstwa Polskiego (Polish Teachers' Union)
ZUS	Zakład Ubezpieczeń Społecznych (social insurance)

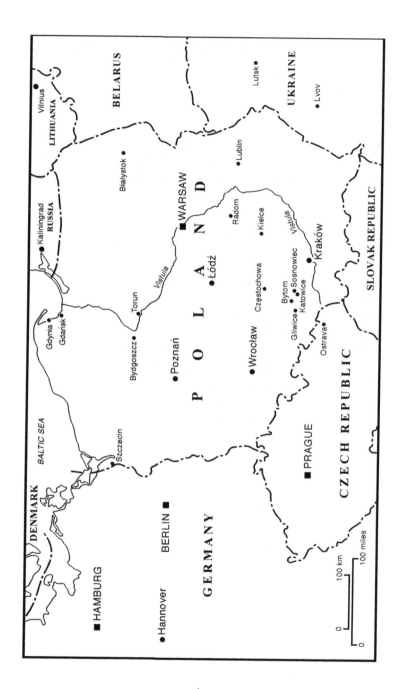

1
INTRODUCTION

'Tiger Economy' of Central and Eastern Europe?

For Poland, and the world as a whole, the decade of the 1990s was one of capitalist triumphalism. The fall of the Berlin Wall and landslide victory of the Polish opposition movement, Solidarity, in 1989 was seen as vindicating the triumph and superiority of one system – capitalism – over another – communism – and hailed in some quarters as the 'end of history' (Fukuyama, 1992). For the people of Poland it signalled the end of a repressive regime and sclerotic economy, which by the 1980s could barely supply even the most basic goods. In 1989, under the leadership of the Solidarity political party and trade union, the road to the new capitalism was implemented by trying to jump start the market. In January 1990, so-called 'shock therapy' was implemented overnight, which comprised draconian policies of reducing public spending and freezing wages. However, there was a lot more shock than therapy, and the early 1990s saw the closure of a large number of factories, which brought high unemployment in its wake. For many people initial enthusiasm quickly turned to disillusionment, which was reflected in a wave of strikes over pay and restructuring in the early 1990s.

By 2008, however, Poland was seen as a success story. With growth rates of 6.2 per cent in 2006 and 6.5 per cent in 2007 (Eurostat), it was deemed to be the 'tiger' economy of Central and Eastern Europe (CEE). After drastic falls in output and employment in the early 1990s, there was high and steady growth, widespread privatisation and the largest flows of foreign investment among European post-communist economies. A walk down Nowy Świat, a fashionable street in Warsaw, with its coffee

1

bars and expensive shops and restaurants seems to be a testament to the success of Polish capitalism and transformation to the market. Indeed a visit to any of the main Polish cities such as Gdańsk, Wrocław, Poznań and Kraków with their restored *ryneks* (market squares) would seem to reflect a new prosperity. Further evidence of improving living standards lies in the constellation of huge shopping malls lying on the periphery of these major cities with their ubiquitous chain stores, food outlets and multi-screen cinemas. The winners and beneficiaries of transformation are clearly evident in the new cars and recently built gated housing developments. Success is writ large in the neon lights on the top of Warsaw's tall buildings advertising major foreign investors and reflected in the refurbishment of public buildings, which have gradually replaced the crumbling and neglected edifices of the communist era.

On questioning the success story of Polish capitalism at a seminar in 2008, I was met with incredulity from another academic who insisted that the 'fundamentals' of the Polish economy were excellent. The rhetoric of 'good fundamentals' is used by the International Monetary Fund (IMF) and the World Bank to measure whether an economy is on track. This is a checklist for properly managing capitalism, which includes low inflation, an acceptable level of debt, low public spending and high growth. If these are satisfactory, then the country is deemed a safe place for international capital and finance.

A thread running through this book is that the transformation of Poland, as well as other economies of Central and Eastern Europe, has been underpinned by neoliberal policies. Emerging at the end of the 1990s, neoliberalism is a relatively new but fuzzy term, which has come to be a catch-all for a set of policies that have come to dominate the management of contemporary capitalism from about the early 1980s.[1]

The revival of economic liberalism, as a way of managing capitalism, has its roots in the crisis of the 1970s at the end of the long boom when Keynesian economic policies were no longer able to secure the conditions of accumulation and prevent falling rates of profit (see Harvey, 2005; Saad-Filho and Johnston,

2005; Harman, 2008, for example). The crisis in banking and finance and the unfolding recession after 2008 are now calling into question the ability of unfettered markets to provide the conditions for capital accumulation and Keynesianism is back on the agenda.

The experience of neoliberalism in Poland has been similar to that of other countries, with a polarisation of income, resulting from a redistribution of income and wealth to those at the top end of society, and the majority of people facing increasing insecurity in the workplace and more precarious access to services as welfare is commodified.

Themes

This books draws on research and writing that I have carried out mainly between 1998 and 2008, although it builds on theory and empirical work from an earlier book, *Restructuring Krakow: Desperately Seeking Capitalism* (Hardy and Rainnie, 1996). In this period I have conducted numerous interviews with managers of previous State Owned Enterprises (SOEs) and foreign investments to look at the process of privatisation, the impacts of foreign investment and restructuring. Extensive interviews have been carried out with national trade union leaders in Gdańsk and Warsaw and regional trade union representatives in a variety of other cities such as Lublin, Białystok, Kraków and Katowice. Activists, shop stewards and women workers in workplaces in all of these cities and beyond were interviewed in a variety of sectors such as manufacturing, health, education and food retailing. Further, interviews were conducted with social activists in new organisations such as Stop the War (*Inicjatywa STOP Wojnie*), and the anti-globalisation (*alterglobalism*) and anti-capitalist movements, as well as leading campaigners in the feminist movement. Some of the research has been exclusively for the book, and in other places I have drawn on the work from projects I have carried out with colleagues on women and migration.[2]

The book is organised around three broad themes. The first traces the Polish economy through the development, crises and collapse of the Soviet-style system to the institution of neoliberalism through shock therapy. The second theme focuses on the impacts of global integration in terms of placing Poland in emerging European and global divisions of labour, and the effects that this has had on work, welfare and people's everyday lives. Third, the importance of resistance to neoliberalism by trade unions and new social and political movements is central to an account of post-1990 transformation.

From Stalinism to Neoliberalism

Chapter 2 traces the imposition and development of the Soviet planned economy in Poland from 1948 onwards and its eventual demise in 1989. The story told here centres on an economy that was prone to crises almost from its inception, where the reaction of the working class to increasingly frequent and deeper crises was one of discontent and rebellion in 1956, 1970, 1976, 1980 and 1988. The Polish ruling class reacted by brutally repressing strikes and protests and imprisoning activists, but at the same time introduced reforms to try and buy the quiescence of the working class.

The increasing inability of the Polish Soviet-style economy to deliver increasing living standards stemmed from the interrelationship of factors both internal and external. The emphasis on heavy industry at the expense of consumer goods in the 1950s and 1960s lay in military competition with the West. However, in the 1970s deeper integration with the global economy in an attempt to resolve the dilemma of escaping from stagnating living standards and placating a rebellious working class had disastrous economic results. This further crisis culminated in the mass protests and factory occupations of 1980/81 and the founding of the Solidarity trade union and political movement.

Solidarity was one of the biggest, if not the biggest working-class movement, in post-war Europe. After the repression of Solidarity in 1981 and the introduction of martial law, further reforms collectively referred to as 'market socialism' were introduced. These failed miserably to extract the economy from deep crisis and the decade of the 1980s saw systemic implosion. By the end of the 1980s the system could not even deliver a decent standard of living for the Polish *nomenklatura* ruling class itself and the stage was set for profound economic and political change.

Chapter 3 argues that the political, social and economic changes in 1989 were not a movement from one system – communism – to another – capitalism, but should be understood as a 'leap' to integration with the global economy, the foundations of which were laid in the reforms of the 1970s and 1980s. The model of capitalism that was prescribed for Poland by sections of Solidarity's leadership and international institutions was based on market-led, neoliberal reforms.

In this book the term neoliberalism is defined as a set of institutional initiatives that have reconfigured the relationship between the state, labour and markets. In Poland, as elsewhere, the aim is to manage capitalism in order to restore profitability, raise the rate of exploitation in the workplace and secure a wider range of opportunities for accumulation by capital. More specifically the policies that comprise this changing relationship between states, labour and capital include, for example, the liberalisation of trade and investment to ensure new markets for capital that needs to expand across national boundaries either to increase production, access new markets or source lower costs. There is a crucial connection between neoliberalism and the integration of the global economy – they are inextricably linked. Neoliberal policies such as deregulation, the liberalisation of trade and investment and privatisation are necessary for wider and deeper integration with the global economy.

Although the United States and Britain led the way with neoliberal, market-led policies at the end of the 1970s, these were introduced incrementally and with varying degrees of working-class resistance. In Poland, however, shock therapy – a package of draconian deflationary policies and liberalisation – was introduced overnight in 1990. In this sense Polish transformation was combined and uneven in that the process and outcomes of transformation have to be understood in the context of the dynamics and development of the global economy. New institutional architecture was necessary to facilitate deeper integration with the global economy, for example property rights, legal structures to regulate competition and capital. If these institutions developed rather chaotically in the early 1990s, then preparation for and membership of the European Union consolidated this process and embedded neoliberalism.

The question of class has been eviscerated from many accounts of transformation. The kleptocracy of state assets, by the Polish *nomenklatura* ruling class, through 'spontaneous privatisation' in the final decay of the communist system, enriched a group of people who were able to take advantage of transformation. Further, workers, far from being a stage army in 1980 and 1988 to overthrow the repressive communist regime and usher in capitalism, have played a key role in resisting and shaping the reforms since 1989.

Chapter 4 examines the huge efforts of international organisations, the US and core economies of Europe, whose activities and 'aid' amounted to an unprecedented campaign to extend and consolidate the ideological hegemony of neoliberalism. It was not the case that instilling neoliberalism in Poland was an external project as some have suggested (Gowan, 1995). Nevertheless, organisations such as the IMF, by financially underwriting the project, were greatly able to influence the options for transformation. States and firms of the core capitalist economies did not subscribe to the idea that the market would simply rise like a phoenix from the ashes of communism. They understood that it would be contested, by workers as well as by sections of the domestic ruling classes, and therefore a plethora of coercive and persuasive measures were taken to promote and maintain ideological support for the market.

Aside from the powerful supra national institutions there was a plethora of other aid initiatives, the largest and most audacious of which was USAID that pumped over one billion dollars into Poland over a ten year period. An ideological onslaught was thought to be necessary in order to prevent any backsliding. The main beneficiaries of the vast resources that were pumped into Poland during the 1990s were consultancy firms, most of whom were from outside the country. The activities of consultants have been neglected and it is difficult to overstate the role they have played in the transformation of CEE and the extent to which these activities comprised a very lucrative part of their portfolios.

Impacts of Global Integration

Chapter 5 examines the way in which Poland is fitting into new European and global divisions of labour. This is set in the context of the rhetoric of the 'knowledge-based' economy where innovation is seen as central to improving national competitiveness. There are competing claims about the Polish economy. The first is that it is benefiting from foreign investment and winning high-level operations and functions of transnational corporations (TNCs), which offer the possibility of the transfer of technology and organisational know-how. The second claim is less optimistic and sees Poland as peripheral to the EU, with its production systems marginally and unfavourably integrated into the trade and production systems of core capitalist economies and minimally in systems of innovation.

The notion of uneven development lies at the heart of the analysis; rapid integration with the global economy has meant the destruction of some production capacity and industrial landscapes while others have been upgraded. This unevenness has had a profound effect on people's livelihoods in terms of the amount and type of work on offer, which has been reflected in a significant shift in employment from the primary to the service sector. The growth of new jobs has been in areas important for global competition, such as finance and business services.

Chapter 6 examines how integration with the global economy has demanded the imposition of a new discipline in the workplace in order that restructured State Owned Enterprises or new greenfield investments can compete. In comparison with Western Europe, workplaces in Poland were characterised by low productivity and considered by Western managers to have overemployment and obstructive workers resistant to change. High unemployment for much of the 1990s and (slightly) higher wages paid by foreign investors meant that they could cream off the most skilled and the youngest workers. An indication of the competition for jobs is that when Opel (General Motors) set up a factory in the mid-1990s in Gliwice (Upper Silesia) there were 20,000 applicants for 2,000 jobs.

Case studies of ABB and Volvo illustrate how capital tried to impose new disciplines and working practices on their workforces. These challenges centred on how to mould existing managers and workers into new ways of doing things, and in particular, getting rid of deeply engrained ideas about full employment and consultation, considered to be a barrier to restructuring and profitability. ABB had established methods for stripping out those with the wrong mentality and promoting what they referred to as the 'hungry wolves' – ambitious young managers eager for high salaries who were willing to adapt.

Chapter 7 looks at the profound impact that this restructuring has had on people's lives, and in particular on work and welfare. Rather than caricaturing neoliberalism, I discuss how the day-to-day policies and practice of transformation in Poland has involved imposing the rule of the market on all aspects of social life. The effects of global integration on the everyday lives of ordinary people are examined through narratives of poverty and supporting statistics, which paint a bleak picture of Poland. This is not only in comparison with the rest of Europe, but also in comparison to some other countries from CEE (particularly the Czech Republic and Hungary), which we might have assumed were at a comparable level of development. Poland has a high (and growing) proportion of people at risk from poverty, one of the greatest inequalities in the distribution of income and the lowest spending on social transfers. To compound this situation the health service, which has the lowest spending in Europe, is deteriorating and lurches from one crisis to another.

For people in work there has been the growth of in-work poverty with low wages and people have moved from the 'shock resulting from empty shelves to the shock resulting from the empty pocket' (Podemski, 2007). A constant theme in interviews conducted in 2007 was the belief that transnational companies regarded Poland as the 'Africa' of Europe. Not only were the wages and working conditions on offer seen as an affront to the dignity of working people, but they were viewed as the cause of outward migration, which was robbing the country of skills and fracturing families.

Resistance and Discontent

Chapter 8 provides an account of labour organisations since 1990. Many commentators and academics have written off trade unions as marginal and suffering from trenchant ideological hostilities. Trade union membership has fallen as its traditional bastions have been closed or restructured, and at the same time incoming foreign investors have shown hostility towards labour organisations, with many instances of workers being sacked for organising or even joining trade unions. However, if we look at the picture of what has happened in workplaces the situation is mixed and uneven, and does not fit with the gloomy prognostications of the miserabalist camp. Labour has been central to contesting or accommodating the new capitalism, and in some workplaces significantly affected the nature and form of privatisation.

The main trade unions have moved from a reluctance to actively recruit new members (Ost, 2002) to much more active organising models, where they have tried to recruit in new sectors of the economy. Recruitment has not only been top down, but grassroots initiatives from local and regional organisations have established active branches in foreign owned car plants, which were deemed to be out of bounds and union free zones. The public sector has seen huge protests, particularly among nurses and teachers, which have erupted sporadically since 1990. In the case of nurses a completely new union was formed in 1996, which organised women who had little or no experience of political involvement. Moreover, partly as a result of falling unemployment, by 2008 trade union disputes were showing a qualitative change from defensive actions against redundancies and unpaid wages to offensive actions for higher pay and trade union recognition.

Chapter 9 focuses on resistance by working-class women and feminists. Many accounts have seen women as victims of transformation, in that they have borne the brunt of restructuring since 1990 in terms of unemployment, pay and discrimination at work. In addition, the double burden carried by women has been exacerbated by cuts in welfare provision, which has shifted care for young children, the sick and the elderly onto families. Unlike other countries in CEE, in Poland this has been reinforced by a small, but vocal reactionary element, who have proselytised the traditional role of women as being in the home and not the workplace.

This chapter points to the role of women as activists and contesters of neoliberalism. Although often poorly represented at the national level of trade unions and political parties, women are active as union representatives at local and regional levels, in schools, hospitals and factories, as well as in wider community organisations. In some cases they have been at the forefront of some of the most militant disputes. In 2000 and then again in 2007, for example, nurses occupied government offices for over a week demanding that their grievances were heard. In 2007 this led to a six-week-long nurses' protest camp in Warsaw, opposite the Prime Minister's office. After a parliamentary bill in 1993 made abortion illegal, new feminist movements have appeared which are demanding equality in the workplace, an end to discrimination and for a woman's right to choose with regard to fertility and sexuality.

Chapter 10 explores disaffection with the main political parties and the parallel rise of new radical parties and social movements. Disillusionment is evident from responses to elections, which, with the exception of the first semi-free elections, have seen huge swings in voting and dismal turnouts. Political parties have shown little stability and have been characterised by splits, regroupings and the rise and fall of populist parties. Whether governments have come from the post-Solidarity or post-communist camps all of their policies have been variations on the neoliberal agenda. Right wing parties have been much more ideological in terms of family values, the influence of ex-communists and corruption, but this has been a useful fig leaf for diverting attention from a deteriorating health service and increasing labour market flexibility.

Resistance to neoliberalism has not only come from trade unions, but is also evident in a new wave of social movements that have sprung up since 2000 which are part of a much wider critique of imperialism and capitalism. In Poland, and other parts of CEE these groups are starting to reclaim the language of emancipation, workers' democracy and women's liberation, which was brutally distorted by the Stalinist regimes.

2
CRISIS, REVOLT, REFORM AND
REPRESSION: POLAND 1945 TO 1990

This chapter outlines the development of the Polish economy
from 1945 to 1990 and examines the way in which Poland's
Soviet-style economy was prone to crisis from its inception.
Before its collapse in 1989 the economy was characterised by a
dialectic of development, which involved increasingly frequent
and ever deepening crises culminating in revolt by the working
class, and the twin responses of reform and repression by the
Polish ruling class.

The period of 1948 to 1989 is one that demonstrates the process
of development and subsequent disintegration of a particular
politico-economic formation – communism – within a world
that was increasingly integrated and crisis ridden. The economic
development of Poland depended heavily on the Soviet trading
bloc. However, the increasing internationalisation of the world
economy outside of the communist bloc meant that the conditions
that allowed for relatively successful autarchic development in
Poland were only possible within a limited time frame. The long
boom that lasted for the two decades that followed the end of the
Second World War sucked larger and larger areas of the globe into
the world capitalist order. This increasing internationalisation and
integration meant that by the late 1960s national development
behind trade barriers became increasingly impossible.

Standards of living for a large proportion of the Polish
population increased, albeit unevenly, until the mid-1960s after
which economic conditions grew increasingly problematic. In the
1970s the Polish economy had opened up to the West as a solution
to its own problems, just as the world economy went into recession.

A series of increasingly desperate measures throughout the 1970s and 1980s only had the effect of exacerbating the problems that Poland was facing, with internal revolt growing stronger and better organised. By 1989 the response of repression and reform by the Polish ruling class became increasingly incapable of either reforming a failing system or deflecting the popular opposition to that system.

From 1945 to the Mid-1960s

Poland emerged from the destruction of the Second World War with many of the characteristics of a developing country. The population was largely rural and mostly employed in agriculture, levels of education were low and birth, death and infant mortality rates were high. Much of the fixed capital had been destroyed or damaged during the war (Schaffer, 1992: 240). An estimated 5 million Poles died between 1939 and 1945,[1] which amounted to 16 per cent of the 1939 population (Piotrowski, 1998: 305). The February 1946 census showed 23.8 million inhabitants, that is about 11 million less than in 1938 (Landau and Tomaszewski, 1985). Further, thousands of Poles were displaced as Poland's national boundaries were redrawn by the United States and the Soviet Union as they carved up the new geography of post-war Europe at the Yalta and Potsdam conferences.[2]

The establishment of the pro-Soviet People's Republic in Poland after 1945 was neither immediate nor unproblematic. This was partly to do with an initial Soviet desire to maintain amicable relations with Western powers. However, a neglected but critical factor was the role of the Polish working class taking social and economic transformation into their own hands. Kenney (1997) provides a fascinating account of the political confusion at the end of the war, when small groups of workers in dozens of factories in liberated Poland began to rebuild and activate their factories in late 1944, as the German army retreated from eastern and central Poland. The movement of workers' councils challenged official ideas of nationalisation, because after defending and rebuilding their factories, workers had no inclination to hand them over either to the Soviets, the government or private employers. Therefore across Poland workers took slogans of nationalisation at face value and took the state to mean themselves – the working class – as they restarted production and elected factory committees.

The imposition of Stalinism and control of the factories by the Polish Workers' Party (PPR),[3] far from being plain sailing, had to cope with major strike waves, endemic labour turnover and insubordination. Workers continually contested wage scales, norm setting and the work rules to challenge managerial control. There was strong resentment at being ignored or mistreated by management and, in particular, anger at the threat that all they had fought for might be taken away. According to Kenney:

> A young sociologist Hanna Swich met such workers in 1950; they spoke to her of 'state capitalism' where added value was taken by the state as it had been before by the capitalist, only now without a shadow of respect for the worker. (1997: 83)

The PPR's determination to impose the Soviet model was symbolised by a declaration by the Minister for Industry and Trade, Hilary Minc, in May 1947: 'We have won the battle over production, and we shall attempt to win the battle over trade' (Kenney, 1997: 192). In keeping with this Soviet model, planning was centralised in the hands of the State Commission for Economic Planning and became compulsory and comprehensive. The number of industrial ministries increased from one in 1948 to six in 1949 and ten in 1954, reflecting the increasing bureaucratisation of decision making (Slay, 1994). Political control over the economy was exercised through the *nomenklatura*. This was the small elite who held key positions in all spheres of the economy, through its appointments of managers, planning officials and trade union leaders. According to Kuroń and Modzelewski this elite transformed themselves into a new ruling class which they refer to as the central political bureaucracy, 'while the state which it ruled was transformed in this process, into a state of class dictatorship by the bureaucracy' (1982: 36).

The structure of the Polish economy was formed at the end of the 1940s and the beginning of the 1950s, during the period of so-called 'accelerated industrialisation'. The whole process was driven by the military demands imposed by the Soviet Union (Haynes, 1992a and 1992b) and based on the Soviet experience. This is described in a resolution of the PZPR[4] in 1956 as a response to the outbreak of the Korean war in 1951:

> Already in 1951, in view of a dramatic worsening of the international situation, the necessity has arisen to build a large defensive industry as quickly as possible and to raise the current expenditure for the national defence. (Landau and Tomaszewski, 1985: 219)

The necessity of building a militarised economy in competition with the West resulted in extreme centralisation, complete state control of distribution, and structurally the development of heavy industry such as steel, mining, heavy machinery and chemicals at the expense of consumer goods. Kuroń and Modzelewski argued that the imperative imposed on the central bureaucracy was 'production for production's sake':

> They [the central bureaucracy] set about realising that task [production] despite the differing interests of the remaining classes and, in a sense against them ... What then is the class purpose of production? It provides both the means of capital accumulation and the investments needed to maintain and strengthen the rule of the bureaucracy. (1982: 36)

This extensive capital accumulation allowed Polish national income to grow (in real terms) by more than 76 per cent from 1947 to 1950, with agricultural and industrial production more than doubling in the same period (Slay, 1994).

Tittenbrun (1993) suggests that these features pertained to a period of socialist primitive accumulation. Growth was generated by increasing inputs of raw materials and labour, in particular involving the large scale conversion of peasants into an urbanised working class. Between 1946 and 1955, 1.8 million migrated from rural to urban areas in Poland (Landau and Tomaszewski, 1985). Readily available supplies of cheap labour and a captive Soviet market dampened any drive to increase productivity or invest in new technologies. This form of growth was predicated on an extremely high participation rate (particularly for women) and low wages, which made workers particularly susceptible and sensitive to increases in food prices.

By the end of the 1960s, the basic structure of the Polish economy was firmly established, dominated by giant and highly integrated firms, principally in the heavy industrial sector. These gargantuan firms, however, lacked economies of scale. While they employed thousands of workers, SOEs included a wide range of social functions and technical specialisation in particular products was very low (Hardy and Rainnie, 1996). Alison Stenning's work provides a rich account of the development of the Nowa Huta town outside Kraków, built in 1949 to house the workers from the Lenin Steelworks (see for example Stenning, 2000).[5] Agriculture, in contrast to other Soviet bloc countries, however, remained mainly in private hands. Services accounted for less than 15 per cent of GDP, an extremely low proportion by market economy standards (Hardy and Rainnie, 1996).

Politically the *nomenklatura* system dominated whereby the Communist Party appointed various positions in all areas of public life, from ministers to health resort staff, from editors of national and provincial newspapers to fire brigade chiefs, bank managers, museum directors, and heads of local administrative bodies. A Central Committee document made the role of the *nomenklatura* clear:

> For the party, the nomenclature is one of the basic tools that guarantee that only people who are ideologically reliable, who are highly qualified and who act in the social, political and cultural interests of the country, will be called upon to fill management positions. (Smolar, 1983: 43)

Although apparently producing steady growth rates that were reasonable by world standards, the industrial dynamism and economic security of the Soviet model in Poland was not matched by a comparable rise in living standards. The first outward sign of working-class discontent after 1948 was the uprising of 1956. The revolt, first in Poznań, closely followed by Warsaw and other large cities, was triggered by demands to subordinate production to consumption. The revolt had its roots in minor reforms initiated in early 1956 by the new Communist Party leader, Edward Ochab, motivated at least partly by Khrushchev's denunciation of Stalin. Political prisoners were released, industrial decentralisation was promoted and measures were taken to improve living standards. However, these were insufficient to placate growing working-class discontent.

Simmering grievances over wage levels erupted in June 1956, and after a series of demonstrations, troops were sent to Poznań. The official figure for the number of workers killed and wounded was 53 and 300 respectively. Initially the PZPR responded with some reforms, prompting the development of workers' councils, particularly in and around Warsaw. However, anti-reform measures, driven by fears of a Soviet intervention, meant that Ochab was replaced by Gomułka. The years 1957 to 1960 saw a period of counter reform as the PZPR reasserted its authority and the thaw that had begun after Stalin's death came to an end (Slay, 1994). The workers' councils that had appeared spontaneously in 1956 were effectively neutralised as they were incorporated in 'workers self-management conferences' controlled by the PZPR and official trade unions.

This is the first cycle of a pattern that would re-emerge with increasing severity over the following decades. A slowdown in the ability of the economy to deliver rising standards of living, followed by revolts triggered by price increases, led to reforms based on decentralisation and worker self-management. Recentralisation, repression and reform followed in its wake. Recurring features which were evident with increasing severity from 1956 onwards included a deterioration in the efficiency of investment, a fall in the average rate of utilisation of productive capacity, a fall in the rate of growth of fixed capital, a decline in the rate of economic growth and growing inflation accompanied by stagflation, which meant a fall in real average wages (Kondratowicz and Okolski, 1993). Typically the ruling class would react by introducing more control in enterprises, a higher turnover of managerial and political cadres, intensified propaganda against ideological revisionism, the suspension of certain investment projects and the reallocation of investment favouring the consumption goods sector and services. By the end of the 1960s, however, it was clear that a policy of extensive growth could no longer deliver positive rates of growth and increasing standards of living.

The 1970 Crisis and the Gierek Reforms

A slowdown in the Polish economy was apparent from the mid-1960s (Maddison, 1991), and in 1970 a political crisis was triggered by an increase in food prices. The context of this was the problem of coordinating production and consumption in an economy that was increasingly prone to cycles of overproduction and shortages. From 1955 to 1970, official statistics show that rates of labour and capital productivity fell (Slay, 1994). Declining capital productivity meant that progressively larger shares of national income had to be devoted to investment in order to maintain growth rates. Declining labour productivity meant that increases in employment exceeded planned rates in order to provide firms with sufficient labour. From 1960 to 1970 the yearly growth in real wages for workers averaged only 1.8 per cent, indicating a stagnation in living standards (Slay, 1994).

By 1970 the Polish state faced revolt on two fronts: first, by the students and intelligentsia who had joined their colleagues in other Central and Eastern European countries in revolt in 1968; and second, by workers. On 12 December 1970 the Gomułka regime announced an increase in commodity prices of up to 30 per cent. This met with violent opposition from workers in the Baltic coast towns. Although initially driven by an increase in the price of food, workers from Gdańsk also demanded open elections to trade unions and workers' councils, as well as increased powers for the workers' councils themselves. Once again the response of the state was twofold. Troops were sent in and the official number of killed was 45. However, on 20 December 1970 Gomułka resigned in disgrace and was replaced by Gierek, who promised to be more responsive to the demands of the working class and to raise standards of consumption.

Import-led Growth

Under strong pressure from workers, Gierek was forced to rescind the announced price rises and the new unpopular 'incentive system', which attempted to intensify work. Promises were made to increase living standards by modernising machinery and reorganising production to meet a rapid growth in consumption. From an economic point of view, however, Gierek faced the same dilemma as Gomułka, namely a choice between high economic growth with massive capital accumulation and modernisation of the industrial structure on the one hand, and a visibly higher standard of living, necessary to pacify rebellious workers, on the other. To circumvent this difficult decision Gierek proposed the *New Development Strategy* based on import-led growth. This involved importing modern machinery and equipment, licences to use particular technologies and grain from the West financed by Western credits. Once the imported capital was in place then exports to the West would earn the hard currency to pay off the debts incurred by the imports.

In the short term these Western credits helped Gierek's policy of consumerism, but political stability and the quiescence of the working class was bought at a high cost. These reforms only temporarily suspended the dilemma between the growth of capital accumulation and consumption, and by 1976 it was clear that these reforms had only placated the working class temporarily. Retail prices increased by 10 per cent between 1975 and 1976 and in 1976 the government decided to reduce consumption by raising the price of meat and other foodstuffs. Strikes, demonstrations and riots broke out again, this time centred in Radom and Ursus, an industrial suburb of Warsaw. The regime quickly withdrew the price increases, but arrested the strike leaders and put them on trial.

There was a steady decline in the growth of industrial production from an average of 10 per cent per year between 1971 and 1975, to less than 2 per cent in 1979 (Nuti, 1982). Furthermore, the burden of debt increased from 12 per cent of export earnings in 1971 to 75 per cent by 1979, with inflation, an unfamiliar phenomenon since the mid-1950s, reappearing (Slay, 1994). This was compounded by a decline in real income for some groups[6] and by shortages of consumer goods, a familiar feature of central planning, but which had now become persistent and endemic. Working hours were extended to Sundays with the extension of systematic overtime (Landau and Tomaszewski, 1985). This led to a rapid growth of black or grey markets within which shortage goods were obtained at high prices or through connections, position or corruption. The population not only resented the shortages, but also the resulting unequal distribution of access to goods and services as the consumer goods and currencies that flowed into Poland brought opportunities for the enrichment of a few at public expense. Smolar (1983) points to a dramatic expansion in the number of the managerial positions in economic and social life that were subject to the *nomenklatura* personnel system.

1976: Slowdown and Revolt

Thus in the first half of the 1970s, after the slowdown and stagnation of the 1960s, the Gierek reforms had started to deliver rising standards of living, but by the middle years of the 1970s these reforms were having disastrous consequences. Part of the reason for this was Poland's increasing integration into the global economy, which meant that the traditional mechanism for insulating a centrally planned economy had been dismantled. International inflation, which reached unprecedented levels in Western economies in the late 1970s, was imported and built into price formulas as the prices of imported consumer and capital goods increased. The prospects for Polish exports, which were intended to pay the debt, deteriorated in the face of a world recession. In addition rising interest rates in the West led to a mounting burden of financing debt, which pushed Poland's ratio of debt service payments to exports to 83.2 per cent by 1980.

These factors external to the Polish economy have been underplayed by those who want to see the breakdown of Soviet-style communist economies as rooted only in the shortcomings of the planned economy. However, there were also internal factors which contributed to the cumulating crisis. The fact that the level of investment exceeded the absorptive capacity of the national economy, especially in construction, meant that projects had long gestation periods. Imported capital was increasingly frozen in unfinished investment projects, which by 1980 was equivalent to about 50 per cent of national income produced that year (Slay, 1994). Moreover, this investment was in greenfield projects which were favoured by the reward system within the *nomenklatura* and therefore failed to modernise existing industrial plants. By the mid-1970s imported machinery and appliances contributed over 50 per cent of the total supply on the domestic market,[7] although only 60 per cent of licences purchased from the West were used to facilitate technology transfer (Landau and Tomaszewski, 1985).[8]

Thus Poland attempted to resolve the problem of a slowdown and stagnation in its own economy by moves to integrate more closely with the global economy, while the world was facing its deepest recession since the 1930s. In response to stagflation, falling domestic demand and increased competition on world markets, the mid-1970s saw the resurgence in the West of free market economics associated with Friedrich von Hayek and Milton Friedman and the Chicago School, which in policy terms was reflected in among other things, deregulation, privatisation and anti-trade union legislation. Competitive pressures between firms drove moves towards downsizing and labour flexibility. Western capitalist economies and units of capital responded to the crisis with varying degrees of success. However, such remedies, although no guarantee of success in themselves, were not even on the agenda for the ruling classes of Central and Eastern European economies. For example, bankruptcy and liquidation, used to discipline capital in the West, simply did not exist. Combined with ossified institutional and political structures and obsolete products and processes, room for manoeuvre and the potential for restructuring in the face of international competition were severely inhibited. For Poland then, the most significant outcome of its strategy of import-led growth was not that it managed to become more efficient, but that the economy was increasingly stagnating and debt ridden.

The Roots of the Organised Opposition

The second half of the 1970s saw the development of an organised opposition catalysed by the prosecution and persecution of the 1976 activists. Fourteen intellectuals announced the formation of KOR (Komitet Obrony Robotników) – the Workers' Defence Committee – to provide help for the imprisoned workers and their families. Most importantly KOR included former communists, such as Jacek Kuroń and Adam Michnik, leaders in the 1968 student rebellion, who had renounced the PZPR and communism as practised in the Soviet bloc.[9] Importantly, KOR helped to forge an alliance between the working class and the intelligensia. By 1980 numerous other unofficial political groups had appeared and the growth of underground printing and publishing networks was beginning to exceed the capacity of the government to destroy them (Slay, 1994).

Market Socialism and Systemic Implosion: the 1980s

The Birth and Repression of Solidarity

On 1 July 1980 a government spokesperson announced that better cuts of meat would be available only in the 'free price' shops where prices were much higher. The announcement was the signal for a wave of strikes that rolled across most of Polish industry for the next six weeks, to reach its climax in the coastal cities of Gdańsk, Gdynia and Szczecin in mid-August (Barker, 1987). Although the strike action was triggered by food price increases, it was symptomatic of a much deeper malaise. Workers were increasingly alienated, both materially and politically, especially as the system was chronically unable to deliver rising standards of living. No longer concerned simply with immediate local issues, the list began with the demand for new, independent trade unions. It went on to call for relaxation of censorship, new rights for the church, the freeing of political prisoners and improvements in the health service (Barker, 1987). On 31 August, the government signed a series of accords, including the right to strike and to form an independent trade union. On 17 September 1980, a coordination committee was formed in Gdańsk, which became the founding committee of the self-governing union NSZZ (Niezależny Samorządny Związek Zawodowy: 'Solidarność') known as Solidarity. Early the following year a network of enterprise-level organisations from Poland's leading SOEs was established, including the Lenin Steelworks, the Gdańsk and Szczecin shipyards and mines. For the first time, there was an independent working-class movement organised against the very state that was supposed to embody the power of the working class.

The PZPR had been forced to make concessions in the face of unprecedented protests, but the leadership of the PZPR was divided over the appropriate response to the rise of Solidarity. Gierek, deemed incapable of dealing with the crisis, was forced to resign, and was replaced by General Jaruselski. Under pressure from the conservative wing of the party, Jaruselski imposed martial law in December 1981 and Solidarity's leadership and activists were arrested, trade unions suspended and the PZPR purged of reformist elements.

Market Socialism

Martial law was used as a means of pushing through major price rises (Lewis, 1994: 187). However, repression was again accompanied by attempts at social and economic reform, which were commonly characterised as a move towards market socialism. This represented a recognition by members of the ruling class that the planned economy, as it had functioned up to 1980, could not only no longer deliver rising standards of living for workers, but now threatened the privileged position of the *nomenklatura* themselves. A central feature of the reform was that enterprises should be independent, self-financing and self-managed. This meant that enterprises had much more freedom about production decisions, and in theory the income of enterprises and their employees were to be determined by the financial performance of enterprises. Self-management meant that powers were given to workers' councils. In addition to giving enterprises increased autonomy, restrictions on small businesses were relaxed and a more positive attitude to foreign investment was encouraged.

The attempt at limited marketisation, however, produced contradictory tendencies in the economy. The centre continued to retain substantial powers through tax liabilities, subsidies and access to supplies and raw materials. In particular, the continued central control of investment had significant implications for the structure and performance of the economy. The pattern of investment, although in theory sufficiently high to restructure the economy, only served to reinforce its traditional structure. For example, a high proportion of investment outlays were expended on the continuation of unfinished projects from the Gierek era, with only a small proportion allocated to replace obsolete machinery. As a result, a growing proportion of capital stock machinery became worn out, unreliable and caused frequent breakdowns (Kondratowicz and Okolski, 1993). This meant that goods were uncompetitive on the world market, and at home there was a marked effect on people's material conditions and access to consumer goods. Progressively more scarce investment resources led to an increase in centralised decision making, while at the same time reforms loosened the control of the central authorities over individual enterprises. Not only had the economy ceased to be a classical planned economy, but decision making had descended into chaos and uncertainty.

Nomenklatura to Property-owning Capitalist Class

There were important changes taking place in the Polish ruling class. During the 1980s managers were able to take advantage of the loosening control of enterprises and call for private enterprise to gain control and ownership of state assets. Typically, these so-called spontaneous *nomenklatura* privatisations involved the selling of non-core operations such as a computer centre, repair facilities or a sales centre to a group of insiders that included managers and party members. State Owned Enterprises were often stripped of their most profitable operations, and their new owners could make a profit by selling the good or service on the black market.

Decentralisation allowed the ruling class the option of shifting their power base, either by acting as owners of small businesses, or as a result of the *nomenklatura* privatisations, or more commonly as increasingly powerful managers in quasi-governmental decentralised enterprises. The *nomenklatura* used their position to become wealthy owners of what used to be state enterprises through two important legal forms: the leasing of state owned companies and joint stock companies (*spólki*). In a well publicised case of Elpol electronic *spólka*, members of the board of directors (who happened to include representatives of the Minister of Interior and Defence, a former vice-premier, and managers of other SOEs) received generous compensation on completion of the conversion from state enterprise status (Slay, 1994).

Many accounts treat the *nomenklatura* ruling class as a homogeneous group with similar interests. However, what emerged was a series of ambivalent and ambiguous positions. For a significant section it became clear that while it was still important to maintain party membership, their interests lay increasingly with involvement with foreign capital. Cieochinska concludes that:

> As a result, towards the close of the 1970s there were more ambitious solutions which allowed the political elite to transform itself into management staff and entrepreneurs. The communist doctrine was dead, and there was only the apparatus which, in the name of the reforms could see to the interests of the *nomenklatura* in getting rich. This philosophy engendered demands for foreign capital and the establishment of the first joint venture companies ... Therefore there were grounds for the thesis that the elite was distributing the benefits of the development of the market economy, outside agriculture, in the final stage of the command economy, which occurred in Poland in the 1980s. (1992: 215)

The outward manifestation of this process was twofold: first, the growth of foreign small scale enterprises grew from 100 in 1981 to 841 in 1989; second, the number of firms in the private sector increased from 351,000 in 1981 to 572,400 in 1988 (Hardy and Rainnie, 1996).

Systemic Implosion

The consequences of these partial reforms and the deepening economic crisis resulted in increasing political instability. Ordinary people experienced a marked deterioration in their quality of life. In the workplace, managerial ineffectiveness, the inefficient organisation of production and frequent shortages of inputs and raw materials served to reduce workers' morale even further. This was reflected in an exodus of Poland's working population as 640,000 people in the 18–65 age group left the country between 1981 and 1988 (Landau and Tomaszewski, 1985). Shortages became commonplace in everyday life and in the early 1980s the average time devoted to shopping, which involved queueing and long searches for the most basic goods, rose to two hours per household every day.

Over time the consumer market became disorganised; large scale bribery, queueing, waiting lists, speculation and the direct exchange of goods between enterprises to access scarce commodities were typical symptoms of this process. A flourishing underground economy played a particularly destructive role and between 1980 and 1986, it is estimated that up to 25 per cent of personal incomes came from secondary activities with foreign trade transactions providing up to 10 per cent (Myant, 1993: 68).

According to Kondratowicz and Okolski societal degradation extended to environmental decay:

> Rampant expansion of the coal-based energy sector contributed to unprecedented air and water pollution. This and other factors ... transformed Poland from an almost environmentally clean country into a conglomerate of lands plagued by biological disaster. (1993:16)

Poland's ecological problems, exacerbated by pressures on the health service and food processing industry, were reflected in deteriorating public physical and mental health. Between 1980 and 1988 reported cases of dysentery and food poisoning quadrupled, and incidents of salmonella increased by a factor of 2.5 (Slay, 1994). Between the mid-1960s and the late 1980s the mortality rate among men between 30 and 60 increased and there was an increase in deaths caused by cancer and cardio-vascular diseases. Further, this impairment of the quality of life manifested itself through mental stress, which could be observed in aggression, depression and neurosis (Hardy and Rainnie, 1996).

The Roundtable Talks and the End of Communism

As we have seen, crisis was endemic in Poland almost from the inception of the Soviet-style system. The reforms of the previous two decades had been a failure at nearly every level. One effect of this was that although Solidarity appeared to be a spent force in the mid-1980s, the failure of the Jaruselski reforms to initiate anything but a holding operation in the face of growing political and economic troubles provided a platform for the reemergence of the movement.

The PZPR feared a social explosion due to the economic malaise and runaway inflation that had depressed Polish living standards and deepened public anger and frustration. After the government increased food prices by 40 per cent a further wave of strikes rocked the country. By this time the movement had gained so much momentum that it became impossible to hold off change. The PZPR was forced to reopen negotiations with the banned trade union Solidarity and other opposition groups in an attempt to defuse growing social unrest.

The Polish Roundtable Talks took place in Warsaw from 6 February to 4 April 1989. In the semi-free elections that year, Solidarity took all but one of the 35 per cent of seats it was allowed to contest in the lower house (*Sejm*) and 92 of the 100 places in the less powerful upper house (senate). The PZPR was a moribund force and after two attempts by the communists to form a government failed, in September 1989, Jaruselski asked Mazowiecki to lead Poland's first non-communist government for 40 years.

Neoliberalism in Ascendance: 1989 Onwards

Solidarity had been transformed over the course of the 1980s and two different ideologies representing 'liberal' (or neoliberal) and social democratic world views competed for the favour of Solidarity's leadership. Solidarity had begun as an organisation committed to some form of democratic socialism, but by the end of the 1980s the dominant ideology was one of neoliberalism. The social democratic element of Solidarity had been routed when the organisation as a mass movement had been destroyed by martial law, repression and the imprisonment of its best activists. By the late 1980s Solidarity came to be represented by a small number of individuals such as Wałęsa, and intellectuals, such as Balcerowicz, who were proponents of the free market.

Gradualism was eschewed and 'third ways' dismissed as unsuccessful experiments. The neoliberal view argued that Western-style capitalism and a complete break with the institutions and policies associated with communism were the only option. In this view the market was the end goal of transformation – that is the implantation of market capitalism – as well as the mechanism for bringing about the transition through creative destruction. Social democrats and other groups, however, had rejected liberalism as excessively libertarian, and inappropriate for the situation in 1989. They envisaged a much stronger role for trade unions, workers' self-management, participatory producer and consumer cooperatives and the welfare state.

Slay points to the emergence of Balcerowicz, an economics professor at the Central School of Planning and Statistics in Warsaw, as the architect of shock therapy:

> Mazowiecki's selection of Leszek Balcerowicz, in August 1989, to head the new government's economic team ... signalled the ascendacy of the liberal view ... [he] brought a degree of credibility in the eyes of Western financial experts. Balcerowicz's dual role as deputy prime minister and minister of finance demonstrated ... the government's commitment to a rapid trans-formation along liberal lines. (Slay, 1994: 91)

In January 1990, a series of economic measures – the *Balcerowicz Programme* – was introduced. This so-called shock therapy took the form of a massive dose of IMF type stabilisation, which comprised high interest rates and tight controls on the money supply and government spending. The share of subsidies in GDP fell from 15 per cent in 1989 to 6 per cent in 1990. Real interest rates increased dramatically for new lending and old loans. The intention was to jump start a market economy (see Lipton and Sachs, 1990) with short-term pain as the price that had to be paid for the speedy adjustment to the benefits of a market economy.

After two decades of incremental integration with the international economy, the liberalisation of trade and foreign investment meant a leap to the global economy with little protection. Although average tariff levels were higher than the European average, reductions in effective protection meant that Polish firms were exposed to the rigours of international competition. Sudden exposure to global competition, accompanied by reductions in internal demand and central subsidies, meant that large numbers of enterprises were uncompetitive and were liquidated with a high loss of jobs.

In conventional economic terms certain aspects of the *Balcerowicz Programme* could be considered a success, including a slowdown in inflation, the elimination of shortages and the stabilisation of the currency. However, the initial costs turned out to be high in terms of output and employment, as Poland plunged into recession. The initial impacts were brutal for many ordinary people. Employment in the state sector fell by 14 per cent in 1989–1990 and output in the socialised sector fell by 24 per cent (Ksiezopolski, 1992). Unemployment rose from 0.05 per cent in December 1989 to 8.4 per cent (more than 1.5 million) by 1991. Real wages fell in the state sector in 1990, and real household incomes decreased by over 30 per cent for pensioners and more than 50 per cent for peasant households in the first quarter of 1990 (Ksiezopolski, 1991). Workers in the public (but not private) sector were penalised by the abolition of the inflationary wage index introduced in July 1989, which amounted to a pay cut.

The losers and winners at the beginning of transformation are clearly illustrated by surveys of the Polish Statistical Office outlined in Table 2.1. This shows the large scale redistribution of income away from workers and farmers and in favour of entrepreneurs. This is the beginning of an emerging picture of the rich getting richer, and a growing proportion of the working class getting poorer, with other groups of workers occupying segments of varying degrees of relative affluence along the spectrum.

Table 2.1 Distribution of Income 1988–1991

Source of income	Level (1985 = 1000)			Composition (%)		
	1988	1990	1991	1988	1990	1991
All income	113.6	102.7	108.8	100.0	100.0	100.0
Wages	111.5	75.5	73.4	46.3	38.2	35.1
Private agriculture	124.4	70.7	57.5	12.7	6.6	5.1
Other private activity	118.8	157.4	170.0	25.6	37.9	38.6
Welfare payments	111.5	95.6	124.0	15.4	17.3	21.2

Source: Gomulka, 1993.

Conclusion

Accelerated industrialisation shifted the Polish economy from having the characteristics of a developing country in 1945 to a Soviet-style economy by the mid-1960s. The subordination of consumption to investment as a result of military competition with the West meant that crises were endemic from the outset. Ever more brutal repression and increasingly desperate reforms failed to deliver higher standards of living and laid the foundation for deeper crises and more entrenched and organised opposition. Opening up to the West in the 1970s and 1980s further exacerbated the economic malaise. The 1980s were characterised by systemic implosion and the system could no longer deliver privileges even for the *nomenklatura* ruling class. Sections of the Solidarity leadership, along with international organisations who would underwrite the changes, set the stage for rapid integration with the global economy through unleashing markets and liberalisation.

3

THE LEAP TO GLOBAL CAPITALISM: 1990 ONWARDS

In 1990 neoliberal economists saw CEE as a laboratory in which they could experiment with the implantation of 'capitalism in the raw' through market driven policies. In another camp were those who could be described broadly as institutionalist, who envisaged a more inclusive and social democratic variant of capitalism. Beyond these two different visions of capitalism, there is a stream of radical and Marxist thinking on transformation, which sees it as combined, uneven and contested. The increasing integration of post-communist economies into the global economy has deepened the combined nature of capitalist development and at the same time shaped the context in which transformation has unfolded. Transformation is uneven in the sense that polarisation and inequality are not temporary aberrations of policy, but intrinsic to capitalist development, and the result of the competition that underpins it. The restructuring of Poland and other CEE economies has not simply been one of the unfolding of neoliberal policies on a blank sheet; rather it was and continues to be a contested process between different sections of capital, the state and organised workers.

This chapter begins by looking at the dominant prescriptions that were put forward to transform the economies and societies of CEE. It is tempting to omit these academic debates, because the ground has been well covered and neoliberalism can appear to be something of a 'straw target'. However, these ideas need to be laid bare and the arguments against them rehearsed, because their deployment has not been confined to the transformation of post-communist economies. The ideas of neoliberals are continually recycled to justify a particular set of market driven policies in both advanced and developing economies by both right wing and social democratic governments alike. The main part of the chapter puts forward a Marxist framework of analysis, which sees the emergence of Poland's new capitalism as complex, dynamic and deeply uneven. Economic restructuring and institutional architecture are outcomes of tensions between the state, labour and capital in the context of Poland's deeper integration with global capitalism.

Different Visions of Capitalism

Neoliberal Fantasies

In 1990, Lipton and Sachs wrote the seminal article summarising the neoliberal[1] position on Poland; in short this was a recipe for installing an economic system similar to those of the capitalist economies of Western Europe. The legacy of communist institutions, and particularly the state, in Poland and CEE generally, was viewed as a problem that had to be sidestepped and circumvented to ensure that existing structures and interests – either those of workers or the incumbent ruling class – would not derail the reforms. The introduction of a market system was seen mainly in terms of the dismantling of the old communist structures, after which market-based solutions would be installed to fill the gap.

This was manifest in shock therapy introduced on 1 January 1990, which comprised a package of policies, implemented overnight, imposing draconian cuts in government spending and the money supply, and high interest rates (see Blanchard *et al.*, 1991; Brada, 1993). This was the macroeconomic package of 'sound money' that underpins the neoliberal project. Therefore, the neoliberal school advocated little less than the complete reconstruction of economic arrangements from the top down. In their analysis economic laws are seen as universal and well understood, as are the ingredients of a successful economy, namely that they are based on the free market, unambiguous property rights, and the unassailable relationship between competition and efficiency. In other words, an attempt to jump start the market would involve institutional measures which were intended to free up entrepreneurship, abolish barriers to entry and exit to the market, and abolish central price controls, with privatisation lying at the core of the policy (Pickel, 1992). History, society and politics were viewed as impediments to the design of the transformation agenda by those who knew best. Thus the 'economists' consensus' advocated a package of policies, which could be transferred unproblematically from the very varied experiences and institutional set-ups in developed and developing countries (Gowan, 1995; Kozul-Wright and Rayment, 1997; Florio, 2002).

Rather than the neutral 'invisible hand' of the market there is a strong class element to neoliberalism. Specifically, these new rules governing the functioning of capitalism included a new discipline for labour to the benefit of lenders and shareholders (Duménil and Lévy, 2005). In Poland, workers in the public sector were immediately faced with a fall in living standards as their wages were restricted (*popiwek*) in the face of high inflation. The 'doublespeak' of neoliberalism was manifest in the fact that, while the role of state as provider of welfare was diminished, it nevertheless remained a staunch defender of capital with regard to its domestic and international firms. There was a dramatic growth of financial institutions in their own right as well as a new relationship between financial and non-financial institutions; and new legal frameworks to facilitate the free flow of capital and the restructuring of firms through mergers and acquisitions.

With hindsight it appears even more risible that these neoliberal economists and policy makers thought that the new capitalism could be instituted according to a textbook blueprint, or sophisticated mathematical models, particularly popular in economics departments. Anyone who has had the merest flirtation with economics will know that its predictive and prescriptive capacity is completely reliant on a set of theoretical propositions known to be true only under highly stylised circumstances (Murrell, 1993). Neoliberal economists are in complete denial about the role played by the state historically in economic development, and its continued crucial role in capital accumulation. The mantra of competitive markets demonstrates blindness to a central feature of contemporary capitalism, which is its domination by a small number of large firms. Further, the rhetoric of the market as an impartial adjudicator was quickly exposed as privatisation got underway. The selling off of vast swathes of assets was not a technical issue, but again an issue of class, which involved squabbling between different sections of the ruling class as to whether their interests lay with domestic or foreign capital and a deepening anger from working-class people as they were excluded from the division of the spoils (Kowalik, 2001).

Institutional Fixes

This 'capitalism by design' was far more problematic than its architects had anticipated. From 1990 onwards, transformation in Poland unfolded in ways that were *unexpected*, in that SOEs did not suddenly become competitive, *unintended*, with high and persistent levels of unemployment, and *uneven*, in the misery that was experienced by large sections of working-class people while others enriched themselves (Gomułka, 1993; Paci *et al.*, 2004). This left the door open for accounts of social change which drew on evolutionary thinking and those that were based on the rediscovery of institutions (Jackson, 1992; Van Ees and Garretsen, 1994; Tsang, 1996).[2]

This broadly institutionalist perspective has several strands.[3] One school of thought argued that the institutions of the state could be used to encourage the development of a 'Western-style corporatist social order' (Amsden *et al.*, 1994: 209), where planning had to be reinvented and capitalism was to be embedded into societies in which, it is argued, for decades it had been unable to fit (Hardy and Rainnie, 1996). Further, it was argued that the lessons of late industrialisation in the Newly Industrialised Countries of South-East Asia could be transferred to CEE (Chang, 1995; Lo, 1995; Kozul-Wright and Rayment, 1997; Henderson, 1998). The clearest expression of this position is in the work of Amsden *et al.* (1994), where it was argued that the activities and prescriptions of the Bretton Woods institutions – such as the World Bank and the IMF – allied to a mistaken commitment to the free market based on simplistic eighteenth-century liberalism have been little short of disastrous in places such as Poland. However, they conclude that this was nothing more than the 'wrong capitalist model' (Amsden *et al.*, 1994: 4).

A second perspective drew on the old institutionalists[4] to argue that markets are socially embedded and politically constructed (Polanyi, 1957 [1944]; Granovetter, 1985; Smelser and Swedberg, 1994). This view was succinctly put by Myrdal:

> The market does not just happen. It is not a natural phenomenon. The market is a set of instituted social relations, a set of rules determining what things can be exchanged, who can exchange them, who will benefit from the exchange, and whom will bear the burden of the exchange. (1957:8)

This emphasises that a pure market simply does not exist because any functioning economy puts in place rules to regulate the behaviour of firms, and the relationship between capital and the state (Chang, 2002). Evolutionary approaches, on the other hand, centre on the behaviour of economic agents as a product of both present and historical social processes (Stark, 1990, 1995 and 1996; Pickel, 1992; Chavance and Magnin, 1997; Grabher and Stark, 1997). In arguing that past behaviours have shaped economic institutions and the response of economic agents, these authors criticise neoliberal zealots for their contempt of historical processes. Further, institutionalists point to the irrelevance of textbook economic theory when compared to the vividness and variety of arrangements evident in past and present capitalist economies (Murrell, 1993; Hodgson, 1996).

A third strand of thinking came from those who had originally invoked the use of unbridled market forces to restructure the economies of CEE, but abandoned this 'red in tooth and claw' approach to capitalism. References to notions such as governance, transparency and institutions began to creep into the vocabulary of the World Bank (1996 and 2002). The nonsense of pumping money into these economies and then expecting the market to arise like a phoenix from the ashes became embarrassingly and abundantly clear in the debacle of the IMF in Russia. The millions of dollars of aid which had been poured in to assist with 'building markets' and 'competitive structures' had actually lined the pockets of the mafia who transformed themselves into even more wealthy oligarchs (Florio, 2002). Although less spectacular, the showering of aid to facilitate the move to 'democracy' in Poland benefited sections of the *nomenklatura* and fed the material ambitions of an emerging ruling class. This brand of institutionalism is evident in the criticisms of dissenters from within the camp of those who were latterly regarded as mainstream economists such as Stiglitz (2002 and 2006) and Krugman (2003), who are supporters of the market but argue that it needed to be reined in and embedded in transparent and accountable institutions and structures of governance in order to provide the conditions for competitive capitalism.

Same End, Different Paths

The debate between the neoliberals and institutionalists could be reduced to one in which the former emphasised the immediacy, speed and simultaneity of reform, while the latter ultimately argued for gradualism, seeing the seeds of change as emerging from within existing institutions and were more tolerant of a wider number of configurations of state, market and firms. In other words, these added up to different visions of capitalism, the first a more brutal version where the market could be invoked to restructure and restore competitiveness to these economies with little regard for the social consequences. The second vision of capitalism recognised a necessary role for the state in regulating markets and trade and acknowledged the need to provide at least a minimum safety net of welfare provision.

Combined, Uneven and Compressed Transformation

There is a body of Marxist literature which has adopted a much more critical stance to transformation (Clarke *et al.*, 1993; Hardy and Rainnie, 1996; Smith and Swain, 1998). Underpinning these analyses is the centrality of class, and the assumption that the 'law of value' and competition should lie at the heart of an analysis of capitalism. Neo-Gramscians have offered an additional radical perspective through their focus on the way in which transformation has been a hegemonic project by the US and Europe to create neoliberal economic regimes that mirror their own (Bieler, 2002; Shields, 2003 and 2004; Holman, 2004; Bohle, 2005 and 2006; Bohle and Neunhöffer, 2006).

The essence of the approach taken here is to argue that the transformation of CEE economies has to be understood in the context of the dynamics and development of the global economy. The analysis draws on the notion of combined and uneven development (Trotsky, 1977 [1934]) in which there has recently been renewed interest (Dunn and Radice, 2006; van der Linden, 2007).[5] By seeing change as a dynamic process of interaction between economic change and political and social forces, the idea of combined and uneven development offers the best analysis on which to build a non-deterministic account of transformation. The account here emphasises the institutional dimension and role of the state as being critical to understanding the varied outcomes between and within economies in CEE in the way that it has mediated the reinsertion of these countries into the global economy. Crucially, the form and content of development, in its widest sense, cannot be known or predicted because the process of transformation has been contested by different factions of the ruling class and by workers.

Combined Development

Rather than seeing the global economy as the aggregation of different capitalisms, capitalism has to be understood as unifying the world into a single interactive productive system under the dominance of capital. If one single law expresses the capitalist form of combined and uneven development it is the 'law of value'. This law has two main aspects. First, competition means that all producers have to produce with the minimum input of labour time and second, it forces a tendency towards a normal rate of profit in all industries. The transformation of Poland and CEE is, therefore, *combined* in the sense that the growth, stagnation and eventual disintegration of these communist economies has to be understood in the context of the dynamics of the global economy.

As we saw in the previous chapter the 1950s and 1960s were regarded as the golden years of world capitalism. Unprecedented rates of growth and consumption were not only confined to the United States, Western Europe and Japan, but were also experienced by communist economies. The retrospective brush with which neoliberals painted a picture of uniform inefficiency in communist economies does not accord with the fact that these regimes were, until the late 1960s at least, able to deliver rising, if uneven, standards of living. Although their development took place behind closed doors in the 1950s and 1960s, the logic of world capitalism nevertheless impinged on the nature and form of their development as they were forced to compete militarily with the West (Haynes, 1987). Production was distorted towards heavy industry at the expense of the production of consumption goods. In other words, they were not immune to the rhythms of the global economy.

By the late 1960s the long boom was ending and this was not only clearly evident in the advanced economies, but was also reflected in a slowdown in the growth rates and profit levels of countries in the communist bloc (Maddison, 1991 and 2001). However, while the advanced economies had well-honed tools for disciplining capital in the face of a crisis, the option of mergers, takeovers, bankruptcy and liquidation were missing from the repertoire of communist economies such as Poland. Using piecemeal reforms, Poland attempted a gradual integration with the global economy, but rather than achieving higher standards of living, it only succeeded in increasing their debt and importing inflation (Haynes and Hasan, 2002a and 2002b).

In Poland the period of 1948 to 1989 demonstrated the process of development and subsequent disintegration of an extreme form of socio-economic formation, that of state-led industrialisation within a world economy that was increasingly integrated and crisis ridden (Simatupang, 1994; Slay, 1994). State-led industrialisation of one variety or another was the dominant form of organising capitalism during the long boom of the 1950s and 1960s. However, it held within it the seeds of its own destruction. As the depth and breadth of linkages in the global economy became greater, national development behind trade barriers became increasingly impossible. Successful and expanding firms, initially from the US, needed to move outside their national boundaries into new territories in order to accumulate. However, this expansion of capital and the internationalisation of circuits of capital (Palloix, 1977) required a number of institutional developments, including the liberalisation of trade and investment, privatisation to free up the assets of other economies and the deregulation of finance. The latter was necessary not only to sell financial services, but also to recycle profits to provide the funds for further expansion. Together these interrelated trends and developments can be loosely termed as 'economic globalisation'.

Uneven Development

The *uneven* development of capitalism, with concentrations of wealth on the one hand and poverty and oppression on the other, is ubiquitous and the evidence incontestable. However, according to neoliberal economics this is a necessary, but transitional stage in the workings of the market in reallocating factors of production to bring about a convergence of income and rates of growth. Other economists see unevenness as the outcome of the wrong policies in a banana skin version of economics, where domestic or trade policy needs to be tweaked by a technocratic state, usually informed by Keynesian thinking. However, this unevenness is neither an accident of economic change and development, nor a shortcoming of policy, rather it is a necessary and central aspect of capitalism.

There is much debate surrounding the origins and socio-economic mechanism of unevenness (Mandel, 1970; Lowy, 1981; Smith, 1990; Dunn and Radice, 2006), but simply put, geographical unevenness represents the diverging returns on investment reflected in different opportunities for profit. The result of competition is the creation and/or destruction of entire built (and natural) environments, as well as the social structures that accompany them. Capitalism perpetually seeks to create a geographical landscape to facilitate its activities at one point in time, only to have to destroy it and build a wholly different landscape at a later point in time to accommodate its perpetual thirst for endless capital accumulation (Harvey, 1996). The exposure of Poland to the vagaries of global competition through shock therapy unleashed a process of 'creative destruction'. However, there was much more destruction than creation in Poland, as large sections of industry and firms remained uncompetitive in comparison to their Western counterparts.

Neoliberal accounts of the restructuring of the Polish economy have characterised transformation as a linear process from a planned communist economy to a capitalist market economy, the ingredients of which are obvious and well understood. Similarly, evolutionary and institutional approaches see development as following a prescribed sequence of stages as 'no part of this orderly process could be mixed up, shifted around, telescoped or skipped over' (Novack, 1972a: 147). Some Marxist accounts, particularly those deriving from the regulation school, have subscribed to this view of linear change by suggesting that capitalism passes through a number of stages, moving from Fordism to post-Fordism, which are characterised by different methods of production and institutional regimes.[6]

Capitalist development and transformation, however, cannot be explained through the unfolding of a series of laws. In contrast to institutionalist and evolutionary accounts which emphasise the incremental nature of economic change, the idea that there are *historical leaps* has been accepted for a long time.[7] Under this process a backward country can adopt what is most advanced, but does not have to take things in the same order. In fact the logic of competition compels firms to try and catch up with the latest techniques, under threat of punishment for non-compliance, with the penalty of economic failure.

Compressed Transformation

At the beginning of the transformation process, Poland, as well as the other CEE economies, can be understood as being backward in the sense that their level of technology and productivity significantly lagged behind Western market economies. From 1990 an intensification of integration with the world economy through trade and foreign investment, oiled by a greater circulation of finance, has made it possible to get hold of technical and organisational improvements much more quickly. Capitalism can be imported into a new country in its most advanced form and is able to exert change much more strongly and in a shorter time period. The role of foreign investment by large TNCs has been critical to this process, the networks of which have either locked in or excluded sections of Polish capital. The decision to locate a greenfield car factory, for example Opel (General Motors), at Gliwice meant the immediate introduction of state-of-the-art technology. However, equally important is the introduction of a range of know-how across the full range of managerial functions, which introduces a lexicon of new material practices and discourses.

Therefore, the growth of productive processes can be faster or slower depending on natural conditions or historical connections (Novack, 1972a). Rather than understanding change as being incremental and predictable, the integration of CEE with the world economy from 1990 onwards should be understood as a leap incorporating changes (partially or fully) that have been *compressed* in time. This is in contrast to changes that took place in Western market economies over a much more extended time period. Although restructuring on broadly neoliberal lines has had a different starting point and pace in each national economy, this form of restructuring took place from the mid-1970s onwards in the non-communist core economies. Therefore, whereas Western European capitalist economies have had 30 years to restructure, these changes have been compressed into only a decade and a half in post-communist economies.

The notion of societal leaps stands in stark contrast to evolutionary and incremental accounts of economic and social change, as well as those that see change as a process of sequential stages. Further, it implies a much less stable capitalism with heightened competition where the advantages of national capitals and states can only be temporary in a situation where other countries can quickly appropriate technology, skills and organisational innovation.

Institutional Architectures

Although the world is increasingly integrated into a unified 'single world market' it is not a homogeneous capitalist milieu (Barker, 2006) and the strong institutional foundations that underpin uneven development have been a neglected part of the analysis. Here we mean institutions in the widest sense, including not simply the different relations among local states, capitals and labour forces, but also the whole political and cultural web of social relations in which these are embedded, as well as the corresponding local forms of civil society (Barker, 2006).

Myrdal (1957) argued that a 'backward country' must have sufficient institutional and cultural capacities to appropriate advanced technology. Even though technologies can arrive ready-made, this would not necessarily overcome the legacy of old ways of thinking, with which they could coexist for a period of time at least (Davidson, 2006). This is well illustrated by Van Zon (1998) in his study of the Zaporizhzhya area of the Ukraine. He suggests that conventions of behaviour such as kleptocracy, corruption and a general atmosphere of distrust that persisted from the previous regime led to low levels of foreign investment. Therefore, despite the introduction of both formal and informal institutional change through foreign investment and Western management techniques, deep structural characteristics in the economy and in business practices have limited the scale and speed of corporate change (Czaban and Henderson, 1998; Whitley and Czaban, 1999).

The imitation and assimilation of elements of advanced culture and technology is selective, therefore a 'backward' country can 'import' some elements of advanced culture while retaining other inherited aspects of its own institutional forms. In other words, within its own internal structures it can combine a mixture of advanced and archaic ingredients thereby generating a new amalgam with distinct characteristics from those found among its rivals. The notion of path dependency views the emergence of differences between the integration of national economies with the global economy as being primarily rooted in the internal developments of economies. However, national peculiarities are not simply a function of inherited differences in starting points, but a product of the world system as these are inflected within each separate state (Barker, 2006). Each country is part of a larger whole, standing in a particular and shifting nexus of relations with other parts and with the whole shaped simultaneously both by the development of social relations within its borders and by the multiple forms of economic, political, military and cultural traffic across those same borders (Barker, 2006).

Therefore, while capitalism is underpinned by specific and universal characteristics (Meiksins Wood, 1997; Screpanti, 1999), namely the 'law of value', individual capitalist systems, in their historical and national development, have all been characterised by a high degree of institutional and organisational diversity (Boyer, 1995; Zysman, 1996; Whitley, 1997 and 1998). Similarly, the economies of CEE have exhibited a rich variety of different institutional arrangements that depart from the models of designer capitalism and blueprints that were urged in the early days of transformation (Stark, 1995). Thus specific and evolving configurations of post-communist economies are characterised by their composite, combined or mixed features, which cannot be viewed as stage-posts as the economy moves from one end point (the command economy) to another (the market economy).

Similarities shared by Central and Eastern European economies include the emphasis on neoliberal policies and their discourses, the globalising trends of capital in the form of foreign investment and the agendas of international organisations such as the IMF and World Bank. Communist economies were not homogeneous with a single logic and this has influenced the routes they have taken to restructuring and reintegration with the global economy. First, there is diversity in the starting point and initial conditions of these economies in terms of the legacies of their industrial structures, the nature and depth of the crisis that pertained in the late 1980s and the degree of integration with the West. A second dissimilarity relates to the 'departure from actually existing socialism' (Altvater, 1998: 593) taken by these economies in response to the economic stagnation that was apparent by the late 1960s (Maddison, 1991). Hungary, for example, instituted widespread and relatively successful market reforms in 1968, in terms of integrating with West European economies, whereas Poland had two decades of disastrous economic reforms. The third factor influencing nationally specific paths of transformation after 1989 was the balance of political forces and the unique political and economic routes taken. In Poland, the central role of the political party and trade union Solidarity in bringing about the demise of the previous regime, and its massive popularity at the outset of transformation, gave the government a unique opportunity to implement a drastic set of reforms (Ost, 1989 and 1992; Rainnie and Hardy, 1995). It should be noted, however, that this honeymoon period was very short-lived and by the early 1990s, strikes rocked the country and brought down the Solidarity government in 1993.

Approaches that observe superficial characteristics in an attempt to pin down capitalism into distinct periods[8] underplay historical complexities whereby modern and archaic features can exist along side each other. The 'varieties of capitalism' perspective, which tries to label and categorise comparative national capitalisms, is a static approach rather than one that emphasises the dynamic and constantly changing nature of the system. This was put succinctly by Novack when he said that 'history plays pranks with all rigid forms and fixed routines. All kinds of paradoxical developments ensue which perplex people with narrow formalised minds' (Novack, 1972b). Rather than a simple straight, single line of direction in social development, what we have instead is economic change that is complex, contradictory and contested. The theoretical task is therefore to analyse the dialectical interplay of action and reaction of the contending forces in their connection with the historical environment.

Poland and the European Neoliberal Project

Neoliberal accounts suggest that the state needs to be dethroned as the owner of assets and stripped of its role in the organisation of economic activity. Lipton and Sachs (1990) suggested that the legacy of the communist bureaucracy made it incapable of intervening even in cases of market failure. However, the state has not withdrawn nor have its activities been diminished, rather the nature and form of state intervention has changed (Shields, 2004). A dramatic reorganisation of institutions was necessary in order for the economies of CEE to integrate with the global economy and the state was central to authoring and instilling new structures consistent with and necessary for neoliberalism. For example, a number of tasks such as the regulation of competition, arbitrating between foreign and domestic capital, reassigning property rights, and contract law needed to be accomplished. New government departments and quangos were elevated in prestige and importance. In Poland, the Ministry of Privatisation was central to the trans-formation project, as the department charged with divesting public assets and selling individual State Owned Enterprises as well as whole sectors of industry. The newly established foreign investment department (Polska Agencja Informacji i Investycji Zagraniczych, PAIZ) was pivotal in taking part in the locational tournaments which characterised the strategies of other European countries in their bid to win a slice of global capital and capture, at least part of, the value chains of large transnational firms.

Changes in the organisation of finance and banking were of paramount importance and were 'a condition of existence for the market economy itself' (Grahl, 2005: 293). Moves towards establishing a Central Independent Bank, a process that had started before 1990, underpinned the macroeconomic framework necessary for the neoliberal project to ensure sound money and disentangle finance from domestic capital and the political influence of the *nomenklatura*. Europe and the US needed new markets in which some of their largest and most profitable financial firms could operate. This was particularly true of the United Kingdom (UK) and the US who dominate global financial services. The outcome of this scramble for assets is reflected in the large amounts of foreign capital in the financial sector, with about 80 per cent of the banking system under foreign ownership (HSBC, 2006). Ten of the twelve large commercial banks in Poland are owned by foreign institutions, with the State Treasury owning the remaining two.

This adjustment of domestic policies and organisations from 1990 was not a straightforward process whereby the nation state transmitted or refracted the needs of global capitalism. The competing interests of different sections of the ruling class, and struggles of organised labour, made the processes protracted and the outcomes a political compromise, particularly regarding privatisation and welfare. Therefore the restructuring of the state was much more complex than simply guaranteeing the conditions for the operation of transnational capital.

If the first stage of transformation can be seen as a rather chaotic and contested attempt to integrate with an increasingly liberalised global economy, then European integration can be seen as a more systematic consolidation of that aim. The European Union's strategy has been to promote neoliberal reform and the influence of European transnational capital through the liberalisation and deregulation of CEE (Smith, 2002; Holman, 2004; Shields, 2004). Dangling the carrot of membership, the EU managed to push Poland and other CEEs towards adopting a specific neoliberal reform model, which was a much more radical variant than the one operated in the economies of existing members. Having to conform to EU norms, regarding state aid and rules on competition policy in particular, wedded these countries to the liberalisation of trade and investment in a way that made it difficult to accede to any demands by members of the ruling class for protection or retreat (Bieler, 2002).

Two projects that have consolidated the neoliberal project in Europe were extended to Poland and the other accession countries. The first was the European single market, a popular symbol used to relaunch European integration in the mid-1980s and implemented in 1992, the aim of which was to restore Europe's global competitiveness with Japan and the US. This opened up all economies and prised open previously protected sectors (for example, services, utilities and telecommunication) to trade and investment. While the rhetoric was of innovation and economies of scale the reality was that it allowed the reorganisation of European capital over a wider territory, which was manifest in an unprecedented wave of mergers and acquisitions.

The second project was that of monetary union with a central bank and single currency. This was the consolidation of the single market as it removed barriers and reduced costs for large firms in providing an undifferentiated terrain on which capital could operate. A further effect was that monetary union disciplined capital (Gill, 2001), and particularly public spending, through the restrictive monetary policy in the convergence criteria of the Maastricht Treaty and Stability and Growth Pact. This 'depoliticised' central policy fields and left little room for manoeuvre for wage increases (for working-class people at least) and social policies. The role of monetary policy was therefore to exert a disciplinary neoliberalism, particularly on weaker economies that would face the highest costs in terms of unemployment (Carchedi, 2001). Moreover, monetary integration in the EU was also driven by a need to overcome the fractured and idiosyncratic finance systems of individual European countries to 'build a huge liquid market in Euro dominated securities arising from the material necessity to compete with the US' with the self-proclaimed aim of the EU becoming 'the cheapest and easiest place to do business in the world' (Grahl, 2005: 293).

The Primacy of Class

The reconfiguration of the Polish state has not been the result of genuflecting to the needs of international capital; it has been the outcome of wider struggles between different sections of the domestic ruling class and labour. Neoliberals had a very simple view of class in Poland. According to this view the old *nomenklatura* had to be disarmed in terms of their political and economic power and the working class were viewed as a stage army who had been usefully deployed in bringing about the downfall of the old regime, but who then needed re-education (literally) in the ways of the market economy. Lipton and Sachs (1990) bristled with palpable irritation at the failure of politicians and workers to understand that they needed to take a back seat so that the technocrats could implement the project of the market unimpeded. The notion of class has been eviscerated from most accounts of transformation, replaced in institutional accounts by obliquely subsuming it in references to social groups and elites whose interests are mediated by a neutral state.

Neo-Gramscians and other radicals, however, have reinserted class analysis into the transformation agenda, but in arguing that there was a bourgeois revolution without the bourgeoisie suggests the absence of a capitalist class in Poland (and the rest of CEE) before 1990 (Kowalik, 2001; Bohle, 2006). The analysis presented here departs from the capitalism without capitalists (Eyal *et al.*, 1998) account by arguing that a ruling class did exist in the communist period, who, even though not having formal ownership of assets, had control over them and reaped the benefits of their privileged position in accessing wide ranging advantages from housing and education to the consumption of material goods (Czbanski, 1983; Smolar, 1983).

The New Ruling Class

The emergence of a new ruling class, or some parts of it, has to be understood in the context of the reforms in the two decades preceding transformation. In the face of a rebellious working class, the Polish state adopted a policy of import-led growth in the 1970s, to try and increase standards of living (see previous chapter). These policies gave some sections of the *nomenklatura* exposure to and experience in dealing with Western firms, as well as all-important access to foreign networks and business opportunities. Some of these opportunities were capitalised on by the new entrepreneurs in the small firm sector; however, it was during the 1980s that opportunities for large scale kleptocracy opened up. The State Enterprise Act (1986) relaxed the stringent controls on the activities of SOEs, and enabled managers and well-placed bureaucrats to siphon off the most profitable activities into new firms of which they became the owners. They were able to obtain inputs cheaply or for nothing, and to use their contacts to establish lucrative markets and contracts. In the post-1990 period they were able to consolidate these gains in what is euphemistically called 'spontaneous privatisation' when they simply declared themselves the owners of these new firms (Schoenman, 2005).

By the mid-1980s the nature of the crisis facing Russia, and therefore Poland by extension, was that the system was no longer able to reproduce the conditions of their own ruling class (Clarke *et al.*, 1993). Their interests therefore no longer lay in preserving a stagnating and uncompetitive economy, but lay in more fully integrating with the global economy. Debates about privatisation have been reflected in the different interests of factions of the ruling class, with a schism between those who perceived their interests in lying with a domestic capitalism and those who had more to gain through international alliances and further integration with the global economy.

After 1990 in Poland, established groups, and more often than not the *nomenklatura*, served as gatekeepers for aid from the West as they were already part of networks in government, business and politics. Many astute individuals from the intelligentsia carved out a triad of business foundations and scholarly activities, as well as serving as consultants, brokers and partners. These opportunities were often fleeting, but their ambitions and activities were not curbed by rules and regulations, which were often non-existent or not enforced.

Anthropologist Janine Wedel (2001) observed the emergence of this new class and the way in which the *nomenklatura* managed to manipulate and take advantage of this new orbit of opportunity offered by Western assistance after 1989. The money that flooded in to support the 'market' and 'democracy' was built on the backbone of these 'energised elites' who cultivated international contacts and set up NGOs and 'foundations' to receive Western aid. Registering as a foundation typically provided favourable legal and tax advantages and by 2000, 5,000 foundations and 21,000 associations had been established, making it possible for private groups and institutions to legally appropriate public resources (Wedel, 2001).

Some have suggested the existence of a social vacuum and atomised behaviour in Poland, but in fact there was a complex system of informal relationships, such as patron-client or horizontal networks, which pervaded the economy and bureaucracy. Cliques of the old *nomenklatura* and Solidarity were therefore able to thrive and survive in a period of uncertainty and previous hierarchies where everything depended on patronage and personal connections were accentuated.

Shields (2004) rightly argues, 'Party membership is a poor predictor of the elite after communism', in other words the *nomenklatura* were not able to simply convert themselves into the new capitalist class. Some Solidarity activists were able to capitalise on this gravy train because by the 1980s they

> had redefined reform by redirecting their efforts from political to economic activity and preaching a new philosophy; form a club or lobby to do what needs doing and finance it through entrepreneurial activities. Some people who had previously exchanged underground leaflets at private gatherings turned to trading software and financial schemes. (Shields, 2004: 88)

The strand of the new ruling class that emerged from the ranks of Solidarity was also facilitated by the privatisation process, which enabled some individuals at least to obtain assets and enrich themselves. Although vigorously opposed by those that had promoted the neoliberal agenda, one of the main forms of privatisation for small and medium-sized firms were worker-manager buyouts. However, these were something of a misnomer as it was usually the managers, often members of Solidarity, who became the owners with token shares going to the workforce. Tittenbrun (1993) looks at the methods used to acquire companies cheaply, either by undervaluing them or borrowing the funds to buy them at low rates of interest. Having tracked companies over a ten-year period Tittenbrun (2005) documents the way in which workers' ownership of firms, measured in terms of shares, has dwindled to a tiny percentage of firms' stocks as ownership is concentrated in the hands of managers of Polish or international firms.

Transformation also created a new layer of managers whose interests were not those of ordinary people because their function was a 'staging post and direct intermediary for the implantation and reproduction of foreign capital' (Holman, 2004: 223). Transformation and the opportunities offered by foreign companies and consultancies have created a well paid and highly rewarded group of people whose interests lay with the new transnational capitalist class.

Workers

With a few notable exceptions, the role of organised labour is missing from or marginalised by accounts of transformation. Evolutionary and institutional accounts see economic agents in general as 'cultural dupes' (Jessop, 2001: 1228), the passive bearers of a set of habits, norms and routines from which they are unable to make a radical break. Other accounts see workers as victims of transformation, the object rather than the subject of history and peripheral to the massive restructuring that was happening. While neo-Gramscians acknowledge the importance of class, they are very pessimistic about the role of organised labour, seeing them as either passively or actively acquiescing to the neoliberal project.

The view that organised labour was only briefly centre stage in 1981 amounts to a dismissive account of history. These accounts fail fully to acknowledge the rich tradition of organised workers in Poland in the post-war period by treating the decades of communism as a homogeneous and undifferentiated epoch. This period was characterised by a sequence of revolt, reform and repression. Workers' rebellions took place in 1956, 1970, 1976 and 1980 (see Barker, 1986; Harman, 1988). These were usually triggered by an increase in prices, and followed by a two pronged approach from the ruling class, which were reforms aimed at pacification alongside brutal repression, purges and imprisonment.

The working class, organised or otherwise, have played a central role in patterning economic change in general, and in the pace and form of transformation in particular (Clarke *et al.*, 1993; Thirkell *et al.*, 1995). Further, post-1990 the role of working-class resistance has been pivotal in patterning the dialectic of change in Poland (Hardy and Rainnie, 1996). Many accounts of trade unions in Poland have cited declining membership, because of restructuring and entrenched ideological differences, as sufficient evidence to condemn them to the margins. Although this may amount to wishful thinking in some quarters it does not accord either with the role that trade unions played in the early days of transformation or with their recent responses to the challenges of the new economy. Organised labour as a force for change has largely been written off or dismissed as either impotent or active supporters of the market (Gardawski *et al.*, 1999; Cox and Mason, 2000; Ost, 2002; Gardawski, 2003; Martin and Cristescu-Martin, 2004) and it is claimed that their frustration has been channelled into nationalism and xenophobia (Ost, 2006). This pessimistic view fails to take account of protests and demonstrations both at workplace or national level, which are not always manifest in strike statistics. Further, from the late 1990s some trades unions have been reinvigorated by a step change as the main players have recruited aggressively in new sectors of the economy. However, since 2006 the most significant development has been the increased confidence workers have shown in fighting for higher pay as a result of a fall in unemployment and tighter labour markets. These themes are explored in much more detail in Chapter 7.

Conclusion

The Marxist analysis presented here sees the development, collapse and subsequent transformation of the Polish economy (as well as other post-communist economies) both in the context of and contributing to changes in the global economy. Not only should transformation be understood as being combined, it is also inherently uneven. Outcomes and endpoints are not predetermined. The state, the institutional architecture of individual capitalist economies and the balance of class forces have been critical in shaping the content and processes of transformation.

The law of uneven and combined development can only serve as a guide to an investigation and analysis of the processes at work in a given social environment. It can help to understand the peculiarities of past history and aid an analysis of unfolding social processes. Echoing Bond (1999) the importance of combined and uneven development is that it allows the exploration of systematic unevenness in spheres such as production, social reproduction and human domination along lines of class, gender and ethnicity, which stresses the social damage associated with uneven capitalist development.

4

'NOT JUST AN INSIDE JOB': CONSTRUCTING CONSENT FOR NEOLIBERALISM

There has been an important ideological dimension to transformation in Poland, which has involved ingraining a particular set of ideas and beliefs associated with the market. Notions of private property, competition for scarce resources and the assumption of individuals motivated by self-interest are presented as unchallengeable assumptions of economic life in neoliberal analysis. The commodification of everything has to become 'an ethic in itself, capable of acting as a guide to all human action, and substituting for all previously held beliefs' (Treanor, 2005).

Even though neoliberalism is neither a coherent nor a self-conscious strategy on the part of the ruling class, they needed continually to justify a particular set of ideas to themselves and also gain broad acquiescence in order to reduce resistance to the restructuring of economies as a whole and individual workplaces. Therefore the ideas and discourses of neoliberalism are 'enabling myths' that aim to create a deceptive clarity that a particular way of organising economic and social life is self-evident (Dugger, 2000). In the context of the transformation of CEE in general, and Poland in particular, the market has been a pivotal enabling myth. The notion of the invisible hand is invoked to suggest that the market will produce economic outcomes that are both efficient and equitable, and that will produce economic growth. However, the discourse of the market and associated enabling myths have not appeared spontaneously, but have been promoted by influential agents who have attempted to shift understandings about economic behaviour, both deliberately and unconsciously. From the national level to the workplace, those in privileged situations have attempted to marginalise old ways of doing things, especially if they involve notions of collectivity, and engender what are regarded as new and appropriate understandings that are compatible with the market and integration with global capitalism.

Creating hegemony is important at all levels of analysis and neo-Gramscians have been concerned with developing this notion in the context of international relations and identifying a transnational capitalist class who perpetuate and spread these ideas (Cox, 1993; Sklair, 1997; Gill, 2001; Shields, 2003 and 2004).[1] Globalising bureaucrats are important for laying the conditions for the internationalisation of capital. These instruments of 'rational', Western modernisation operating in CEE include some of the most perfectly honed weapons of global governance that have evolved in the post-war period (Baker and Welsh, 1999); most notably these include the World Bank, IMF, G7 and the EU. Within certain limits powerful countries try to create international regimes that favour particular firms and sectors by setting the rules of engagement (Hollingsworth and Boyer, 1997).

By USAID's own admission, 'The idea of aid to Poland, and all of central Europe, was seen as the new Marshall Plan designed to revitalise post-Cold War Europe, but reconstructing perceptions would prove a lot harder than the brick and mortar post-World War Two' (USAID, 2002a). Therefore the task of reintegrating these economies with global capitalism required investment in winning 'hearts and minds' as well as the nuts and bolts of laying the groundwork of the market economy. Western aid and the proliferation of agencies who queued up to deliver it need to be understood in the context of powerful national and supra national organisations that seek to mould productive systems in their own image, establishing ideological consensus to demonstrate the viability of capitalist systems. Grandiose claims about pouring in aid on the scale of the Marshall Plan at the beginning of transformation turned out to be more hot air than substance, and according to an Organisation of Economic Cooperation and

Development (OECD) study in 1995 aid had fallen dramatically short of what was needed (Smith and Hardy, 2004).

This chapter begins by looking at the activities of the IMF and the way that conditionality imposed a strait jacket on the options for transformation; it then compares the enormous efforts by US and European capital to secure the 'right sort of capitalism'. The second part of the chapter examines the role of consultants, who played an unprecedented role in implementing the policies and projects of their paymasters and to some extent became the unacknowledged authors of transformation on the ground.

IMF: Carrots and Sticks

In the early 1990s the IMF was the primary vehicle of US and leading European capitalist economies for integrating a vast new territory with the world economy along neoliberal lines. The doublespeak of neoliberalism usually meant exhorting or coercing weaker states into opening their markets, while protecting their own. In its role as banker of the last resort the IMF provided debt ridden countries with the financial liquidity they needed, but stringent conditions were always attached. The IMF eventually signed conditionality agreements with every country of the former Soviet Union and Eastern Europe.[2]

In Poland the IMF had been one of the main authors of shock therapy in 1989, which comprised the usual package of cuts in government spending, particularly in welfare, and high rates of interest to control inflation. Initial enthusiasm quickly evaporated as unemployment increased and poverty and hardship grew. In these circumstances the role of the IMF was to keep weak and fragile governments in the first parliament on track and push through further reforms. More than one governing coalition was prevented from retreating from harsh economic policies in order to implement a budget that was perceived as 'objectively' necessary to establish credibility in the eyes of global capital and currency markets. Therefore governments hewed to an orthodox conception of macroeconomic stabilisation. Stone points to the way that the IMF used both conditionality and coercion to continue to drive through reforms and bolster the position of those Polish politicians who were wedded to a neoliberal agenda:[3]

> the IMF did not budge from its role as the enforcer of programmatic details. In 1990 and 1991 it suspended programs immediately when Poland missed its targets and insisted that the programs be brought back on track before new lending could begin. In 1992, while Poland did the hard work of finishing the macroeconomic stabilisation begun two years before, the Fund waited for positive proof that the budget was on track before restarting the program. The result was that, in Poland, the IMF bolstered the position of reformers. The reformers always insisted that they were carrying out Polish reforms, not IMF agendas, but they were able to argue that the IMF seal of approval carried weight with international capital markets as with the Paris and London creditors' clubs and was essential to establish the credibility of Polish programs. (2002: 114, 115)

Rachel Epstein (2005) gives a fascinating insight into the tactics used by the IMF and other organisations when they consider that one of their protégés has eschewed their advice. Even before 1990 Poland had begun restructuring its financial sector and USAID affiliates had advised Poland on how to redesign its structures to create the National Bank of Poland (NBP) and nine state owned commercial banks (Stirewalt and Horner, 2000; Johnston, 2001). The NBP was underpinned by the principle of Central Bank Independence (CBI), which had the effect of subjugating monetary policy to international financial markets and wresting it from the political influence of governments. However, the election of the post-communist SLD[4] government in 1994 threatened to upset this.

Under pressure from a working class angry at the effects of shock therapy, the SLD government wanted to implement less draconian monetary policies and to this end wanted the NBP to surrender its 'independence' so that it could be more influenced by the government and harnessed to reforms. This was a complete anathema to USAID, the IMF and World Bank who moved into action to support their allies, the Polish opponents of the legislation, to ensure its defeat. They argued that although CBI was relatively new this was a natural form of organisation and reflected the norm for industrial democracies (Grabel, 2002). USAID and the IMF held meetings with the officials of the NBP to brief them for their performance before the *Sejm* (parliament) so they could argue that low inflation should be maintained at the expense of competing policy goals. Also, this strategic coalition discredited the SLD legislation by using the EU's prestige to narrow the definition of what constituted appropriate policy, even without using explicit conditionality. The president of the European Monetary Institute visited Poland to cast doubt on the SLD's claim that their legislation was consistent with that of the EU. The political conflict over CBI was ultimately resolved with the SLD legislation being 'quietly shelved'.

The Panacea of Privatisation

After 1990 the most pressing task from the point of view of neoliberal economists, international institutions and national governments was privatisation, which was urged with messianic fervour as the universal panacea for transformation. A USAID official based in Central Europe remarked that 'privatisation is our first, second, and third priority'. USAID's Action Plan for US Assistance to Central and Eastern Europe of 1991 envisaged that

> a large portion of assistance for economic restructuring will be targeted at the privatisation process which is essential to the success of overall macroeconomic reform ... Large scale privatisation of these SOEs is essential to the success of economic reform. The US has excellent capability to provide assistance to this end, and the governments of several Eastern European countries. (USAID, 2002a: 50)

David Ellerman (2001) from the World Bank writes:

> The Western advisors were marketing themselves as the intellectual saviours of the benighted East by putting the scientific prestige of neoclassical economics behind one of the most cockamamie social engineering schemes of the twentieth century ... Only a mixture of American triumphalism and

the academic arrogance of neoclassical economics could produce such a
lethal dose of gall. (quoted in Appel, 2004: 5)

Privatisation was a way of 'constitutionalising capital' through
securing property rights and freedom for investors and putting in
place measures which ensured that free enterprise was the primary
vehicle for accumulation (Gill, 2001). Privatisation was trumpeted
as the bedrock of a market economy, but more expediently the
international ruling class were anxious that the 'crown jewels'
of these economies were put on sale for the predations of their
transnational firms as soon as possible. This was reflected in the
fact that one of the first projects financed by 'aid' from the World
Bank, European Union and US was to carry out an inventory of
exactly what there was in the bargain basement of the Polish
economy. In 1994 I was shown 'catalogues of capital' which
comprised a large number of thick reports gathering dust on the
shelves of the PAIZ, which provided the details of firms that were
ripe for the picking.

The UK method of privatisation was used as the template for
selling assets. However, problems with converting SOEs into joint
stock companies and selling the shares soon became apparent.
The institutional architecture was lacking, and in addition a low
level of savings meant that the vast majority of people simply
did not have the resources to buy shares. Undeterred by early
teething problems, the government spurred on by its advisors
used an array of front and back door methods to privatise these
firms and indeed whole sectors. The desire to sell off these assets
quickly led to a version of buy one get one free in some sectors.
When a large British TNC, BOC,[5] wanted to buy two factories
that made industrial gases they had to take ownership of other
smaller and less profitable ones that were in the bundle (Hardy,
1998). When large foreign firms were forced to buy state owned
Polish companies that they regarded as surplus to requirement,
they were quickly closed or disposed of.

The link between aid, privatisation and foreign investment
was explicit in some programmes. Under the *Stabilisation,
Restructuring and Privatisation Programme* (SRPP) the European

Bank for Reconstruction and Development (EBRD) sanctioned 80 million USD funding for restructuring 40 companies to improve their situation in preparation for privatisation (Smith and Hardy, 2004). The stated goal of the SRPP was to make the companies attractive to foreign investors by imposing Western-style governance. USAID threw their financial resources behind the privatisation of flagship large industries in the belief that it would have a demonstration effect. However, funding of 3.7 million USD led to only four SOEs being privatised (Wedel, 2001).

Not all the techniques used to transfer capital to the private sector were so transparent and Amsden *et al.* (1994) cite an example of backdoor privatisation. While there was public debate about mass privatisation in the *Sejm* and wider society, the World Bank with the Polish government introduced the *Enterprise and Bank Restructuring Privatisation Programme*. This transferred the debt of insolvent SOEs to the Polish banks (soon to be privatised by foreign investors themselves), which meant that with a sleight of hand they became significant owners and major agents of restructuring.

Despite these and other ingenious initiatives the process of selling off firms was painfully slow. The reality was that Polish firms considered strategic for TNCs, either because of their domestic market (confectionery and detergent firms) or because of their technological capability or potential (power transformers and automobiles), were snapped up right at the beginning of the 1990s. This left a rump of unsellable and uncompetitive firms. The vast majority of SMEs were sold through the worker-management buyout method, while 500 companies were privatised through the *Mass Privatisation Programme*. This method bundled the firms into 13 National Investment Funds, which were managed by a consortium of foreign and Polish consultants and foreign banks (see Hardy and Rainnie, 1996).

The claims of neoclassical economics were parroted by reformers to suggest that privatisation would restore firms to the invisible and neutral hand of the market to form the foundation of a competitive economy. However, privatisation did not lead to competition, rather it has led to the concentration of key sectors and their domination by TNCs, as well as the enrichment of a small group of Poles. Production targets have been replaced by privatisation targets, and in both cases success was measured by the number, not the quality of these activities.

There were ample opportunities for corruption and shady practices as both consultants and local government officials had abundant openings for deal making based on insider information. One serious conflict of interest lay in the fact that Western firms doing asset valuations for the government often also had clients who were potential buyers at the prices that consultants established (see Tittenbrun, 2005). This meant that there was an incentive to undervalue some firms. There was huge anger directed at the corruption of insiders such as high officials in the Ministry of Privatisation. For example, the Deputy Minister in charge of joint ventures from 1989 to 1992 also owned and operated a consulting firm that specialised in joint ventures, and when this was outlawed he simply handed over the firm to another close associate (Wedel, 2001).

Charges of industrial espionage were common, and managers of the Huta Sendzimira steelworks in Kraków suggested to me that visitors arriving under the guise of potential foreign investors were actually sizing up the extent to which they represented competition. A recurring theme in interviews about aspirations for transformation was that a sort of Polish capitalism was assumed and people were unprepared for the extent of foreign ownership and way in which TNCs had so quickly bought up the 'family silver'. This was reflected in a banner with which trade unions decorated the entrance to the Ursus tractor factory: 'A foreign elite steals from us while the Polish people are at the bottom'.

Making Poland Safe for US Capitalism

Although donors of 'aid' from all organisations and governments were enthusiastic and convinced of the centrality of privatisation, the intervention of the US stands out as trying to put in place much deeper and far reaching initiatives to reconstruct Polish capitalism. These attempts to shift the political and ideological climate in profound ways had their most naked manifestation in the form of USAID. According to Donald Presley, the then Assistant Administrator for Europe and Eurasia, this ideological onslaught was deemed necessary because 'we thought that democracy was very fragile and could easily roll back' (USAID, 2002b).

Between 1990 and 2001 USAID were involved in 400 activities as they pumped a billion dollars of assistance into Poland. In the first few years this involved financing a range of activities that lacked coherence and focus. They admit that, 'Those involved in the aid process ten years ago say there was not much of a plan of what to do first as much as a recognition that a broad approach was essential' (USAID, 2002b).

By the mid-1990s there were 85 US-based governmental organisations scattered across 1,500 locations, the management of which was handled out of Washington. By the end of 1996, after throwing dollars at many disparate projects, the priorities for US capitalism became clear. Efforts were concentrated on four areas: private sector development, financial sector development and local government reform as well as continuing efforts to imbue Polish trade unions, or at least Solidarity, with a commitment to a free market model of capitalism.

The Polish American Enterprise Fund (PAEF) of 254 million USD accounted for nearly one quarter of the total USAID budget. Its primary aim was to encourage private enterprise by taking shares in Polish firms or engaging in joint ventures. From their point of view the PAEF had two advantages: it accelerated the privatisation process and returned a profit of 120 million USD by 2000.

The financial sector was the second target for aid. Poland simply lacked many of the instruments of finance that had developed in Western capitalist economies and USAID went about providing the resources to construct the institutions that would allow it to integrate with global financial markets. This included projects to ensure that Poland's rules of the game were compatible with those of international finance, which included assistance with bank supervision, technical assistance to the Stock Exchange and developing new financial instruments such as OTCs (Over

Table 4.1 Selected USAID Projects (over 5 million USD), 1990–2001

Name of activity	Polish counterpart	Implementing partner	Time period	Funding USD
Polish-American Enterprise Fund	Various private enterprises	Polish American Enterprise Fund	1990–2005	254,500,000
Restructuring agriculture and agribusiness	Private agribusiness, private cooperatives & government agencies	US Department of Agriculture, ACDI/VOCA, Land O'Lakes	1990–98	25,717,00
Regional energy and restructuring programme	Ministry of Industry and Trade, power distribution sector, municipalities	Bechtel, RCG Haggler, Bailley & Company, Electrotek US energy association, New York state electric and gas	1991–99	16,700,152
Privatisation and enterprise restructuring	Polish Banks, LOT Polish airlines, Polish securities Commission	Coopers and Lybrand, KPMG, Price Waterhouse, Deloitte Touche	1991–96	24,680,000
Local government partnership scheme	Gminas nationwide	Cheminoco Ltd	1997–2001	25,912,247
OTC (Over the Counter market)	Polish brokerage houses	KPMG/Barents	1995–98	5,087,984
Support to Solidarity BKN	Solidarity Bureau for Consultation and Negotiations	Free trade union institute	1994–99	5,883,955
Georgetown University Training Programme	Various trainees from public and local sectors	Georgetown University	1990–99	10,116,060

Source: Adapted by author from USAID, 2002b

the Counter market in derivatives).[6] This was driven by the fact that the US (followed by the UK) is home to the largest global financial institutions meaning that it is the main beneficiary of liberalisation. This has been reflected in the way that both the US and the UK have consistently and vigorously lobbied for the opening up of the financial sector at World Trade Organisation (WTO) negotiations.

A more sophisticated financial system was also important to support the realisation of surplus value in the real goods sector – in other words, to ensure that consumers and intermediaries had the wherewithal to buy US goods and services. In 1996, this was well illustrated by the way in which the General Motors Acceptance Corporation (GMAC), with the PAEF and the Polish Private Equity Fund, bought a controlling share in Polbank SA (formerly Bank Ogrodnictwa Hortex) (General Motors, 1996). Although the bank continued its original business its main reason for existence was to offer finance to Opel (owned by General Motors) dealers and their customers in Poland. According to General Motors, 'The Polish market is an important one for GMAC due to the great potential for automotive production and growth of consumer financing' (General Motors, 1996). Therefore the financial means was provided for dealers and consumers to purchase their products.

One of the most substantial grants from USAID was given to aid the reform of local and regional government. The perceived weakness of central government in Warsaw made regional and local government the prime movers in the reforms (Chowaniec and Harbinson, 1994). Large projects in local and regional government were driven by two agendas, first that in the event of a left turn or the election of an unsympathetic government the regions and localities, if carefully nurtured and inculcated with the right ideas, could act as a bulwark against a policy reversal at national level. Further, the regions and localities would be the space in which privatisation could be given a further impetus in the areas of health, water and transport. The *Democratic Governance and Public Administration Project* (DGPA) was given a budget 12.8 million USD on the basis that 'a promising partnership could be nurtured between local governments in Poland and the American government itself'. It was aimed at training and bolstering a regional and local level of government with intensive and extensive training. This included technical training, installing internet software and implementation of local finance (previously controlled by national government) with over 300,000 Polish employees trained in America.

USAID provided finance to test the new regional structures in Nowy Sącz in the south of Poland, and these became the model for the legislative reform of regions in 1998. The USAID agenda was to give the private sector a central role in public sector provision, and in 1999 consultants financed by the scheme helped one small *gmina*[7] privatise six village clinics. However, not all localities were so enthusiastic about privatisation. In 1994 workers in Łódź organised a local campaign backed up with strike action and successfully prevented the privatisation of water and sewage by the French firm Generale d'Eaux. Similarly the proposals to privatise water and sewage were defeated in Poznań in 2002 (Hall *et al.*, 2005).

As Table 4.1 shows, another strand of aid was focused on trade unions. In the early 1990s many resources had been put into developing links with Solidarity's leadership whose rhetoric about markets and opposition to the communist regime appeared to make them obvious allies in the Polish labour market. This included taking Solidarity leaders on long all expenses paid visits hosted by the AFL-CIO Free Trade Unions to the US.[8] For example, between 1996 and 2000 at least three groups of Solidarity leaders from leading SOEs in Wrocław went on these trips. From 1994 direct support was given to Solidarity to establish 'bureaux for consultation and negotiation in different regions to deal with workers lay offs' (USAID, 2002a).

In the Huta Sendzimira steelworks finance had been provided to run courses for trade unionists to educate them in the workings of the 'market economy' using orthodox economics texts. These initiatives were designed to reinforce the message that redundancies and unemployment were an unfortunate, but necessary aspect of the new times and central to the workings of the market.

Increasingly workers became less and less convinced, if they were ever convinced in the first place, that they should be making sacrifices where others were clearly reaping the benefits.

Taken together these initiatives by USAID amounted to huge traffic across the Atlantic. The *East Central European Scholarship Program* (established in 1990) provided training in the US for thousands of Polish 'democratic' leaders in the areas of public policy, administration, health reform, finance and banking, business administration and education. In the other direction armies of volunteers, mostly with no knowledge of Polish or Poland, ranging from MBA graduates (through the Peace Corps) and retired business people, arrived in Poland to dispense advice. However varied the origins of these helpers they all possessed an unshakeable faith in the correctness of the ideas they were proselytising, which was singing from the song sheet of neoliberalism.

Making Poland Safe for European Capitalism

In some quarters US imperialism and Anglo-Saxon capitalism have been viewed as the main dangers to democratic processes in the emerging economies of Central and Eastern Europe. The corollary of this was to press the advantage of a 'return to Europe' and membership of the European Union as the lesser of two evils. However, as we saw in the previous chapter increased integration with Europe, either through the *ad hoc* arrangements of the 1990s or full accession to the EU in 2004, has deepened and strengthened the neoliberal agenda (Holman, 2004). Further, notwithstanding occasional trade spats, an integrated Europe rather than being a threat to America represents the culmination of its efforts (Callinicos, 2001). Earlier notions that EU enlargement provided the best way to ensure democracy in *all* of post-communist Eastern Europe was immediately undermined by the inclusion of only the first five states and the exclusion of the remaining applicants.[9] It was considered by the ruling classes of current EU members and representatives of capital that the costs to European capitalism outweighed the advantages they would reap in terms of new markets for goods and new destinations for foreign investment in the excluded countries.

Initially, aid to CEE was through PHARE (Poland and Hungary – Assistance for Economic Restructuring) (1996). PHARE offered a similar package to USAID with the explicit aim of economic restructuring, privatisation and helping 'build democracy'. The first phase of aid in the early 1990s was aimed at basic macroeconomic stabilisation, humanitarian assistance and the supply of basic imports necessary to sustain agriculture and industry.

The Association Agreements in 1992 were a high profile initiative on the part of the EU, which purported to liberalise trade with Partners in Transitions. However, at the same time as espousing the benefits of free trade and cross-border investment the reality was one of protectionism on the part of the EU. Trade was severely limited in those goods in which Poland had comparative advantage, namely steel and agriculture (which accounted for 35 per cent of exports) (Messerlin, 1992). Rules of origin placed restrictions on importing anything to the EU whose content was less than 60 per cent Polish. This is part of a consistent pattern of rhetoric whereby the EU and its individual states have tried to proselytise a variant of free market capitalism that departs sharply from the 'real existing capitalism' practised in their home economies.

If the first stage of aid from the EU was unfocused, after 1993, the main thrust of PHARE shifted to preparing countries for membership as agreed in the Copenhagen Criteria. The accession negotiations involved ensuring that each applicant state was able to take on the full commitment of EU membership as defined in the 31 chapters and 80,000 pages of the *acquis communautaire*. The main element of the enlargement strategy of the EU demanded more measures of deregulation and liberalisation. The small print of the neoliberal agenda involved the harmonisation of legislative frameworks and laws along with a dose of social protection in case social discontent derailed reforms.

The Role of Big Business

The institutions of transnational business such as the Transatlantic Business Dialogue, the World Economic Forum, the International Chamber of Commerce and the Competitiveness Advisory Group played an active part in trying to mobilise economic interests, governments and trade unions in their desire to make CEE safe for US and European capitalism. The European Round Table of Industrialists (ERT) in particular played a pivotal role in trying to secure the interests of capital and exerted a strong influence on policies that were in its interests. This included most obviously the implementation of the single market, the creation of the Trans-European Network infrastructure scheme, the restructuring of European education policy and the whittling away of social protection measures (Doherty and Hoedeman, 1994). The ERT agenda was clear:

> What industry cannot accept is that the pursuit of other objectives is used as an excuse for damaging the wealth creating machine itself, whether by raising its costs or blocking its development. There can be no healthy society or healthy environment without a healthy economy to pay for them. (ERT, 1993)

The pre-accession strategy was devised by the EU Commission with the support of the ERT. The latter consisted of the chief executives of European TNCs and represented the interests of transnational capital (Bornschier, 2000; van Apeldoorn, 2000 and 2003). There was a symbiotic relationship between the EU Commission and big business, with the former relying on the structural power and cooperation of the ERT, and the ERT needing the Commission to initiate appropriate legislative proposals within the EU. From 1997 the ERT intensified its lobbying, urging the EU to reform its institutional structures to facilitate enlargement and to work closely with the governments of applicant countries towards meeting the EU conditions for membership.

Therefore the EU Commission and the ERT gave an ideological direction to the overall process of European integration including unleashing market liberalisation for candidate countries. Bieler (2002) concludes that overall, the promise of membership ensured a restructuring of CEE in line with the EU's neoliberal trajectory and satisfied the need of European transnational capital for the further expansion of capitalist accumulation. In turn, it has fulfilled the objective of the Polish ruling class to secure external restructuring.

One initiative that was trumpeted as filling the role of a development bank for the post-communist countries of Russia and CEE was the establishment of the EBRD in 1991.[10] For the first few years the EBRD was mired in scandals with reports of extravagant office parties, private jets, marble clad buildings and exorbitant salaries for directors with very little to show in the form of lending. The EBRD's aims repeated the usual mantra of structural and sectoral reforms, competition, privatisation and entrepreneurship.

The difference between the EBRD and other institutions was its focus on the development of an infrastructure that could support the activities of other sections of capital. In short, it has provided the finance to oil the wheels of large scale capital privatisations, which were too expensive and too risky for a single firm. For example, it provided 63 million euros over 14 years to Pątnów-Adamów-Konin SA – Poland's largest power company. However, far from promoting competition, this company is owned and controlled by Elektrim SA, a huge Polish conglomerate with activities in a wide spread of sectors (see Hardy and Rainnie, 1996). The EBRD also provided the resources to upgrade and clear the debts of the PKP (Polskie Koleje Państwowe), the Polish Rail company, so that it could be made attractive for private capital. This exhibits a similar pattern to British privatisations such as British Airways, where it was not privatisation *per se* that produced so-called efficiencies, but millions of pounds of public money used to restructure the company in advance to make it more attractive to private capital.

The Marriott Men

As important as the new managerialist discourse itself has been the growth of agents responsible for its spread across the globe who form an emergent and increasingly powerful group. Consultants have found rich pickings in their role as intermediaries between the donors and recipients of aid. They have introduced material and discursive practices, tried and tested in the many other countries in which they operate, and often transferred unadapted 'off the shelf' solutions. Gramsci anticipated the role of these organic intellectuals:

> If not all entrepreneurs, at least an elite amongst them must have the capacity to be organisers of society in general, including all its complex organism of services, right up to the state organism, because of the need to create the conditions most favourable to the expansion of their own class; or at the least they must possess the capacity to choose deputies (specialised employees) to whom to entrust this activity of organising the general system of relationships external to the business itself. (Gramsci in Hoare and Nowell-Smith, 1971: 6)

There are hard and soft aspects to the operations of consultants. The former include tools of restructuring such as the transfer of accounting systems, logistics and quality control, while the soft aspects include the production and distribution of new management techniques and fads. Thrift argues that consultants provide 'a kind of grammar of business imperatives' (Thrift, 2001: 416), which constitute general principles of business life, and gather intelligence through continually monitoring new organisational innovation and best practice.

Table 4.2 gives a flavour of the level of involvement of the big six consultancy services and the degree to which they were deeply involved in the process of restructuring in Poland. It also gives some idea of the way in which 'aid' money largely and directly benefited these large transnational firms.

Aid abroad meant lucrative business back home. A US firm, Chemonics, won a 26 million USD contract to promote local democracy in Poland, which was described as 'one of the most ambitious aid programs in the former Soviet bloc' (Dobbs, 2001). An analysis of the project shows that the bulk of it was spent on aid consultants, many of them Americans, for salaries, airfares, cars and support staff in Washington. The USAID website proclaims that 'the principal beneficiaries of America's foreign assistance programs has always been the United States'. Keeping money

Table 4.2   Consulting Firms in Poland

Consulting Firm	Major Projects	Foreign Clients
KPMG	• Preparation of the financial part of privatisation prospectus for Bank Slaski • Advising Privatisation Ministry on sale of ZCP paper mill, privatisation of the furniture sector • Advice for PepsiCo for their investment in Wedel SA	Nestle, Henkel, ABB, Gillette Cussons, Union Carbide, Ahlstrom Phillips, Saatchi & Saatchi, Cargill
Arthur Andersen	• Preparation of restructuring programme for coal mining • Efficiency improvement programme FSM car company • Production scheme for Cinquecento • Consulting for government on sale of FSM Fiat	United Distillers, Cadbury Schweppes, Sarah Lee Corporation, Colgate Palmolive, Levi Strauss, Alcatel, Polish-American Enterprise Fund
Deloitte Touche	No information provided	Chrysler, Coca Cola, General Motors, Hambro Bank, Procter & Gamble, Reynolds Tobacco International
Ernst and Young	• Public sale of TONSIL company • Analysis of meat and potato industries for Ministry of Privatisation • Market research for Holiday Inn • Consulting for Gerber and ABB on acquisition of enterprises	Gerber Basic American Foods, ABB, Holiday Inn, Gianni Versace
Cooper Lybrand	• Restructuring programmes commissioned by World Bank on power and electricity sectors • Preparation of new management system for Polish railway (PKP) • Auditing AT&T, Unilever, ING Bank • Pre-privatisation studies in paper, paper products, automotive spare parts, industrial gases commissioned by Ministry of Privatisation	AT&T, Unilever, ING Bank, Polish American Enterprise Fund
Price Waterhouse	No specific information on Poland but widespread involvement on restructuring and privatisation of various industries worldwide	British Rail Engineering, Telecom Australia, Rover Group, Skoda, Hungarian State Property

Source: Adapted by author from British News from Poland, 1993

firmly in American hands is reinforced by laws that obliged USAID and Chemonics to use American sub-contractors and firms.

A Polish consultant recalls 'dozens of Americans arriving with their wives, dogs, cats and children, causing many more problems than they were able to solve' (Wedel, 2000). He noted that the cost of employing an American in Poland was around 200,000 USD a year – many times higher than the salary of a Pole with equivalent qualifications. Reactions from Poles ranged from qualified praise to outright hostility. The mayor of a lakeside resort town said, 'When we agreed to cooperate with them, we thought we would get something concrete out of it ... we were looking for tangible results, but all we got was a lot of paper and books' (Wedel, 2000). Even Poles who were well disposed to USAID had reservations about the manner in which the know-how was delivered. A leading Polish expert on local government reform and a former cabinet minister described the approach as colonialist; the attitude of foreign experts was, 'We have the money, we are wise, we know what to do' (Wedel, 2000).

Most aid was focused on privatisation and the development of the private sector. Consultants were initially welcomed and then the pejorative term 'Marriott men' entered popular Polish vocabulary to describe 'experts' who arrived for short periods of time and rarely left their luxury hotels, let alone Warsaw. These advisors developed weak links with recipients and at best had a very scanty understanding of the countries in which they were dispensing advice. The US General Accounting Office (GAO) confirmed reports of Polish officials that early technical assistance in the banking sector involved many consultants coming to Warsaw for one or two day stays, and producing reports that simply repeated what they had been told by Polish officials (US GAO (1995) quoted in Wedel, 2000). However, whatever the Marriott brigade failed to deliver in terms of expertise, they compensated for in terms of the hard currency they contributed as they patronised the best hotels and restaurants.

Many of the policy recommendations coming from those prevaricating from the comfort of their offices in Washington or Warsaw, or the consultants who took off-the-shelf solutions, were oblivious to history and the specific local conditions in which these prescriptions were applied. A Polish Ministry of Industry official who compared consultants to 'a surgeon who comes, does his work without talking with the patient, and leaves without checking to see whether the operation was successful' reflects the fact that advisors did not have to face up to the consequences of the policies that they foisted on people. Jeffrey Sachs has been a particular target for criticism. He was a prominent advisor and architect of shock therapy who jetted into Warsaw for a few days at a time, in between trips to Prague, Moscow and São Paulo, during the crucial period of its initial reforms in 1989–90. Professor of Economics, Grzegorz Kołodko, director of Institute of Finance (and later Deputy Prime Minister and Minister of Finance) said:

> If there's a difference between Professor Sachs and myself, it's that I'm not from outside. I could have a cynical, purely professional ... relationship, like [with] Argentina – I travel there, live in a five star hotel, and I say 'lower real wages by 20 per cent overnight. And you have to stand it because you don't have any other way out [and] this results from my economic analysis' ... If it works then I will take the credit. If it doesn't work, then I can say: 'You Argentinians, you have screwed up again'. (Wedel, 2001: 57)

Conclusion

The efforts of international organisations, the US and EU bolstered by a myriad of smaller initiatives amounted to an unprecedented campaign to extend and consolidate the ideological hegemony of neoliberalism to support the large scale restructuring of these economies and their integration with the global economy. However, the role of international organisations and their advisors and consultants are important, but should not be privileged in the overall analysis of Polish capitalism. For Gowan (1995) the drivers of neoliberalism were almost completely external, but this neglects the importance of domestic classes in collaborating with, acquiescing in or resisting these ideas and practices.

There are two perspectives on the huge ideological intervention made under the auspices of aid in Polish transformation. The first focuses on the greed and arrogance of the people and organisations that delivered these so-called aid packages and the complete inappropriateness of the policies that they peddled. The second perspective locates these interventions within a much wider political economy, where the ruling classes in the US and Europe, and the institutions they dominate, have extended the ideological conditions to support a particular variant of free market capitalism.

5

CATCHING UP OR LAGGING BEHIND? POLAND IN THE GLOBAL DIVISION OF LABOUR

By 2000, the 'red in tooth and claw' view of capitalism, underpinned by a faith in unbridled market forces, was replaced with a new orthodoxy and panacea for economic success that went beyond the neoliberal agenda. Market forces were no longer regarded as sufficient to shift the trajectories and integrate developing economies, or those in transition, successfully with the global economy (World Bank, 2002). Under the banner of the 'new economy' academics and policy makers have seized upon recent changes to suggest that we are living in an entirely new phase of capitalism. This view characterises contemporary capitalism as technology driven, where 'creating assets depends less and less on physical mass, and more and more on intangibles such as human intelligence, creativity and even personal warmth' (Coyle and Quah, 2002: 8). It is this 'knowledge economy' that countries need to sign up to if they are going to compete successfully in the global economy. This view is reinforced from a European perspective by the Sapir Report in 2004 (Sapir *et al.*, 2003; Sapir Group, 2005; Sapir, 2006), which views the poor performance of European capitalism as a symptom of its failure to transform into an 'innovation-based economy'.

In some quarters a new spin is being given to the deindustrialisation story. In 2004 a British economist and journalist, Will Hutton (2004), declared that mass production in the advanced developed economies was dead. He argues that there is a new global division of labour with advanced market economies becoming 'weightless' as they concentrate on knowledge-based functions, while production moves to China and South-East Asia. This has very strong echoes of the New International Division of Labour Theory which suggested that, while some countries are 'post-industrial' and at the highest stage of development in high skill, knowledge-based service production, others are lower down this hierarchy, at the stage of specialising in low or high technology goods (Froebel *et al.*, 1980).

With regard to debates about restructuring the global economy there are two competing claims as to how Poland might fit into the emerging European and global divisions of labour. One story is that Poland is benefiting from the fragmentation of the value chains of large TNCs and integrating into their production and marketing arrangements, which is enabling it to upgrade on the basis of having high levels of education, human capital and technical capacity (Kaminski and Smarzynska, 2001). A less sanguine view is that Poland is tentatively linked by a few outposts of foreign capital and therefore only marginally integrated into Western production systems and minimally into innovation systems (Martin, 1998). Others have suggested that the post-communist countries are integrating on the basis of becoming sites for low cost wage production – sort of 'maquiladoras' of the European Union (Ellingstad, 1997).

This chapter examines the particular meaning of the 'new economy' in the case of Poland's transforming economy, and the way it is the product of new disciplines and imperatives that have been imposed as a result of rapid integration into the global economy. The pivotal role of foreign direct investment (FDI) is discussed in relation to how far foreign capital is locking Poland into global flows and, in particular, the role it plays in the restructuring of the value chains of transnational corporations. Further, I discuss the way in which the growing unevenness of the European economy has seen Poland emerge as a supplier of a reserve army of labour to economies such as the UK and Ireland.

Restructuring Work

Expanding the Service Sector

In the last 15 years the Polish economy has undergone a profound restructuring that has fallen into roughly three phases. In the early to mid-1990s exposure to the international economy brought about the bankruptcy and closure of large SOEs and in some cases whole sectors, such as textiles. The collapse of the Soviet Union and the disbanding of its trading system (CMEA)[1] in 1992 meant the disappearance of the main market for relatively advanced technological goods, which affected key sectors of the economy, and defence in particular.

In 1999, the so-called 'second wave' of reforms introduced the market into public services and restructured welfare with profound implications for workers and users alike (Kolarska-Bobińska, 2000a and 2000b; Stenning and Hardy, 2005). Pensions have been privatised along the lines of the World Bank model and left providing for old age to the vagaries of the stock market.[2] The most dramatic of these reforms was in the health service, which resulted in hospital closures and job loss of nearly 30 per cent in the sector between 1995 and 2003 (Table 5.1). By 2005 the third round of restructuring was underway, primarily in areas that EU competition policy had prised open for the predations of large transnational corporations. This new round of reforms was primarily focused on telecommunications, airlines, railways and the post office. In each of these sectors job losses and/or deteriorating working conditions have been threatened.

Table 5.1 shows the profound impact of restructuring on the labour market.

The two sectors that have experienced the biggest decline in employment are agriculture and mining. In just less than ten years the number of people earning a living from the land has fallen from 27 per cent to 16 per cent of the population. The fall in the number of people working in mining and quarrying seems to be much less dramatic in terms of the proportion of the population affected. However, the loss of 158,000 jobs in this period (GUS,

Table 5.1 Changes in Employment in Poland, 1995–2006

	% of total employment			% change in employment
	1995	*2000*	*2006*	*1995–2006*
Agriculture, forestry and fishing	27	28	16	– 49.0
Mining and quarrying	2	1	1.3	– 43.9
Manufacturing	20	17	20	– 21.0
Construction	5	5	5	– 25.5
Trade and repair	12	13	16	+ 5.2
Retail	7	7	9	+ 7.3
Hotels and restaurants	1	1.5	2	+ 15.6
Real estate, renting and business	3	5	8	+ 67.1
Education	6	6	8	+ 9.0
Health and social work	6.5	6	5.5	– 29.8

Source: Adapted from GUS, 2007a: 126

2007a: 126) left some mining regions such as Wałbrzych with an official unemployment rate of 24 per cent in 2006 (GUS, 2007b). The real unemployment rate is estimated to be much higher as only one in six people, mostly long-term unemployed, are eligible for benefits.

Although the decline of jobs in manufacturing over this period is 21 per cent, nearly one in five of the working population continued to be employed in manufacturing, which is a high figure compared with only 13 per cent in the UK for example (Office for National Statistics, 2005). Overall the most marked trend is the expansion of jobs in the service sector. Table 5.1 shows the increase in the number of people employed in the retail, hotel and restaurant sectors. The biggest growth is the 67 per cent increase in employment in business services, which grew from 554,300 to 926,100 jobs; and went from employing 3.5 per cent to 7.3 per cent of the labour force.

These changes in employment have to be understood in the context of the new discipline and new imperatives to which the Polish economy was exposed as it opened up to international competition from 1990. Whereas Western capitalist economies had undergone periods of restructuring from the mid-1970s with weak economies and inefficient sections of capital undergoing 'rationalisation' – a euphemism for closure or downsizing – this process in Poland was compressed into a much shorter period of time. Before 1990 economic reform in Poland had been piecemeal (Simatupang, 1994; Slay, 1994; Hardy and Rainnie, 1996), but rapid integration with the global economy after 1990 brought deep restructuring in its wake.

Compressing Time and Space

In 1990, at the point of transformation, the structure of the economy was distorted and characterised by a high degree of vertical integration in large SOEs, but low levels of economies of scale and specialisation. Once exposed to intense competition from 1990 onwards, parts of the production process that were either very basic or missing completely had to be developed in a short space of time if individual firms and the economy as a whole were to integrate with the global economy. A whole raft of activities central to the circulation of capital became important, such as accounting, storage, marketing, information gathering and advertising, which mediate and abbreviate the exchange process.

The British manager of Cussons, which took over a factory producing washing powder, describes how unprepared some Polish workplaces were for international competition:

We found very little quality consciousness. As long as the boxes were full everything was OK. What's more they occasionally substituted ingredients! Marketing was non-existent. There was no market research. We didn't know who our customers were; we didn't even know where they were. Sales organisation was limited to a man who sat by the telephone, which occasionally rang. There were no growth plans. Sales plans were measured against what happened last year. Furthermore there were no exports. Export to the east, to former Soviet countries had been a very important market ... Teamwork was completely lacking. All decisions were sent to the president. I remember large queues of people from the ground floor to the first floor (where my office was) all awaiting decisions. Organisation was extremely centralised. Nor were there any pay differentials. Some

> supervisors got even less than the operatives. We found lots of data, but little useful information. For instance there were no cash flow forecasts or daily sales analysis. There was not much money, nor was there much English. One engineer in the factory spoke a little English ... When we arrived there were six Russian computers still in their boxes and a workforce that was computer illiterate. (Hardy, 2002)

In Cussons quality management was introduced with improvements in packaging and soap powder formula. The research and development department in the UK used 'value engineering' to achieve significant cost reductions, market research was introduced and the number of sales personnel increased from zero to 125 people. In firms that produce directly for the consumer market, skills associated with market research, marketing, product differentiation and sales are critical areas of competition.

Another group of activities were also necessary for reducing geographical barriers and speeding up the circulation of capital – what Marx referred to as the 'annihilation of time through space' (Harvey, 1996 and 2005). Activities focused on reductions in time and effort, such as warehousing, transport and logistics, are essential dimensions of competition. In Poland before 1990 managers worked with time frames that were far longer than those of Western firms. A Senior Manager from BOC noted:

> They can't believe in the future until it becomes the past. Even when it's the present they can't quite believe that it's happening. Before the lorry is parked outside they can't believe it exists. This presented problems for planning because they couldn't understand that you could plan a deal in four months time and simultaneously get the equipment. They were locked into a linear way of thinking, which meant that first they had to have the equipment and get it going and then they could start thinking about planning and how to sell it. (Hardy, 2002)

In this firm a major task of the foreign investor was to restructure the firm and bend the mindsets of its managers and workers to submit to the discipline of the competitive markets in which time had to be compressed.

What emerged from case studies in Wrocław (Hardy, 1998 and 2002) was that Polish enterprises were not uniformly poor and backward in relation to Western counterparts in terms of the hard technology employed. There were significant variations both between and within sectors (Amsden *et al.*, 1994; Hardy and Rainnie, 1996). In all cases, however, what was missing was tight managerial control over the full range of the production process, and in particular Western managerial practices in the areas of financing, accounting, marketing and human resource management. While improvements in hard technology could be described as incremental, changes in managerial practices had taken a quantum leap.

The Pivotal Role of Foreign Capital

Evidence of global TNCs in Poland is ubiquitous, they are visible in retailing, banking and the plethora of production sites that they operate across the country. At the top of Warsaw's tall buildings the names of Toyota, Citibank and VW are emblazoned in neon lights. Neoliberal and conventional economists believed that foreign investment would be 'the engine of growth' (Lipton and Sachs, 1990; Dobosiewicz, 1992; Donges, 1992; Hunya, 1992) in post-communist economies. This claim was premised on the argument that, not only would foreign investment bring a vital injection of capital to economies where domestic individual and institutional savings were low, but that there would also be an automatic transfer of technical and managerial know-how to firms. Further, neoliberal accounts point to the role of FDI in bringing about a competitive stimulus that would force all firms to restructure both their management and production activities, according to some sort of economic Darwinism. In Poland, as in other countries, FDI has been central to the development strategies of regions and localities (Hudson, 1995; Phelps and Fuller, 2000). Each region and town had a department charged with place marketing and the production of glossy brochures that extol the virtues of the area in a bid to capture a share of global capital.

A second set of arguments has suggested that the days of TNCs as 'slashers and burners', coming into localities attracted by financial incentives and then leaving when they dry up, are gone. They suggest that new corporate dynamics have led to the emergence of qualitatively new and essentially superior forms of manufacturing investment by TNCs in Less Developed Regions (Amin *et al.*, 1994; Dunning, 1997; Fynes and Ennis, 1997; Rugman and D'Cruz, 1997). Such 'quality' investments were seen as the product of a number of organisational changes, which included increased autonomy for firms from their headquarters, a shift from defensive strategies related to cost to offensive strategies associated with asset and knowledge seeking in the locality and the need for aftercare. This amounts to a much more optimistic view about how TNCs might benefit localities in terms of the sort of jobs on offer and their stability.

It is important to set the experience of Poland in the context of flows of foreign investment in the global economy, which grew inexorably between 1986 and 2006 at an average annual rate of 27.9 per cent (UNCTAD, 2007). Among post-communist countries, Poland, the Czech Republic and Hungary, in that order, received the strongest flows of foreign investment. Between 1995 and 2004 stocks in these countries grew fivefold (twice as fast as the stock of world FDI) and together they accounted for three quarters of the total inward FDI to new EU members (UNCTAD, 2005: 86). The scale of global restructuring and turbulence is indicated in Table 5.2 by the number of cross-border acquisitions as weaker sections of capital were eaten up by those that were more profitable. Further, a marked increase in workers employed in foreign affiliates was evident in 2005 and 2006.

Although this might appear to bode well for Poland in terms of the possibilities of capturing a share of global foreign investment, Table 5.3 provides a sober antidote to accounts that point to catching up in terms of volumes of FDI. In the EU the three strongest economies – UK, France and Germany – account for 44 per cent of FDI stocks, whereas the three strongest post-communist economies only accounted for less than 5 per cent between them. This pattern is also reflected in the comparatively tiny share of flows of FDI that these three countries received in 2006.

Table 5.2   Selected Indicators of FDI and International Production in the Global Economy, 1986–2006

	Annual growth rate (per cent)						
	1986– 1990	*1991– 1995*	*1996– 2000*	*2003*	*2004*	*2005*	*2006*
Inflows of foreign investment	21.7	22.0	40.0	–9.3	31.6	27.4	38.1
Cross-border acquisitions	25.9	24.0	51.5	19.7	28.2	88.2	22.9
Employment of foreign affiliates	5.3	5.5	11.5	5.7	3.7	16.3	13.9

Source: Adapted from UNCTAD, 2007: 9

Table 5.3   FDI Stocks and Flows in CEE Accession Countries as a Percentage of GDP

	Stocks of FDI as a percentage of EU total			*Flows of FDI as a percentage of EU total*
	1990	*2000*	*2006*	*2006*
United Kingdom	27	20	21	26
France	12	12	14	15
Germany	15	12.5	9	8
Italy	8	5.6	5.4	7
Czech Republic	0.2	0.9	1.4	1.1
Hungary	0.07	1.0	1.5	1.1
Poland	0.02	1.6	2.0	2.6

Source: Adapted from UNCTAD, 2007: 251 and 255

In terms of capturing a share of global flows of FDI Poland is on the periphery of Europe.

Restructuring Networks

Firms now operate in a context of 'hypercompetition' and 'disorder' where CEOs (Chief Executive Officers) are quoted as describing the new situation as 'brutal', 'intense', 'bitter', 'savage' and 'where only the paranoid survive' (Ilinitch *et al.*, 1998: xxi). This is the background in which the opening up of Poland and CEE offered a new terrain upon which capital could restructure its operations, in terms of increasing sales, rationalising production and cutting costs, with mergers and acquisitions being a major weapon in the restructuring and consolidation of many sectors. Although the idea of the learning firm and the knowledge economy are privileged in much academic literature (Asheim, 1997; Amin and Cohendet, 1998; Antonelli, 1999; Maskell and Malmberg, 1999a and 1999b), this 'hypercompetition' means that firms are constantly reviewing their strategies at every point in their circuits of capital. The knowledge content of production is increasingly a crucial element in competition and firms attempt continuously to innovate products and processes. However, seeking lower costs across all their operations and realising surplus value through selling in new markets are still of paramount importance.

In the early 1990s, there was an unseemly scramble as large transnational companies picked off the 'jewels in the crown' of the economies of CEE. TNCs seeking market access, such as those involved in food processing, detergents or cigarette production, were in the forefront of grabbing new markets. Nestle 'snatched' Poland's second largest chocolate factory from another investor by taking out adverts in local papers in Poznań and sending their executives to the factory gate with megaphones. Such was their desperation for a slice of the action that they gave incumbent management and workers guarantees regarding work and wages and made a generous donation to the local hospital.

From the mid-1990s the biggest investment has been in finance, the retail sector (and particularly supermarkets) and automobiles. Most global car makers have factories in Poland. The biggest investor is still Fiat, which has invested almost 1.64 billion USD, the second largest share of any foreign capital. Korea's Daewoo is in third place, investing more than 1.5 billion USD in car production and General Motors has invested 800 million USD in the Opel plant in Gliwice. The presence of major assemblers has spawned a large number of component producers, who supply Poland and other parts of the firms' networks. Volvo has established its global sourcing centre in Wrocław where it assembles trucks and buses. Other major car firms such as VW and Toyota do not assembly cars, but produce sub-assembly for their global networks.[3] Between January and September 2005 Poland produced 76 per cent more cars than in the same period the previous year. The fact that 84 per cent of passenger cars and 90 per cent of vans were exported suggests that Poland is becoming a major export platform for car production (Poland Economic Newsletter, 2004).

After EU accession, despite the expected burst of investor interest, risks persist for capital in the new EU economies. Low costs can be a short lived and fragile comparative advantage, particularly in sectors such as textiles, which are notoriously footloose, and where some subcontractors have already relocated outside the EU. A recent survey suggested that corporate investors perceived poor infrastructure, corruption and the gradual erosion of low cost advantage as leading threats to the competitiveness of the eight new post-communist EU members (UNCTAD, 2005). Although EU reforms were expected to bring infrastructure, investment and the regulatory stability of the EU single market, economic and social costs were expected to be high. EU law adds a new layer of regulation and may undermine relative FDI advantages in areas such as tax costs and labour costs. These factors could push investors further east and south outside the new EU.

'High Tech' Panaceas?

The Logic of Trade

It has been argued that Poland is integrating successfully into the global economy on the basis of four claims: that trade has expanded; that the composition of trade has changed as a result of successful restructuring; that there has been a shift to more skilled labour intensive and capital intensive products; and that there is a break away from sunset goods towards trading products where demand is growing (Kaminski and Smarzynska, 2001).

Poland has integrated into the global economy through what Martin (1998) calls the 'logic of trade'. There have been marked changes in terms of what Poland trades and its trading partners. The collapse of the CMEA and trade liberalisation produced a huge shift away from trade with old Soviet bloc countries and towards the European Union. In 1989 the EU accounted for 32 per cent of Polish exports and 34 per cent of imports, with these figures rising to 68 per cent and 61 per cent respectively by 2003. Within the EU Germany is the main trading partner accounting for 24.4 per cent of imports and 32.3 per cent of exports in 2004 (GUS, 2004). In terms of the content of international trade Poland has shifted to importing relatively high technology goods and exporting raw materials and semi-processed goods, such as coal, timber, cement, copper and clothing.

Much has been made of Poland 'catching up' by capturing the high value added end of firms' value chains, by winning research and development (R&D) facilities. However, the global context in which Poland is trying to upgrade its economy is one where R&D is highly concentrated with the top ten countries (led by US) accounting for four-fifths of the world total of R&D. Half of the world's R&D is accounted for by large TNCs and concentrated in a handful of industries such as IT hardware, automotives, pharmaceuticals and biotechnology. Traditionally R&D functions in host countries have been associated with adapting products and processes to new markets, but competitive pressures mean that TNCs are increasingly interested in tapping into knowledge centres, sources of new technology, recruiting skilled workers and monitoring competitors (UNCTAD, 2005). The rising costs of R&D and scarcity of skilled labour in some advanced capitalist countries coupled with lower wages and skilled workforces in post-communist economies means that they are now candidates for locational tournaments to try and win higher grade and skilled operations from foreign investors. Therefore, while in the past R&D has mainly been confined to developed countries with strong systems of innovation, there is an increasing trend in offshoring these functions, particularly to countries like India and China.

Islands of Innovation

According to the Polish Agency for Foreign Investment (Grycuk, 2005) there has been a flow of high value added investment into the country. Their statistics report that in 2004 75 per cent of TNCs announced expansion plans for their R&D centres in Poland and a number of new research units have been established.[4] There are three sectors that have got either relatively high levels of R&D or the potential for innovative activity which could be viewed as 'pockets of innovation'; these include the automotive, IT and aircraft industries.

As we saw in the previous section the automotive industry, in terms of both assemblers and component producers, has invested heavily in Poland. According to UNCTAD (2005) some of the new EU members' foreign affiliates have emerged as important R&D players in sectors such the automotive and electronics sectors. However, the extent to which technology has been transferred is highly variable depending on the nature of the activity undertaken and the particular corporate strategy of the firm. In 2007 Volvo still undertook core research and engine production in the home country. In 2002 Volkswagen produced a large percentage of engines for its global network in Poland, but all parts were imported from Germany and there was no local sourcing. On the other hand, Opel (General Motors) in Gliwice has transferred technical know-how to certain of their key suppliers. The point here is that these technology spillovers cannot be automatically assumed and claims of technology transfer have to be treated cautiously. The outcomes are highly mixed, and range from examples of high level 'knowledge-based' production to the manufacture of simple components for the global networks. Further, research and development may be little more than simple adaptation to local markets.

Less attention has been paid to the IT sector as it is largely comprised of Small and Medium-sized Enterprises (SMEs) and indigenous firms rather than flagship, high profile foreign investments. Micek (2005) claims that the growing number of IT firms around the Katowice and Kraków regions make up an early stage cluster. The source of new IT firms has been the spillovers from academic institutions in the majority of cases (82 per cent in Katowice and Kraków), but also the spin-outs created by the restructuring of large firms. This 'cluster' is due to specific geographical conditions, which according to Micek (2005) includes a pool of abundant IT skills and experienced professionals. Five out of the top ten universities in computer science are in southern Poland. While IT carries the promise of being high tech, how far this constitutes an upgrading of activities depends on the nature of the work. IT includes software programming, but it also may include much more routine work such as data processing.

Whereas the IT cluster in south-west Poland has largely been self-generating and received little institutional or regional assistance, the other embryonic cluster 'aviation valley' has been widely promoted internationally. Rzeszów and Mielec in south-east Poland were two of the centres of the defence industries pre-1990, specialising in producing military aircraft and helicopters. The collapse of the Warsaw Pact severely reduced its market with the possibility that this area would become an economic disaster zone if demand collapsed and government support was withdrawn. Interest by major global defence firms such as Pratt and Whitney in sub-contracting part of aircraft production has led to Rzeszów and Mielec being designated as a cluster with the aim of building a low cost supply chain on the basis of a network of SMEs.[5] This is at a very early stage of development and it is too early to say whether it can deliver on its aspirations to be engaged in high tech production or whether these functions will simply be confined to low skilled operations, while high technology processes are carried out outside of Poland.

'Third Division' in European Technology

Despite these islands of success and the plethora of EU and government initiatives, a broader view of Poland is less sanguine.

Bakowski (2004) lists the weaknesses of research and innovation in Poland as including:

- Primary emphasis on basic research
- Complicated Research and Technology Development system with a large number of industrial institutes
- No integration between research and production
- Low contribution of research carried out within companies
- Low interest of industry in innovation
- Low competitiveness and innovativeness of enterprises
- Slow growth of high tech based SMEs
- Low level of information and technology transfer between the public and the private sectors and within the private sector itself

In particular, the idea that Poland is catching up in terms of technology is not reflected in an increasing proportion of high tech imports, as Table 5.4 shows.

Table 5.4   High Tech Imports as a Percentage of Total Imports

	High Tech Imports as a Percentage of Total Imports
United Kingdom	26
Germany	14
France	18
Ireland	29
Hungary	21
Czech Republic	13
Slovakia	5
Poland	3

Source: Eurostat

This is further reflected in low spending on research and development where Table 5.5 shows that Poland is nearly at the bottom of the league table in the amount of GDP spent on research.

Table 5.5 Highest and Lowest Spending on R&D: Selected EU Countries in 2006

	Percentage of GDP spent on R&D
EU (27) average	1.8
Finland	3.5
Germany	2.5
Denmark	2.4
Czech Republic	1.5
Hungary	1.0
Poland	0.6
Bulgaria	0.5
Romania	0.5

Source: Eurostat

Exporting Labour

Since accession to the EU in 2004 Poland has emerged as a supplier of a reserve army of labour to the core economies of Europe. The accepted figure is that 2 million Poles have left to seek work in other parts of Europe.[6] Poles are by far the largest group from CEE, and make up between 60 and 70 per cent of migrant workers in receiver countries. Although it is a free world for capital, the mobility of workers in seeking better lives elsewhere is severely constrained. This is not simply the case for workers trying to enter from outside the European Union, but also within the EU itself. In 2004 only three EU countries, the UK, Ireland and Sweden, opened their labour markets to new entrants from CEE, although by 2008 other countries had opened up their markets to varying degrees.

The pull and push factors of migration, and the continual redrawing of boundaries by European states to create a hierarchy of privilege and security in the workforce, are the outcome of the unevenness of European capitalism in terms of wages and employment opportunities. In 2004 the average rate of unemployment in Poland was 20 per cent, and almost double for young people. The UK and Ireland, on the other hand, have been deemed to be successful economies in Europe; Ireland as a recipient of significant EU structural funding and large amounts of investment by global IT companies, and the UK because of the critical role played by the City of London in recycling global surplus value. The decision to open the UK labour market in 2004 had nothing to do with altruism, but a shortage of labour in low wage sectors of the employment market. In 2007 the UK labour market was not fully opened to the most recent EU entrants from Bulgaria and Romania as there was deemed to be a sufficient supply of reserve labour.

A film shown on Channel Four in the UK in September 2007, *It's a Free World*, was excellent in highlighting the exploitation of migrant workers in the UK. However, it was focused on 'bad apple' employers on the fringes of the labour markets, whereas the reality is that CEE migrant workers are central to British and Irish capitalism and indirectly (or directly) employed by some of the largest companies. Although there is no doubt that some employment agencies are run on a semi-criminal basis, others such as Adecco are large transnational corporations themselves.

The widespread employment of migrant workers, in the UK and Ireland particularly, has to be linked to the neoliberal agenda of flexible labour markets as a way of driving up the rate of exploitation. It is more profitable to employ migrant workers on lower wages and poorer contracts. Privatisation of welfare provision, such as care for the elderly, has driven down wages. Further, the deregulation of other areas of the economy such as transport services, particularly buses, means that there has been an intensification of competition through the use of low cost labour. Therefore migrant workers fit into the bottom of the employment hierarchy doing the worst paid and least secure jobs.

The impetus for importing Polish migrant workers (and others from Central and Eastern Europe) in the UK has to be understood in the context of increased competition between capitals. One example of this is the food retail sector where migrant workers are involved in 'picking it, plucking it, packing it and moving it', through their employment in agriculture, food processing and supermarkets. In the East Anglia area of the UK there is widespread use of Portuguese and Eastern European workers, often employed in terrible conditions, with gangmasters running some small towns. However, it is not simply that employers in this region are particularly nasty, but rather that exploitation has to be understood in the way that food suppliers are locked into highly competitive markets. Supermarkets, who control the food chain in the UK (more than any other country), continually try to drive down prices and costs with sophisticated techniques like online auctions, and this pressure is passed down to individual suppliers.

Migration has had a significant impact on the Polish economy. While it has contributed to lowering the unemployment rate, which by 2008 had fallen to 11 per cent (GUS, 2008), migration has also brought about a significant drain of well-educated people and skilled workers. Table 5.6 shows that Poland is in a strong position in terms of the education of its labour force, having improved its position from 27th to 15th place between 1995 and 2001 and being significantly ahead of Hungary (35th) and the Czech Republic (38th).

Table 5.6   Human Capital Index (selected countries)

Country	1995		2001	
	Position	Index	Position	Index
Australia	1	0.99	3	0.97
UK	7	0.95	6	0.95
Spain	14	0.90	12	0.89
Korea	16	0.88	16	0.87
Greece	24	0.81	30	0.79
Ukraine	25	0.80	27	0.81
Russian Federation	26	0.80	24	0.82
Poland	27	0.80	15	0.87
Hungary	36	0.71	35	0.76
Czech Republic	38	0.70	38	0.70

Source: Adapted from UNCTAD, 2005: 291

There has been a trend of younger educated people migrating to find work, unsurprising with unemployment of 40.2 per cent among workers in the 20 to 24 years age group in 2003 (GUS, 2004: 249).

The situation is very dynamic. In 2008 the decreasing differential between wages in the UK and Poland, and the falling value of sterling, led to some Poles returning home (Morris, 2008). By the beginning of 2009 the haemorrhaging of thousands of jobs in the UK as the recession deepened compounded the uncertainty that faced migrant workers.

Conclusion

There is little evidence to support the view that Poland is being integrated with Europe on the basis of a low cost 'maquiladora' economy. However, the story that Poland is upgrading its economy on the basis of having captured high grade foreign investment is overly optimistic. The picture we have to make sense of is complex. Since 1990 undoubtedly Poland, along with Hungary and the Czech Republic, has been a forerunner among post-communist economies in attracting FDI, but these flows of FDI are peripheral and significantly lagging behind those of 'old' EU members. Poland is well placed in terms of a skilled and educated workforce to receive higher level parts of the value chains of TNCs, but domestic spending on R&D in general and business R&D in particular is very poor. In this sea of peripherality there are islands of innovation in relation to automobiles, IT and defence, for example. However, we cannot assume the automatic transfer of technology as it depends where individual production units fit into the complex chains of the global firms. In the cases of IT and defence, these are proto clusters but it is too early to say whether these amount to wishful thinking or have the potential to transform into locally based centres of dynamism.

The development of Polish capitalism since 1990 has been *combined* in the sense that there has been a rapid integration with the global economy in terms of trade, investment and financial systems. The restructuring of the economy, however, has been highly *uneven* as some parts of the productive capacity and the industrial landscape have been destroyed while others have been upgraded as they are locked into the activities of TNCs. This unevenness has had a profound impact on the opportunities for working-class people, as the work on offer in their regions and localities and the future of their workplaces are determined by vagaries of global capitalism.

6

THE 'SHOCK TROOPS' OF FOREIGN CAPITAL

In 1981 the Polish government sent tanks into factories up and down the country that had been occupied by workers to crush the wave of protests that led to the formation of Solidarity. From 1991 onwards, however, a different type of 'shock troops' arrived in the workplaces of Poland and these were men (usually) in dark suits, armed with a different set of weapons such as downsizing, quality control and just-in-time management to restructure Polish workplaces. Chapter 4 discussed the huge resources that were put into trying to create a new ideological climate to secure the conditions for market-based, neoliberal capitalism. Less attention, however, has been paid to the role of foreign capital, transnational corporations and their executives who have played a very important part in trying to establish new material and discursive practices through the deep restructuring of workplaces and workplace behaviour.

The way in which capital has tried to impose a new discipline on labour and reconstitute power in the workplace is missing from most of the radical and Marxist accounts of transformation. In both conventional management and radical literature firms simply arrive in new places and this neglects the way in which capital crossing borders is a highly political process (Phelps *et al.*, 1998; Phelps, 2000; Tewdwr-Jones and Phelps, 2000). It may be that certain sectors are closed to foreign capital in which case they will need to be prised open for the predations of foreign firms through organisations such as the WTO, or as part of IMF imposed conditions. In the case of large scale privatisation TNCs had to enter into negotiations with 'host' states, which involved some combination of coercion and persuasion to acquire new assets at bargain prices. For some firms, regional and local states and their ruling classes were important for acquiring land, the necessary infrastructure and legal permissions – in some cases in ways that bordered on illegality (Hardy, 2002). Imposing new practices in the workplace is equally political, as long standing practices of work are usually regarded as a 'problem' and deemed to be unsuitable for global competition.

Tensions in the workplace amount to more than simply a clash of cultures. Workplaces are inherently contradictory, as the pressure of competition continually forces managers to find new ways of extracting surplus value from their workers. This could be effected through an intensification or reorganisation of work, or through enhancing the skills of individual workers (Bowles and Gintis, 1981; Powell and DiMaggio, 1991). In turn workers will, actively or passively, resist attempts to impose harsher working conditions or deteriorating salaries, but may be more acquiescent when their productive potential is enhanced through training, as at least this will help them individually in the labour market. From the perspective of the firm, conflict and hostility are not conducive to increasing productivity or learning, and bosses prefer to 'get their workers on board' by creating an atmosphere where employees are encouraged to share the corporate culture of their employers in the belief that they are 'all in the same boat'.

This task of establishing hegemony in the workplace (Burawoy, 1985) poses a different challenge for foreign capital in CEE, because of the legacy of the large SOEs that dominated the industrial landscape. In Poland this was because SOEs had been centres of intense political activity and opposition, in the early 1980s particularly, and because they were a repository of work practices that were incompatible with the new competition (Swaan, 1996; Swaan and Lissowska, 1996). In the early 1990s the manager of a brand new foreign owned confectionery factory told me that when he first arrived he found that workers left every day with pockets bulging with sweets and chocolate, because this was seen as an acceptable way of compensating for low wages. The first September the factory was opened he was rebuked for challenging the large number of women who failed to turn up for work for three days. He was told, 'Didn't you know it is the plum harvest. We are too busy to come to work!', which reflected the practice of workers returning to their families in rural areas to help with the harvest.

This chapter begins by looking at the legacy of SOEs and how they were inappropriate for the intense competition that resulted from integration with the global economy. The main part of the chapter contrasts the way that two well known TNCs, ABB and Volvo, tried to shift the thinking and behaviour of management and workers as they undertook deep restructuring projects in the factories that they had taken over. The analysis draws on the idea of 'enabling myths' (Dugger, 1989 and 2000) and 'circuits of intellectual capital' (Thrift, 1998 and 2001), which have been particularly salient in transferring new discourses across national boundaries. 'Enabling myths' are a special form of institution and control mechanism to consolidate or justify a particular set of ideas by legitimating certain kinds of organising work or labour over others. As firms cross national boundaries, circuits of intellectual capital are necessary not only to smooth the path of circuits of productive and financial capital, but also to effect rapid change in situations where managers need to react within a short time scale. In the context of Poland and CEE capital needed to develop strategies to dismantle the old legacies of the planned economy and supplant them with a set of ideas viewed as being consistent with the market and global competitive practices.

The Legacy of State Owned Enterprises

In Poland, as elsewhere in CEE, giant SOEs had dominated industrial development in the 1950s and 1960s. They were the product of extensive accumulation which was characterised by relentless growth and hunger for investment that was not moderated by fear of loss or failure. The managers of these gargantuan firms were not held accountable for any costs or inefficient use of resources, and their success was gauged by their ability to meet output quotas. The budget constraint was 'soft' as there was no bottom line or limit for credit, and managers could always try and win extra raw materials to fuel higher growth through bargaining with other firms or central government.

These firms were all encompassing and, in many cases, provided cradle to grave welfare services. Factories often housed, fed and clothed their workers, and were sometimes the only place where things could be obtained at affordable prices. Kenney describes the Pafawag train factory in Wrocław in the 1950s:

> Even the available entertainment was provided by the factory; the largest ones organised and supported the city's first cinemas, theatres and sports teams. Pafawag's social and cultural programs were among the most developed in all of Poland. In 1946 it published the first factory newspaper in the country, an eponymous biweekly with a press run of about three thousand; a factory radio broadcast in the cafeteria. Pafawag had three *siwelicas* (cultural centres) in districts where the factory owned apartments; from 5–9 pm workers could play chess or ping pong or read magazines. Many workers participated in the drama circle, band or choir. Many more played for the factory soccer team (Pafawag was then building its own stadium) or the boxing, cycling and track and field events. (1997: 164)

The onset of the economic crisis at the beginning of the 1970s led to reforms to bring about the partial integration of Poland with the global economy,[1] and during this period many SOEs shed some of their welfare facilities and particularly their ownership of housing.

Table 6.1 compares the characteristics of SOEs in 1990 with those of large firms in Western Europe that had already undergone 15 years of intense restructuring in response to the crisis of the early 1970s.

At the beginning of the 1990s most SOEs were monopoly producers in their country or the CMEA as a whole, and this lack of competition and a shortage economy, coupled with the 'soft budget' constraint, meant that there were no incentives to efficiency. Further, a high degree of vertical integration meant that, although these firms were large, they were unable to benefit from specialisation. Whereas Western firms had outsourced and offshored some of their functions to concentrate on their 'core activity', high levels

Table 6.1 Characteristics of State Owned Enterprises Compared with Western European Firms in 1990

		Large Western European firms	SOEs in CEE
Structure	Nature of competition	Oligopolies (small number of large firms) – market characterised by competition and collaboration	Monopolists – the only producer of a particular good in the country or the trading bloc
	Supplier networks	Outsourcing and offshoring and concentrating on core competences	High degree of vertical integration and few economies of scale
Cultural features	Rent seeking and enrichment of managers	Ability to award themselves high salaries and remuneration linked to profits	Personal gain through 'grey economy' and kleptocratic behaviour rather than maximising efficiency or profits
	Competition	Intense competition on quality, cost and additional services	Poor quality production due to lack of competition
	Management, governance and trade unions	Clear distinction between activities of management and trade unions. Unambiguous governance – could be consensual or conflictual	Triangle of trade union, workers council and board of management. Ambiguous governance
	Full employment	Downsizing and redundancies – a frequent response to competition in public and private sector	Commitment to full employment and reluctance to make redundancies
Knowledge requirements	Human resource management	Techniques to enhance human capital, implement downsizing and individual wage structures	Absence of knowledge about HR techniques. No wage driven incentives, little training
	Finance and accounting	Strict control of finance, centralised accounting, profit centres within firms	Absence of knowledge of accounting. No understanding of cost structures at different points of production
	Business knowledge	Range of management training and fads. Knowledge in-house or bought in from consultants	Engineering rather than business training. Lack of exposure to full range of management functions and techniques

Source: Author

of social provision and a lack of outsourcing meant that SOEs did not reap the benefits of economies of scale.

Other legacies were deemed to get in the way of making SOEs globally competitive. In the chaos of the 1980s, decentralisation and increased autonomy for SOEs provided opportunities for enrichment of the *nomenklatura*. Energy went into kleptocracy and carving out profitable niches in a chaotic system, rather than focusing on the efficiency of the firm that they managed. At the same time ambiguous structures of governance had evolved as workers were given increased rights to participate in decision making processes in the firm as part of the post martial law reforms of 1981. The existence of these workers' councils,[2] which could fire managers and often did, meant that there was resistance to restructuring.

Conquistadores: ABB and Volvo

It was much more by luck than design that I was able to gain access to ABB and Volvo during the late 1990s. I was able to investigate how they set about transferring work practices and, more specifically, how these firms attempted to get compliance for a whole new set of ideas and ways of doing things that were compatible with an intensification of competition and integration with global markets.

Volvo was one of the largest industrial enterprises in Scandinavia with sales exceeding 26 billion USD in 1998. After extensive investment in developed markets, it turned its attention to opportunities in the emerging markets of Asia, CEE and Latin America, which had opened up to the global economy. Initially Volvo's entry to the Polish market had been to avoid protectionism in the form of excise duties on trucks and to this end they invested 20 million USD in developing bus and truck assembly on a new greenfield site. Lower cost production conditions in Poland meant that the site changed from an assembly site to an industrial centre with substantial additional investment to produce for the European market.[3] This was part of a wider rationalisation, which involved the closure of five factories in other European countries.

The second firm, ABB, is a multinational corporation headquartered in Zurich. It was formed in August 1987 by a merger between the Swedish ASEA, flagship of Swedish industry since 1890, and Swiss Brown Boverei (1891), which held a comparable industrial status in Switzerland. Both were already middle level players in the international electrotechnical or electronic engineering industry. ABB had been a central player in the restructuring of the power production and servicing in CEE, where it had some presence in the two decades prior to trans-formation, through licensing agreements as these economies had begun to open up and import Western technology. ABB was the single largest investor in the former CEE and Russia and ranked as the twentieth largest investor in Poland, where it had acquired factories all over the country. Percy Barnevik, the then president of ABB, made his motive explicit:

> We must stop looking at eastern Europe as a potential burden, as a risk area which dumps products on us. They have a gigantic market where whole industries need to be rebuilt. I truly believe we are in a 'win-win' situation.
> (Obloj and Thomas, 1998: 391)

As with Volvo, ABB's activities in Poland were a response to wider competitive conditions. Pressures in the power generation market and the need to internationalise came from both push factors in the domestic market and pull factors in international markets. The market for power transformers had matured, with stagnating demand in established markets, while the need to modernise obsolete equipment through privatisation had created a high level of demand in emerging economies. Thus the transforma-tion of former SOEs and the deregulation of monopoly product markets had opened up new markets and intensified competition between big players. The high level of investment by ABB in Poland was driven by both market access and securing lower cost sources for components such as turbines and switchgear, which were 40 per cent cheaper to produce in Poland than in Western Europe.

Bringing in the 'Shock Troops'

Cherrypicking

One source of resentment towards foreign investors in Poland was the way that they quickly gained ownership of the most profitable sections of capital – the jewels in the crown – leaving the less competitive sections of capital as a burden on the state. When ABB purchased Lodmel it was one of the largest firms making power generators in the Soviet bloc. The purchase of the company was controversial because ABB used cherrypicking tactics. The former SOE was split into three parts: Lodmel (core area of generator production) employing 400 workers, Lodmel Drives (engine production) employing 1,200 workers and Lozemal, which owned the land, buildings and social assets. ABB bought Lodmel (power generators) and Lodmel Drives (engines), while Lozemal remained as an SOE that leased the land and buildings to ABB. This was entirely consistent with entry tactics used by ABB in other parts of Poland and CEE, which were to negotiate in advance precisely how much of the business it wanted to take on and cede control of the rest to the state.

In some acquisitions in Poland, workers were picked by individual interview. As one ABB executive put it, 'we don't want the lazy ones, or the ones who are set in their ways. We leave them to the State' (*Financial Times*, 1993: 17). Financial risks were controlled by buying into existing capacity, which kept costs low and made it rare to spend more than 20 million USD on an acquisition (Batchelor, 1997). In some cases the state received no direct payment for the acquired firm, but rather in-kind payments such as technology transfer were used. Entry by the brownfield privatisation route meant that capital was not tied up with land and buildings. These tactics enabled ABB to get access to skilled labour and embedded technological expertise. Leasing rather than owning assets meant that it was much more footloose and could operate on shorter time horizons if it wanted to sell or switch production elsewhere.

In contrast Volvo quickly abandoned the brownfield joint venture route. After discussions with the Polish government a joint venture between Volvo and Truckski, the leading Polish bus and truck producer, was agreed and assembly production began in 1993. However, the joint venture with Truckski collapsed after one year when the Solidarity trade union would not agree to the large number of redundancies that were demanded as a condition of further cooperation. Subsequently Volvo built a new factory and started production on a greenfield site 20 kilometres away in order to avoid old institutional legacies and start with a clean sheet on which it could imprint the corporate culture of the firm and impose new working practices. Volvo was also seen as having 'cherrypicked' when it took the Truckski workers who had been employed on the joint venture production line to the new factory; they were regarded as the most skilled and dynamic workers.

ABB and Volvo had different ways of dealing with what they regarded as the deep-rooted nature of rigidities in former SOEs inherited from the previous regime. One senior manager at Volvo explained:

> In June 1994 negotiations [with Truckski] were falling to pieces and we decided to go for our own site, my task was to find a greenfield location ... The problem was that they had a lot of people, 3,500 at that time and one of the remarks from the authorities was that we should take on all of them. We said we can only take 2,000 and that is all. Then Mercedes came on the picture and promised to take care of all of them. It was one of the best decisions we ever made. (Senior Manager A, Volvo)

This view was echoed by other members of senior management:

> Greenfield gives much more control of the business ... we can run the business the way we want. I can't think of any successful joint ventures, especially big ones, maybe smaller ones. You just inherit a bag of problems with a joint venture. (Senior Manager B, Volvo)

The rhetoric of Volvo's corporate culture was that it relied much less on hierarchical authority, formal measurement and explicit internal markets (Hedlund, 1991). Rather, Volvo purported to rely on socialisation, rotation of managers and the emergence of shared views of the company's strategy and identity. Whereas ABB's managers were generally older, Polish and inherited from the previous company, Volvo was dominated by a small number of Swedish managers and young Polish middle managers. The ultimate goal was to imbue middle and senior managers with the 'Volvo way of thinking', and the route taken to embedding their corporate culture was very different from that of ABB, which had all procedures for HRM and supply management codified in manuals. Volvo's style purported to appear less hierarchical and, on the surface at least, looked more flexible. Proximity, personal contact, coaching and a very hands-on approach on the part of the Swedish management were seen as preferable to formal training. A shared canteen with management and badminton tournaments for all workers were designed to give the impression that everyone was 'in the same boat'.

If Volvo appeared to take a gradualist and pragmatic route to restructuring, the ABB approach to the transformation of management culture was much more akin to shock therapy. In ABB Lodmel, the traditional structure of the SOE was immediately changed into divisional (product oriented) structures, which had responsibility for supply, production, quality assurance, research and development, marketing and sales. Tight budgetary constraints and responsibility for economic performance were delegated down the hierarchical chain of the division. Physically, the amount of space utilised was contracted as the firm concentrated on its core operation.

According to the then CEO, Percy Barnevik, these global managers were required not only to understand the local culture, but also 'to sort through the cultural debris of excuses and find opportunities to innovate' (Taylor, 1991: 481). Therefore, 'shock troops', comprising ABB global managers and consultants, were sent in to administer a short sharp shock and effect rapid change in the structure and culture of the organisation.

ABB corporate-approved solutions were transferred and forcibly implemented into Polish firms, immediately replacing the former well-established routines, recipes, procedures and structures of the centrally planned economy ... They did not initially perform any sophisticated diagnosis or analysis of local conditions or develop a strategic vision for the transformation process. Rather they forcefully implemented market enterprise discipline in the acquired former state-owned forms by a series of high speed actions. (Obloj and Thomas, 1998: 392)

One of the main tasks was to create a small group of Polish managers who could be left to run the firm once the 'agents of change' had moved on elsewhere. The process of creating new managers or remoulding existing managers took place by increasing material rewards and promoting the enabling myths of the company. First, as with other ABB acquisitions in CEE, this included extensive training sessions to identify and select managers from the acquired SOE, who were described as the 'hungry wolves' (Taylor, 1991) – that is, those most likely to adapt and change and take advantage of the higher salaries on offer. These individuals were then put through intensive education and training to expose them to the principles and practice of the market economy in general and ABB management systems in particular. This privileged group of Polish managers was sent on benchmarking tours to other firms in the ABB Business Area to understand best practice and become imbued with company culture. The material incentives and prestige of managers were substantially increased with large wage increases, company cars, remodelled offices and the possibility of foreign travel.

This intense restructuring took place in the four-year period from 1990 to 1994 after which ABB Lodmel (power generators) reverted to all Polish management, the consultants having moved on and the expatriate managers transferred elsewhere. Constant financial reporting and manuals supplied to the HRM and supply managers regarding ABB policy meant that there was strict arm's length control with little room for manoeuvre for incumbent managers. The rhetoric was of autonomy and learning, but the ABB Business Area decided which market the firm could sell in, and the amount of investment it received. The reality was one of constant pressure to reduce costs and individual factories were not only in competition with other firms, but they also had to compete with other divisions in ABB for new contracts.

Reconfiguring Capital–State Relationships

Globalisation literature, which assumes that TNCs are footloose, underplays the symbiotic relationship between the state and capital. In the case of ABB and Volvo, not only did they need to negotiate entry, but also to cultivate an ongoing relationship with the Polish state. The ability to glean information from national departments and lobby appropriate ministers and functionaries was crucial to their ability to operate competitively.

The existence of a headquarters in Warsaw reflected the fact that both firms needed to have a base near the decision making centre, with the potential for political links with relevant ministers and government departments. A presence in Warsaw was important for lobbying the government regarding the rules pertaining to foreign investment. In the mid-1990s, for example, there was ongoing concern about the classification of industrial assembly, with rules under discussion on exemption from customs duties, which related to the number of people employed and the value of investment and production levels. Pressure to tighten rules on foreign assembly investment came from domestic producers of trucks and buses such as Truckski, who demanded a degree of protection from competition and also from other large foreign investors such as Daewoo who had committed large sums of money. Further, there was antipathy to foreign investors from individual politicians.

A second reason for Volvo needing a high and positive profile in the country and being regarded as a good corporate neighbour lay in the demands of the new competition. In the sale of buses purchased by municipalities and city councils Volvo had extended the package that they offered beyond the provision of finance. From 1998 onwards they offered a wider service relating to trans-portation and planning, providing an overview of the transport needs of a locality and worked with local officials and planners to make adjustments and improvements. In 1999 this strategy had not yet been adopted by other bus makers in Poland, because it required high levels of resources and finance which were beyond the resources of weaker competitors in the market.

In the case of ABB, a presence in the national economy was formalised in their matrix structure. This matrix system meant that senior management in each subsidiary was answerable to a country manager usually based in the capital city, and Business Area managers based outside the country. The purpose of a country headquarters was intended to ensure not only access to decision makers, but to disseminate information regarding national issues, particularly when, in the case of CEE, there were a large number of firms and profit centres operating within each economy. Therefore, when there was a new ABB acquisition managers could benefit from local knowledge embedded in other companies in the group operating in the same country. Important information would include where to recruit, links with universities, building an efficient distribution and service network across product lines, circulating managers among local companies and maintaining good relations with top government officials. Therefore, ABB needed a base inside the country in order to gain local knowledge and a national focal point for collecting tacit knowledge and codifying it for new and existing operations. An understanding of labour relations, banking systems and the establishment of high level contacts with customers were crucial to the operation of the business.

Creative Destruction?

Neoliberal economists assumed that foreign investment in transforming economies would have a competition effect that would stimulate existing firms to restructure and become more efficient. Some evolutionary accounts have suggested that the expertise of incoming foreign investors combined with the knowledge and skills of local firms could produce a beneficial outcome. However, these optimistic scenarios ignore a central feature of capitalism, which is the way in which it simultaneously creates new productive capacity at the same time as destroying the old capacity.

Incoming foreign investment adversely affected indigenous firms who were unable to compete in the case of Volvo and asset stripped in the case of ABB. Truckski was Poland's largest producer of trucks and buses, which was in direct competition with Volvo. The accumulated learning of international oligopolistic TNCs, such as Volvo, in a global market, coupled with the inappropriate corporate culture and learning abilities of previous SOEs, meant that the playing field for indigenous firms was not level. The rhetoric of restructuring and competitiveness to gain ownership of firms and the acquiescence of the workforce were used to mask the intention to asset strip and close the company.

In the case of ABB, between 1990, when it took over the Lodmel SOE, and 1998 the number of workers at ABB Lodmel (power generators) had increased by approximately 25 per cent from 400 to 513 workers. However, employment at Lodmel Drives fell from 1,200 in 1990 to 450 by 1998 and was closed by 2000 with the loss of the remaining jobs.

Truckski: Not a Level Playing Field

After the beginning of transformation in 1990 the privatisation process at Truckski was protracted. Negotiations with Volvo, who wanted to take a bigger share of the firm, were blocked by the trade union Solidarity on the grounds that they wanted to make redundancies. The shares were eventually sold to Sobiesław Zasada Centrum (SZC), a firm owned by a Polish racing driver and backed by Mercedes in 1996. This foreign investor was seen by Solidarity as offering a better long-term future and guaranteeing the necessary level of social provision. A much coveted aspect of the social package was the opportunity for workers to take subsidised holidays in Monte Carlo. The connection with Monte Carlo was the racing driver and owner of SZC and by 1999 500 workers had taken advantage of this subsidised vacation.

Alongside the privatisation negotiations, Truckski began the process of restructuring in 1990 by spinning off non-core activities such as social functions and other small and medium production and service firms. In 1989, total employment stood at 10,000 and by 1999 it had fallen to 2,400 workers. According to senior management there were investments to lower costs, increase efficiency and quality that included: changes in painting technology; technology to lower emissions; cooperation with Mercedes on a new design of city buses and working with Iveco (Ford truck producers) to improve components. However, *Business News from Poland* (1993) claimed that, despite frequent declarations to restructure, SZC has not launched any serious investment projects. By 1998 Truckski's share of the domestic market had fallen to 38.2 per cent, while Volvo's had increased to 14.3 per cent (*Business News from Poland*, 1993).

Truckski's ability to restructure in the face of intensified competition was severely limited. This was reflected in the fact that Truckski vehicles, according to their own management and workers, had a poor reputation for quality and reliability. Their traditional market to the East was severely affected by the Russian financial crisis in 1997. Diversification into Western markets was severely constrained, because they were already saturated. Further, Truckski lacked established service networks to support sales, and crucially competitors were able to offer much better terms of payment through their own credit companies.

Truckski faced problems in the labour market with a large turnover of young management due, at least in part, to the relative geographical isolation of the factory and its inaccessibility without a car. More importantly, Truckski could not compete with the salaries offered by other foreign investors to attract high calibre, well-qualified young professionals. Most of the existing management were internally recruited and had worked for the firm for 20 years or more. Further, Truckski had a relatively old manual workforce with an average age of 43. Solidarity claimed that Volvo had been poaching workers in order to expand, the effect of which was to further deplete the quality of human capital in Truckski.

In mid-1999 the prognosis for Truckski was not good; only a contract to supply a large number of bus chassis to China ensured its survival in 1999. It is clear that this SOE had limited possibilities for competing in an open market, particularly against Volvo's extensive experience of operating in international markets, supported by tried and tested production methods and, importantly, finance and after care facilities. Although it should be noted that other Polish bus producing companies have been more successful. In 2007 Truckski submitted a motion to court for bankruptcy (Infobus, 2008). However, parallel to the decline of Truckski in the town of Truckski-Laskowice has been the arrival of Toyota Motor Industries in 2005, which has invested 250 million euros and created 1,112 jobs in diesel engine production. This is part of a wider pattern of Toyota locating in low wage cost economies (Poland, Czech Republic, Turkey) or those with flexible labour markets (United Kingdom) (Toyota, 2006).

Lodmel Drives: Asset Stripping

The competition effect of ABB on the previous SOE Lodmel was of a different nature. In short, while ABB Lodmel (power transformers) was made internationally competitive, any changes that took place in ABB Lodmel Drives fell far short of making it a serious contender either in the external market or the internal market of the ABB industrial group. ABB Lodmel Drives came from the same parent SOE as ABB Lodmel and was established in 1990. Situated adjacent to each other, the firms shared the same canteen and social facilities. Initially ABB had bought 20 per cent of the shares in the company with the other 80 per cent remaining with the State Treasury. The company made engines for railways, city transport, mining and shipbuilding. In 1990 there was a willingness and enthusiasm from the Solidarity trade union to 'open to the West' and have a foreign investor, and after the agreement was signed with ABB the prospects for the firm were regarded as favourable. Employees' wages were 50 per cent higher than the local average and it was believed that ABB had promised to develop the company and introduce new technology.

By 1993 the workers were already concerned that there had been no new investment or technology transfer, which was reflected in a letter to the management asking for a statement about the future direction of the company and the way in which it was to be developed:

> So far the management has not presented a reliable plan for the Company ... Particularly we badly lack for a clear position of ABB (as shareholder) on its commitment to the Company's future (investment, new technology, licence documentation and marketing support). The continuation of this state is very distressing and may result in a decline of the technological potential of the company and a loss of highly qualified people, which in the future will make it impossible for the company to develop and increase production. (Letter to the Management of Lodmel Drives Ltd, 15 March 1993)

In 1996 ABB purchased 80 per cent of the remaining shares (without informing or consulting with the employees) and the restructuring process was accelerated, but not in ways that the workers had expected. By 1998 there had been six rounds of redundancies reducing the workforce from 1,480 to 460, and production of the second most profitable product discontinued. There was disinvestment in capital equipment with machines simply being moved out of the factory.

The Solidarity trade union supported the idea that restructuring was necessary, but at a meeting held in 1998, management from Zurich argued that there had been no new investment because productivity was low. Solidarity felt that this was disingenuous because workers had not been given the resources or know-how to improve productivity. The firm was operating with exactly the same equipment that had been in place in 1990 and the new technology and technology transfer had failed to materialise. Rather, a process of asset stripping had occurred and I was shown a huge hall that used to employ 400 people in 1994, which, by 1998, was completely empty. The machinery had either been sold or gone to junkyards. In order to save good machines, workers switched labels putting old labels on new machines in the hope that they would remain in the plant. All goodwill had dissipated and great bitterness was evident because Solidarity said that they had gradually realised that ABB had not bought the factory to improve it, but simply as a way of gaining a foothold in the market.

The workers said that they felt emotional about the company, they had fought for it (literally) and wanted it to succeed.[4] The significant wage increase in 1990 was now viewed as a 'sweetener', because although this meant that wages were 50 per cent higher than the average in 1990, it was claimed that they had failed to keep pace with inflation and wage levels were below the average in 1999. Social benefits had also been reduced with the two-week holiday provided for the children of workers scrapped in 1996.

After further rounds of redundancies, in 1998 Solidarity wrote to the Prime Minister to draw attention to what had happened, but felt in a weak and hopeless position in terms of defending jobs. They wanted a third party to look at the accounts as they no longer trusted the information they had been given by ABB.

Today, eight years after the foundation of ABB Lodmel Drives and eight years after ABB's management, the company is more technologically and technically impoverished than it was in 1990. With only 460 employees (in 1990 the company employed 1480 people) and the production space reduced, the company is at the brink of total disintegration. Our continuous intervention and warnings have always been categorically dismissed. The only explanation for the status quo is the company's too small ownership capital. Its growth we are told, is expected with the purchase of Pafawag, the company which could have been our biggest client ... Solidarnosc ABB Lodmel Drives considers these actions to be conscious acts aimed at the destruction of Polish markets and the elimination of Polish companies. In view of this fact we ask the Polish government of the Republic of Poland to verify its policy contributing to the growing poverty and unemployment in Poland. How can we tolerate the situation where Polish companies are being sold for minimal sums and without any support plans? Agencja Rozwoju Przemyslu [Department of Industry] sold 80 per cent of Lodmel Drives secretly, not bothering to inform the company employees. The big question we ask is who really benefits from this kind of privatisation. It is certainly not our country and its citizens. (Letter to the Prime Minister of Poland from NSZZ Solidarnosc (Lodmel Drives), 7 April 1998)

By September 1999 the firm was declared bankrupt and all workers were in the process of being made redundant. It was suggested to me by members of senior management in ABB Lodmel (power generators) that, in 1990, ABB had reluctantly been obliged to acquire Lodmel Drives by the government in order to get the quarry of Lodmel, the power transformers firm. ABB already owned many other firms that made engines and ABB Lodmel Drives was simply surplus to the requirements of ABB's global operations from the beginning.

Conclusion

This chapter has looked at the way that foreign capital tried to impose a new discipline on Polish firms, either those that had been privatised, or new greenfield production, in order to make them competitive in the global economy. However, ABB and Volvo used very different ways of trying to instil new collective understandings by replacing what were deemed to be unsuitable work attitudes carried over from the previous regime. In Volvo, employees were subject to an ongoing process of engendering worker identification with the company, which included close contact with senior management and the use of enabling myths that centred on teamwork, personal development and familial metaphors. In contrast, rather than attempting to get employees to internalise company culture, ABB used blueprints and highly codified procedures to transfer practices relating to HRM, finance and supply management.

Investment by both ABB and Volvo in CEE and Poland was a zero sum game. Between 1990 and 1998 over 54,000 jobs were eliminated in ABB in the US and Western Europe as 46,000 new jobs were added in the Far East and CEE through the acquisition process (*Financial Times*, 1997). A similar story is evident with Volvo. The advantage of lower wages coupled with economies of scale in terms of logistics, supply distribution, the use of high tech equipment and financial and support services in Poland led to the closure of the three European factories in Scotland, Austria and Germany with a loss of 5,300 jobs (Tagliabue, 1998). In 2008

Volvo closed its last bus production facility in Europe in Tampere, Finland (*EuroInvestor*, 2008).

In the case of Volvo and ABB, learning and autonomy have been central to organisational change, but related to coercive rather than liberatory processes. The pace and content of work, and the permanence of these firms in the locality are subject to both the external coercion of the market and the internal coercion of inter-firm competition. The future of ABB Lodmel (power generators) depends on its ability to compete and win contracts within ABB, which relates to its capacity for continual improvements in quality and maintaining low costs relative to other firms within the network. In the case of Volvo, the Polish factory was the 'winner' of inter-company locational tournaments. The ability to deliver on lower cost production led to the closure of three factories elsewhere in Europe in the late 1990s and the closure of the last bus production facility in Tampere, Finland in 2008. However, in the context of new possible production sites opening up further to the East, the viability of that factory within the firm's industrial network in the long term depends on it being able to constantly not only maintain but also improve its performance.

7

EVERYDAY LIFE UNDER NEOLIBERALISM: WORK AND WELFARE

New prescriptions for welfare and work have been at the heart of neoliberal reforms. Full employment and universal benefits are castigated as notions associated with the communist regime, and no longer appropriate to the conditions of global competition. It is argued that these outdated welfare institutions need to be dismantled so that post-communist economies can compete in terms of social and labour costs. Workers are told that high spending on welfare and a lack of flexibility in labour markets are incompatible with winning their share of global mobile investment, viewed as central to the development of Central and Eastern European economies.

Under the tutelage of the IMF cutting public spending was a major pillar of shock therapy in Poland. Since 1990, social policies have undergone many reforms by consecutive Polish governments of different political persuasions. All of these reforms have been marked by drastic budget cuts and reduced welfare, and accompanied by decentralisation of state responsibility for social and family policy. There has been a focus on reducing unemployment rates by cutting benefits, providing 'incentives' to work, and labour market liberalisation through labour law reforms.

Restricting access to benefits, cutting public spending and the drive towards flexible labour markets are a way of trying to impose discipline on labour. Flexible labour markets, in particular, have been advocated by the World Bank, arguing that:

> EU countries may need to err on the side of greater flexibility and lower
> security. This may be the case for newer EU members in particular, because
> they have much poorer business environments, lower employment rates,
> and far greater disparities in employment. (Rashid *et al.*, 2005: 59)

As in Western economies that have gone further down the path of
neoliberal restructuring, a collective interest in and responses to
poverty have been replaced by disinterest (and often denial) and
accompanied by notions of individual responsibility. The cutting
of progressive taxation and welfare spending, enshrined in EU
targets for reducing public sector deficits, has meant a massive
redistribution of income and wealth towards a small layer of
people at the top and the impoverishment of many at the bottom
(Duménil and Lévy, 2005; Harvey, 2005).

The rationale behind these changes in Poland is to increase the
rate of exploitation by making people work harder and longer
for less money, with the minimum safety net and protection, and
the maximum constraints on trade unions in trying to resist these
policies. The 'Marriott men' – the army of consultants, who have
undertaken restructuring on behalf of capital – have pointed to
'problems' of overemployment and excessive welfare provision
by weak governments in the face of popular opposition and
recalcitrant workers who resist new work practices.

This chapter is concerned with how neoliberal policies on work
and welfare have unfolded in Poland since 1990, and the impact
that they have had on the lives of people in terms of what type
of work is on offer, the security of employment, conditions of
work and levels of poverty. However, it is important to note that
these policies have not been simply imposed on an acquiescent
working class; there has been resistance in the workplace and
the wider community by both labour organisations and new
political movements.

Poverty, Inequality and Work Under Communism

Despite an ideological embargo on any discussion of inequality
and poverty under the communist regime, both had existed from

1945 onwards. Podemski (2007) paints a fascinating picture of poverty and class under communism in terms of differences in income, living conditions and lifestyles:

> Membership of the *nomenklatura* guaranteed more than higher incomes. It included retirement benefits, family supplements, special health care benefits, access to spas and hunting resorts ... Such individuals have access to commodities that ordinary men can acquire only after years of waiting and self denial: automobiles, apartments, almost all goods not available on the domestic market. (Smolar, 1983: 47)

The extent of poverty and inequality varied according to how successfully, and usually temporarily, reforms could be introduced to buy off popular protests, usually triggered by increases in food prices. For example, between 1975 and 1979, as Gierek tried to spend his way out of economic crisis, the number of people not reaching the social minimum decreased from one third to one fifth of the population (Podemski, 2007). By 1980, however, living standards were once again on the decline.

There were differences within the working class in terms of salaries, as well as the level of welfare that could be accessed at work, largely through employment in large SOEs (Domanski, 1997). The biggest gap, however, was between the *nomenklatura* and ordinary working-class people. Podemski points to a spectrum of privilege, power and wealth with the 'real owners of the Polish People's Republic' at the top. This meant the party elite, who directly governed, 'having comparable categories of power, wealth and opportunities and monopolising the control over the state's means of pressure and propaganda' (Mach, 2001: 22). Their privileged position was shared with the 'real disposers of the State's means of work' who were the managers of state companies, and exercised power and control over work and the accumulation process. At the bottom was the vast majority of industrial and farm workers who existed on low wages. This polarisation between ordinary workers and the *nomenklatura* sharpened in the 1980s when the managers of SOEs managed to enrich themselves by taking over the assets of their firms, as state control over companies was loosened. The majority of people faced empty shelves and hours of queuing to obtain even the most basic goods (Hardy and Rainnie, 1996).

Poverty was deemed not to exist under the previous regime and levels of poverty were not registered by official statistics (Golinowska, 2000). Therefore we do not know how many people were unable to meet their basic needs under communism, although some authors claim that poverty was widespread (Podemski, 2007). The existence of poverty under the previous regime has to be offset by the fact that full employment (even with low wages) and subsidised food, rent and energy provided a safety net, albeit at a low level. Since 1990 poverty has become an intrinsic reality of transformation and is highly visible in public places. The sharp end of neoliberalism is homeless people living in railway stations, the proliferation of begging and reports in newspapers of the tragedy of old people unable to survive on pensions. In-work poverty is a growing and serious problem as employment is increasingly insecure, casual and badly paid.

Work and Employment

Under the communist regime work was badly paid, but it was relatively secure; full time with high participation rates. Much production took place in large SOEs, which to varying degrees provided a range of leisure and welfare activities, although these had started to diminish in the 1970s.[1] This relative stability in employment came to an abrupt end with the implementation of shock therapy in 1990. Rapid exposure to the global economy from 1990 onwards meant the closure, downsizing or breaking up of SOEs and the large scale bankruptcy of other firms. In the early 1990s this led to a sharp rise in unemployment, and an increase in insecurity and uncertainty for those in work.

A television documentary looked at former workers at the Gdańsk shipyard, Stocznia Gdańska, the birthplace of Solidarity, which at its height had employed 17,000 people (TVP1, 2007). These workers had lost their jobs after working there for 36 years. The shipyard workers spoke about their enthusiasm during the strike in 1980 and how this gave them hope and a vision about the future. They were pictured standing against a background of the ruined remains of buildings, broken empty windows and loose bricks. In 1998 the shipyard was split up and its assets sold to different companies, some of the machinery was taken to a scrap-yard, the ground was divided and sold. This story could be retold about any number of large workplaces that had taken part in the huge Solidarity protests of 1980, only to be downsized or closed after 1990.

The experience of Poland is typical of the experience of the restructuring of labour markets across Central and Eastern Europe (Rainnie *et al.*, 2002). Job security has been replaced by insecurity, through casual contracts and an increase in self-employment. Greater differentials in the value of formal wages have emerged, while the unemployed rely on low value state benefits, disability pensions and informal, legal and illegal income-generating activities.

Unemployment

Table 7.1 shows the impact of shock therapy as unemployment rose sharply between 1990 and 1994. A return to positive rates of growth brought about a fall in the unemployment rate between 1994 and 1998, after which unemployment rose to a new high of 20 per cent in 2003. From 2003 unemployment fell dramatically to 11.6 per cent by 2007 (GUS, 2008). This is partly the result of the boost to demand from Poland's accession to the European Union, which brought about the receipt of structural funds to the tune of 14,000 million euros. Further, the estimated 2 million Poles who left the country to seek work elsewhere in Europe also helped to reduce unemployment.[2]

Claims of success in reducing unemployment need to be treated with caution. In 2007 Poland's unemployment rate of 9.6 per cent[3] was still the second highest in the European Union, even after the exodus of such a huge number of workers. Some economists have suggested that this unemployment figure is exaggerated, because of people working in the informal economy as well as claiming unemployment benefits. In fact, the unemployment figures are artificially low because of people who have opted out of the workforce by taking disability benefits or early pensions, who are not reflected in unemployment figures.

Table 7.1   Unemployment in Poland, 1990–2007

Year	% unemployed	Year	% unemployed
1990	6.5	1999	13.1
1991	12.2	2000	15.1
1992	14.3	2001	17.5
1993	16.4	2002	19.0
1994	16.0	2003	20.0
1995	14.9	2004	19.0
1996	13.2	2005	17.6
1997	10.3	2006	14.0
1998	10.4	2007	11.6

Source: GUS, 2007a: 30

Table 7.2   Six EU Countries with the Highest Unemployment Rate, 2007

Country	% of unemployed
Slovakia	11.3
Poland	9.6
Greece	8.9
Germany	8.4
France	8.3
Bulgaria	6.9

Source: Eurostat

Another important aspect of unemployment is that the overall average figure masks some stark geographical variations. There is a substantial difference in employment opportunities between Poland A in the west of the country, which has a more diverse industrial base and foreign investment, and Poland B in the east, which is more rural and has low levels of foreign investment (Gorzelak and Jalowiecki, 2000). The real distinction, however, is between the big cities such as Warsaw, Wrocław, Białystok and

Kraków, for example, where unemployment in 2007 was between 5 and 8 per cent, and small towns that were dependent on one industry or one large firm with rates of unemployment as high as 32 per cent (GUS, 2008).

The picture is even more complex than this, because particular groups have faced higher rates of unemployment in all regions. In a later chapter I look at how women have lost out in terms of labour market restructuring. They have often been the first to lose jobs and have found it more difficult to find new work, experiencing longer periods of unemployment (Pine, 1995 and 1998; Hardy and Stenning, 2002). As a result, women comprise 60 per cent of the unemployed (GUS, 2008: 25). Generational differences have also emerged – at both ends of the age spectrum. Unemployment has been persistently high among young people, including graduates, such that many of the young unemployed have never had a 'proper job'. In 2006 the 35 per cent unemployment rate for 15 to 24 year olds was approximately double the average rate of unemployment in Poland as a whole (GUS, 2006a: 247). Large numbers of older workers (over 50) have also been laid off, more often through early retirement than redundancy, and have found it difficult to re-enter the labour market (Smith and Stenning, 2006). This is evident in the fact that 48 per cent of those unemployed have been looking for work for over a year (GUS, 2008: 27).

The experience of long-term unemployment is common, especially for those with particular barriers to employment, such as single mothers and those with disabilities. For the majority, unemployment benefits have long since ceased – older workers wait desperately for when they can start receiving their pensions and younger workers are forced to rely on their families, one-off emergency benefits or informal work.

The Polarisation of Wages

Differentials in income did exist under the previous regime, but there has been a profound polarisation in wages since 1990, both within the private sector and between the public and the private sectors. Sectoral restructuring has been connected with an expansion of service sector activity, creating new jobs at one end of the spectrum, in the highly paid finance and business sectors, and at the other end a raft of less secure and low paid employment in lower status sectors. Many of these new growth sectors, especially food retailing, have driven changes in employment contracts, resulting in increasing insecurity in the labour market. This has led to the creation of labour markets characterised by much greater differentials in terms of pay, employment, conditions of work and security.

The key labour market issue has not only been unemployment, but the emergence of in-work poverty. Cities like Wrocław and Warsaw share the same characteristics as other global cities, where the very high salaries of a small group of workers generate a demand for luxury consumption in terms of expensive shops and restaurants. Therefore on the one hand there is a concentration of people working in finance earning high international salaries, and an army of people on low and sometimes poverty wages that service them (Smith *et al.*, 2008). Table 7.3 shows the big gap between those who work in financial intermediation and those who minister to their needs in the health, education and service sectors. Even these figures understate the gap. For example, the average wage for the health sector includes the salaries of doctors and nurses; nurses earn 250–300 euros per month which is much lower than the sector average. Similarly the fact that a layer of people will earn modest administrative salaries in the finance sectors masks the fact there are some very high salaries.

Table 7.3 A Comparison of Wages in Four Sectors, 2006

Sector	Average gross monthly salary			
	Złoty	*Euros*	*USD*	*£*
Hotels and restaurants	1473	412	326	296
Financial intermediation	4096	1146	1685	825
Education	2348	657	965	473
Health	1866	522	767	376

Source: Adapted from GUS, 2006a: 327

In the early 1990s there was an attempt to hold down the pay of public sector workers with the *popiwek*, which limited pay increases in the public sector while allowing those in the private sector to rise. Interviews that we carried out with nurses in the late 1990s showed that their day-to-day experience of making ends meet was a constant struggle. Younger nurses could not afford to leave home and older nurses were dependent on their spouses (Stenning and Hardy, 2005). It is not surprising that teachers and nurses in particular have been involved in several waves of major strikes and protests for better pay.

Many public sector workers suffer from appalling low pay, but do, nevertheless, receive a pay packet. According to the *National Labour Inspectorate* irregular wage payment is a widespread occurrence (Solidarity, 2006b). There have been large numbers of sporadic disputes that have arisen when workers in the private sector have simply not been paid or have had to wait for weeks and sometimes months for their pay. In August 2006 300 women in the Delia textile factory in Zamość went on strike, because they did not receive their wages in June and July. It was the second strike that year because wages in March and April were only paid after a seven-day strike at the beginning of July (Solidarity, 2006a).

Precarious Work and the Drive to Flexibility

Work has become increasingly precarious and casual, with a plethora of different forms of flexibility. The uncertain legal status of temporary contracts, reflecting their relatively recent appearance in CEE labour markets, has seen employers resort to the use of self-employment contracts, enabling avoidance of health and safety responsibilities, regular pay increases and payment of social contributions, and allowing them to dismiss staff more easily (Smith *et al.*, 2008). Sula (2006) estimates that up to 2 million workers may be self-employed through coercion rather than choice.

Using the language of autonomy and flexibility, self-employment is sold as a positive aspect of labour markets, but the experience of self-employment varies according to a worker's position in the labour market. While self-employment can have advantages for workers in higher skilled industries such as IT, it is not an advantage when it has been imposed by employers, in order to give them flexibility and a reduction in costs. In the case of self-employment the payment of social insurance (ZUS) falls disproportionately on the employee.

In Poland as elsewhere, employment agencies have emerged as 'purveyors of flexibility' (Peck et al., 2005; Peck and Theodore, 2007); between 2002 and 2004 the number of temporary employment agencies grew from 80 to 138 (Coe et al., 2007). One interviewee, Maciek, worked in a factory, but was employed by an employment agency, which supplied labour to that workplace. He could be moved on to another workplace, or not given work at all – all at short notice. Further, Maciek was often coerced into working overtime without any additional pay, and faced problems in joining a union because of the temporary nature of the job.

Stenning gives another example of the experience of flexibility in her interviews in Nowa Huta[4] (Smith et al., 2008). Mrs Sasnowicz, a woman in her fifties living with her husband and daughter, had worked in a printing firm through a temporary agency on a series of 355 one-day contracts for a year and a half (four days on, one day off). When the work dried up and she tried to register as unemployed, she found that she lacked one day's work to be eligible for unemployment benefit. Despite these significant difficulties, agencies often provide the easiest way for those with the lowest qualifications and without work to find short-term work. For workers in many of the poorer households periods of unemployment were interspersed with periods of moving in and out of temporary work, and trying to exist on a combination of jobs – formal and informal, temporary and permanent.

The Employers' Offensive

Employers have tried to drive up the rate of exploitation not only through paying low wages, but also by getting workers to work longer and harder with the minimum of protection. This has been reflected in the widespread and systematic flouting of labour laws documented in the *Annual Report on Labour Law Violation in Poland 2006* (Solidarity, 2006b). Supermarkets and hypermarkets have been notorious for poor working conditions and flagrant abuses of labour codes:

> irregularities concerning legal protection of labour related mainly to inaccurate records of working time, failure to provide employees with due rest time, and non-payment of remuneration for overtime work ... and non-observance of binding norms in case of manual handling of loads. There were instances of women transporting loads which weighed 390 kilograms and 304 kilograms by means of a handcart (while the maximum permissible weight limit is 80 kg). (Solidarity, 2006b)

Employers in some workplaces have been quick to dismiss workers who try to join or organise unions. In December 2006 the management of one of Selgros' chain stores near Wrocław dismissed workers who were organising a trade union. Forty out of 350 workers joined and legally registered the organisation. The management refused to accept this and on the same day the shop steward was visited at home and handed a dismissal notice (Solidarity, 2007). Even showing an interest in joining a union can endanger someone's employment. In 2007, the Stokrotka shop in Lublin sacked two women when someone from the management had noticed they were talking with a woman who was a chairperson of a trade union. Wages in these shops are particularly low with 80 per cent of workers earning less than 1,200 PLN gross, that is 620 PLN net (Solidarity, 2007).

The relationship between casualisation and threats to safety at work was evidenced by the Halemba (in Ruda Śląska) coal mine accident in 2006. Twenty-three miners were killed in the biggest tragedy in Polish coal mining for almost 30 years. Trade unions complained that a lack of investment and extensive redundancies had resulted in falling safety standards (Komorovsky, 2006). In 2007 an investigation showed that the methane detectors, which were supposed to warn miners if methane concentration is too high, did not work. Further, the management of the coal mine had taken on unqualified workers who were employed by small private companies in an outsourcing arrangement. The wages of these workers were much lower than those of miners who were directly employed and they lacked other privileges such as earlier pensions (*Kodeks Pracy*). If they had an accident or died at work their families got less help from the coal company or state than the families of miners who were directly employed. In Halemba, out of the 23 miners who died, only eight of them actually were employed by the coal company; 15 were temporary workers from a small private company, some of them with no experience, and the youngest was 21 (Akai, 2006; Easton, 2006). There have been other accidents with temporary workers from agencies, such as an agency worker who was killed in the Łódź Indesit factory. His head was crushed when the safety system that stops the machine working if somebody comes too close was turned off because it halted work too often (*Gazeta Wyborcza*, 17 October 2005).

Migration

One escape from unemployment and low wages has been migration. When Poland joined the EU in May 2004 only the UK, Ireland and Sweden fully opened their labour markets. The commonly accepted figure is that around 2 million Poles have left to seek work elsewhere in Europe. There was not a Polish person that I talked to who did not have a son, daughter, brother, sister, niece or nephew working in either Britain or Ireland. There are no accurate numbers about how many Polish workers are in the UK, but the estimates range between 700,000 and 1 million.[5] Accession to the EU opened up the possibility of working legally in a wide range of sectors in the UK, Ireland and Sweden. Polish newspapers are full of adverts from agencies quick to profit from the new situation, offering jobs in a range of industries such as care (for the elderly and disabled), nursing, engineering and general factory work in the UK.

For some Polish migrant workers this has meant opportunities for skilled work and well paid jobs, particularly in London and Dublin. For others, migration has been motivated by the need to send money home providing short-term support for stretched household budgets.[6] There is overwhelming evidence that Polish migrant workers are being exploited in low paid jobs without security or access to trade union rights – a problem exacerbated by the low level of protection that exists for some categories of workers, such as agency workers (TUC, 2003 and 2004; Donaghey and Teague, 2006; Kropiwiec and King-O'Riain, 2006; Dundon *et al.*, 2007; Hardy and Clark, 2007). However, legal status in the labour market has not removed the threat of abuse by employers. Problems with recruitment and temporary labour agencies are substantial, with some agencies charging workers in their home countries for finding them jobs. A trade union report in the UK found that half the workers surveyed had encountered problems at work in the UK: nearly a quarter had no written contract (this figure was even higher for agency workers); over a quarter had problems with payments, including not being paid for hours worked; discrepancies between pay and payslips; and unauthorised deductions and errors in pay calculations (Anderson *et al.*, 2007). In some instances wages were withheld for months and excessive working hours were commonplace – in some cases with no rest day being provided or inadequate breaks between shifts.

In housing, migration has reintroduced the 'tied cottage system', where the employer providing accommodation gains much more control over workers. Forty per cent of those working for more than 48 hours a week were in accommodation provided by their employer and reported that they had little control, working excessive hours because their employment was linked to their accommodation – which was often very poor and overcrowded (Jordan and Düvell, 2002). In the UK Polish workers tend to be employed in the private sector, which has poor trade union organisation compared with the public sector. Difficulties with the recruitment and organisation of migrant workers are exacerbated by the casualisation of work where workers are often employed, not directly, but by agencies.

Janusz, one migrant worker I interviewed, described how a private transport firm from the UK organised an information session in a prestigious hotel in a major Polish city in 2005. This was attended by Polish bus drivers employed in Warsaw, who were told that they could expect to earn £300 per week in the

UK, after deductions. It would have taken them a month to earn this amount in their current jobs. Within two weeks 22 drivers and two mechanics from the same bus depot left their families to work in the UK. Their initial rate of pay was £4.50 an hour rising to £6.20 after a few months. However, they had to pay £80 a week for accommodation and the amount they earned per week was never as high as the £300 a week they had been promised. When they complained about the difference between what they had been led to expect and their actual earnings an impromptu English exam was organised. Five drivers failed and were immediately sacked, which was intended to warn other drivers about the consequences of complaining. Apart from pay, which was only just above the minimum wage, complete flexibility was required. The so-called 'contract', which was little more than an information sheet, stated, 'There are no regular hours of work, employees are expected to work the hours required for the job'. Drivers could be called at a moment's notice, including the middle of the night. However, despite these conditions the money earned that could be sent back to families was still higher than they would earn in Poland.

Migration provides opportunities for earning money, learning a new language and gaining experience. For young people, in particular, who face 40 per cent unemployment in Poland, it allows participation in the job market for the first time. However, in many cases highly qualified young people with master's level education are working far below their abilities, in employment that has little protection and no structure for development or promotion. Other workers have ended up on the streets when temporary work dries up, and a recent survey found that 18 per cent of London's rough sleepers are now Central and Eastern European (Broomby, 2008).

The migrant workers from South-East Asia who have come to fill gaps in the Polish labour market have even worse pay and conditions. North Korean workers are being used in Polish agriculture and the Gdańsk shipyards under the supervision of the North Korean Communist Party. According to one Polish foreman in the shipyard:

They weld perfectly ... they don't make any trouble. They never come to work hung over ... A Korean even lights a cigarette without taking any break from welding. They work 12 hours a day. When we have a lot of work and a tight deadline, they work even 16 hours a day. Don't write any bad things about them. If those Kim Ir Sens (Korean Labour Party) take them away, the whole production will be stopped ... One Korean worker is worth as much as five Poles. (Chrzan and Kowalski, 2006)

Poverty and Polarisation

When I lived in Warsaw in 2005 I was puzzled to see the same elderly, well-dressed man everyday looking in the communal dustbins. I now realise that he was looking for food or things to sell. A friend told me that this practice of rooting in rubbish for things to sell is widespread. These *nureks* (Polish for divers) 'dive' in dustbins in the streets, local garbage dumps and household rubbish looking for things to sell. They look for paper, and all sorts of cans (especially beer cans because 'they are made of aluminum and you can get a good price for it'). Mrs Tadowska explained:

My husband works not in a centre of Warsaw, but in Wola, that is in the West part of the city. There are not so many banks and posh shops as there are in the centre, more blocks of flats (but they are not slums). He told me that he sees 'divers' every day, some of them with characteristic push-carts (often adapted from baby-carriages), loaded with paper, junk, sometimes a broken fridge or a gas-cooker (that is real luck). Many of them are homeless, mostly alcoholics, but alcoholism isn't usually a cause of their homelessness, it's a way of surviving the dreadful conditions of homeless life. He also told me that some of the people who search through garbage are dressed quite decently, in clean clothes, he said that the same person could be standing in a queue in a bank and would not be out of place. I saw a woman about 50 or 60 years old, she wasn't dressed in shabby clothes, just normal, plain, clean clothes. She had a small stick in her hand, she walked to a street dustbin, quickly searched it through, pulled out an empty can (it was a soft drink), threw it on a pavement and stepped on it (to make it smaller, more convenient for transport), put it in a bag and quickly went to the next dustbin. You need about 65 aluminum cans for 1 kilo and you get about 3 PLN for this.

Professor Hanna Palska confirms this picture of poverty and adds that people do not only search rubbish for things to sell, but also for food (Dyszel, 2006). She relates a conversation with a woman who says:

'You can't even imagine what good things you can find in a scrap heap. Once someone threw away a frozen chicken leg and we had five dinners' says a woman apparently proud of her trophies and on the other hand concealing the source where they came from because searching through rubbish is something you are rather ashamed of ... 'It takes a lot of work and time, but women can really make something out of almost nothing'. They mix milk with water, when they make meat rolls they are mostly made of bread crumbs. (Dyszel, 2006)

The important point that Palska makes is that these are not just exceptional or 'pathological' families, but people who live in constant fear of sickness, hunger or of some sudden catastrophe that they will be unable to cope with:

The world of the poor is a world where you don't earn money, use money (buy or sell goods), you take what they give you, you exchange goods and services with others. A main economical activity is borrowing and trying to get a social benefit from social service. Borrowing isn't easy because the neighborhood is also poor. There are some post-state farm settlements where 95 per cent of inhabitants live only on money they get from social service, and the wealthiest people there, are those who receive old age pensions and a Catholic priest from a local parish. (Dyszel, 2006)

Gazeta Wyborcza carried a report by doctors from Korczak hospital in Łódź, which looked at cases of sick children treated in the paediatric clinic in 2006 (Czerwieński, 2007). They came to the conclusion that one in 20 of them end up in the hospital because their families are poor. In some cases the parents cannot afford to buy medicine or go to a doctor and therefore minor health problems such as asthma are neglected and become serious. In other cases children develop physical symptoms unrelated to an identifiable illness (somatic neurosis), caused by hard living conditions and lack of proper care. For example, one girl of 14 lived with her unemployed parents and sister in one room in the centre of Łódź, and the toilet was shared with other families in the corridor. The doctors suggested that every tenth young patient treated by them last year lived in one room with four other people and 40 per cent of the children live in households without a bathroom, hot water, toilet or central heating (Czerwieński, 2007).

These narratives from interviewees and the press paint a grim picture. However, this anecdotal evidence is well supported by the statistics. Table 7.4 shows that Poland has a high number of people at risk from poverty after social transfers in comparison with the Czech Republic and Slovakia, for example. Rather, Poland is bottom of the league table with countries such as Lithuania, Latvia and Romania, where risk from poverty is higher than the average for the EU.

Table 7.4   At Risk of Poverty Before and After Social Transfers

	Percentage of people at risk from poverty after transfers	
	2000	2006
Latvia	–	23
Lithuania	17	20
Romania	17	19
Poland	16	19
Hungary	11	16
Slovakia	–	12
Czech Republic	8	10
Average EU 25	16	16

Source: Eurostat

Along with Latvia, Lithuania and Romania, income inequality is higher in Poland than other European post-communist economies. Table 7.5 shows the ratio of total income received by the 20 per cent of the population with the highest income compared to that received by the 20 per cent of the population with the lowest income. Therefore the 20 per cent of people with the highest income had an income that was 6.6 times higher than the 20 per cent of Poles with the lowest income. This inequality has increased since 2000.

Table 7.5   Inequalities in Income Distribution in Selected Countries

	Ratio of total income received by 20% of population with highest income compared to that received by 20% of population with lowest income	
	2000	*2005*
Lithuania	5.0	6.9
Latvia	5.5	6.7
Poland	4.7	6.6
Romania	4.6	4.9
Hungary	3.3	4.0
Slovakia	na	3.9
Czech Republic	3.4	3.7
Average EU 25	4.5	4.9

Source: Eurostat

At the other end of the scale the number of Polish multimillionaires increased from 16 in 2006 to 25 in 2007. Even more spectacularly, the percentage increase in the wealth of the top 100 Poles rose from 18.5 per cent in 2006 to 53.7 per cent in 2007 (Wprost, 2007).

Dismantling Welfare

In 1989 the post-Solidarity government immediately replaced universal and work-based welfare policies with limited and targeted measures. Protective laws existing under the old regime, which provided special entitlements for the mothers of young children and single mothers, were the first to be questioned. Any notion of welfare and public care that existed under the previous regime has disappeared from the political agenda and resurfaced in terms of personal responsibility and incentives.

In the late 1990s the post-Solidarity AWS [Akcya Wyborcza Solidarność: Solidarity Electoral Action] government turned its attention to injecting market forces into the public sector and public administration (Kolarska-Bobińska, 2000a and 2000b). This comprised four interrelated reforms – of pensions, local government, health and education – which were driven in large part by the bureaucratic and neoliberal preconditions for European Union accession.

Reform of local government established 16 *voivode* (previously 49) to bring it into line with European Union territorial units, irrespective of whether this made sense in the Polish context (Smith and Hardy, 2004). This has meant that the organisation, management and financing of social services, including child care centres, nursery schools, primary schools, centres of culture and sports centres, have been delegated to territorial communities (*gmina*), which in turn have had to cut many facilities or raise the price of services due to a lack of resources (Glass and Fodor, 2007). At the heart of all of these reforms was an attempt to decentralise, to rationalise and to introduce the market into public institutions. The implementation of the World Bank's pension formula has obliged both public and private sector workers to organise pension provision through the private sector (Stroinski, 1998). When privatised pensions were introduced in 2000 the main towns and cities were full of billboards with pictures of kindly looking elderly gentlemen, encouraging you to place your pension for safekeeping with their financial institution. It is too early to tell what the impact of this will be, but it leaves workers relying on the vagaries of financial markets to provide their main income in old age.

In Poland there has been a focus on reducing unemployment rates by cutting benefits, providing 'incentives' to work, and liberalising labour markets through labour law reforms. The Polish government's 2002 *Entrepreneurship, Development, Work Programme*, including its *First Work* initiative and its plan to ease the Labour Code, have made it easier to both hire and fire workers. In Poland, while successive governments, on the left and right, did move to make the Labour Code more flexible and to control government spending, the biggest assault on welfare was the 2003 Hausner Plan.[7] This was driven by the public spending cuts demanded by the European Union. The proposals would have pushed the retirement age up to 65 for women, excluded large numbers of people from receiving disability pensions and from the right to a minimum pension. The most important type of income support for those out of work is not unemployment benefit, but social pensions and disability pension in particular, which is disimbursed to 3.2 million people – roughly 13 per cent of the working age population (Danmarks National Bank, 2005).[8] The Hausner Plan represented a significant attack on welfare and social security and was dropped in the face of massive opposition to cuts in social expenditure, not only by the public and trade unions, but from the SLD (Sojusz Lewicy Demokraty-cznej: Democratic Left Alliance), Hausner's own ruling party and its junior partner in government, the UP (Unia Pracy: Union of Labour). The Hausner proposals were in line with the demands of foreign capital and its representatives. The level of public debt in relation to GDP was considered too high against EU benchmarks and corporate commentators suggested that plans to water down the Hausner Plan 'jars badly with the view in financial markets' (Capital Market Research, 2004). However, the percentage spent on social protection is hardly generous and Table 7.6 shows that Poland spends significantly less per head than Slovakia, the Czech Republic and Hungary.

Table 7.6   Percentage of GDP Spent on Social Protection: Selected EU Countries in 2006

Country	Euros per head spent on social protection
Poland	555
Slovakia	623
Hungary	689
Czech Republic	1149

Source: Adapted from Eurostat

This move from universalism to tailored policies limits access to benefits for the poorest members of society. In Poland neither parental nor family benefits may be claimed on the basis of universal rights, both are means tested, and parental leave and allowances can only be claimed by women who have spent a year in the labour force. The number of people in receipt of welfare is very low. In 2000 only 5 per cent of women received child care or maternity leave, 3 per cent of families received poverty assistance, 34 per cent received old age or disability benefit and 10 per cent received unemployment benefit (Glass and Fodor, 2007). By 2006 only those families whose per capita income fell below one fourth of the average wage were entitled to benefits (Heinen and Wator, 2006).

The Case of Health

Market Driven Reforms

Market driven reforms in the health service have been chaotic, chronically underfunded and have provoked a series of high profile industrial disputes and protests from health workers since 1999 (Czarzasty, 2003, 2006 and 2007). In the summer of 2007, nurses protesting against low wages and underfunding camped outside the Prime Minister's office for four weeks. From the perspective of patients the widespread need to pay for 'extras' (Grodeland et al., 1998; Lewis, 2000; Miller et al., 2000) leaves those with less money waiting longer, without access to the drugs they need and with worse access to doctors. The financial chaos has been reflected in the bankruptcy of several hospitals and the near bankruptcy of many more.

The 1952 Constitution guaranteed the Polish health care system as free and comprehensive, albeit of much better quality for the party elite and their families. In the last two decades of the communist regime, increasing crises in the Polish economy meant that comprehensive care became progressively less dependable for those without party contacts or enough money to buy care outside of the official system. The immediate period after transformation in 1990 saw the privatisation of pharmacies and the entry of big pharmaceutical companies from the West, which pushed up the prices that people paid for drugs (Kozek, 2006). Abusing their monopoly status and corrupting officials and the managers of medical institutions were common methods used by these companies (Kozek, 2006: 6). The funding for hospitals, on the other hand, came from a patchwork of voluntary contributions and local and national health care taxes.

The 1999 health reforms introduced by the AWS separated the management and financing of health care and introduced a compulsory insurance premium (collected through income tax) paid to new regional health funds (*kasa chorych*) (Tymowska, 2001).[9] This introduced previously unknown concepts of managerialism and cost accounting to the delivery and organisation of health care, introducing market mechanisms into the management and financing of health care. These reforms also set the stage for privatisation by opening up health provision for private contractors. The outcomes of these reforms were hospital closures and the highly uneven provision of health services, which were dependent on the revenue base of each region. Some health funds were much better off than others because they had access to a higher earning and/or larger working population; therefore access to and the quality of health care was something of a lottery.

The SLD government, elected in 2001, inherited a hugely unpopular system, which had seen nurses occupying the offices of the Health Minister among other militant protests in 2000 (Stenning and Hardy, 2005). However, the SLD were equally wedded to the neoliberal reforms of their predecessors, and the fiscal austerity required by the EU. In April 2002, the then SLD Health Minister, Mariusz Łapiński, announced a set of proposals to restructure the administration of the health care system and improve access. The main change in the system was the replacement of the 17 health funds with one National Health Fund (Narodowy Fundusz Zdrowia, NFZ). However, delays to the reform exacerbated the situation in the health care system with, and according to the government itself, the majority of health care institutions ending 2003 in deficit.

Rising debts coupled with a problematic transition from the old to the new system resulted in chaos in the health care system and, among other problems, fears of the non-payment of wages. The reforms did not tackle the underlying problem of chronic underfunding as the government was equally committed to holding down public spending. Łapiński himself was accused of destroying the health care system and was, in January 2003, replaced as Minister for Health. These problems sparked a new wave of militancy among health care workers. Nurses and midwives (through the OZZPiP nurses' union[10]) took part in local occupations of municipal offices to protest against the bankruptcy and closure of hospitals as well as national protests calling for the payment of outstanding wages (including the increases promised in 2001 and still not paid), and an end to repeated and damaging reforms (Czarzasty, 2003).

Problems continued to beset the health service and in a high profile case in February 2007 a court ruled that lenders could sue hospitals to collect 100 per cent of their debts, which endangered the existence of many hospitals. The most high profile case was a major hospital in Wrocław (Poland's fourth largest city), which lost its main source of cash after creditors seized money that was allocated for the hospital by the state fund (NFZ). Parents of children being treated in the hospital for cancer appeared on the TV accusing the creditors of dooming their children to a slow death (Kruk, 2007).

Poland's health care system compares badly with other European and OECD countries (Table 7.7). Spending per head on health is significantly less than two comparable post-communist economies – Hungary and the Czech Republic – and only Slovakia is lower in terms of the proportion of GDP spent on health.

This poor comparison with the rest of Europe and OECD countries is supported by figures from the government showing a deterioration in provision, with a 10 per cent fall in the number of doctors between 2000 and 2005 (GUS, 2006b: 375). Further, Poland has the lowest number of doctors per 100,000 people in the European Union. This figure is 213 in Poland in comparison with 278 in Hungary, 292 in Latvia and 354 in the Czech Republic (Eurostat).

Table 7.7   Health Care Spending in Selected OECD Countries, 2004

	Health care spending per capita (USD)	Health care spending as a % of GDP	% of health care publicly financed
US	6,102	15.3	45
UK	2,508	8.1	86
Greece	2,162	10.0	53
Spain	2,094	8.1	71
Czech Republic	1,361	7.3	89
Hungary	1,276	8.0	73
Poland	805	6.5	69
Slovak Republic	777	5.9	88
Turkey	580	7.7	72
Average (excluding US)	1,445	7.7	75

Source: Peterson and Burton, 2007

Creeping Privatisation

Growing privatisation is reflected in the fact that by 2004 only 69 per cent of funds for health came from the public sector (see Table 7.7). Between 1995 and 2005 there was a clear contraction in public health facilities and sharp growth in the private sector, with the number of public hospitals falling from 696 to 611 (12 per cent), and an increase in private hospitals from 9 to 170 (GUS, 2006b: 383). In the same period there has been a fall in the number of publicly funded beds from 214,000 to 171,000 (20 per cent), and an increase in private beds from 143 to 8,215 (GUS, 2006b: 383).

Chronic underfunding, marketisation and constant reforms have had a deleterious effect on the experience of and access to health care. It is estimated that the out-of-pocket contributions made for health care in 2004 is 28 per cent of the total (Peterson and Burton, 2007: 141). Kozek (2006) claims that: 55 per cent of patients seek out private practitioners; 41 per cent pay for medicines while in hospital; 37 pay so-called 'tokens of gratitude'; 29 per cent pay for their surgery; and 10 per cent pay to have waiting times shortened (Kozek, 2006). The number of public consultations in 2006 was 94,230 compared with 167,022 private ones, and this suggests that many ordinary people may feel driven to the private sector to get treatment (GUS, 2006a: 381).

Conclusion

By 2008 unemployment had fallen to 11.6 per cent, and while this was a substantial decrease from 20 per cent in 2003, it was still nearly the highest rate in the European Union. This average rate of unemployment masks the fact that younger and older workers, women and people living in small towns and rural areas, face greater difficulties on the labour market. In some sectors where there were labour shortages wages rose between 2004 and 2008, but many people face in-work poverty and those working in the public sector struggle to make ends meet. The drive towards flexible labour markets means that work has become more casual and precarious and many people eke an existence in the informal economy. A deterioration in the quality and availability of public benefits, particularly in child care and early childhood education, has exacerbated social polarisation.

The health service has been at the centre of controversy, particularly since 1999. Underfunding and chaotic reforms have led to uneven and uncertain access to health care for patients, and poor wages and working conditions for health workers.

Creeping privatisation means that those who can afford it (as well as those that can't) take out private health insurance, others make payments on a one off basis and the rest simply have to accept what is on offer. This reflects one of the primary features of neoliberalism, which is the marketisation and commodification of welfare stretching into all aspects of everyday life.

Since 2004, migration has offered an escape from unemployment, poverty wages and/or a lack of opportunities. The uneven development of capitalism leaves individuals between a rock and a hard place, when the choice is between poverty at home and working in the UK or Ireland in poor conditions. Leaving children at home, either in the care of one parent or grandparents, or moving the whole family to a new environment isolated from wider family and friends is not an easy decision. In contrast to a successful minority who make up a new affluent class, for most people everyday life is hard and getting harder.

8

WORKERS' ORGANISATIONS IN A GLOBAL ECONOMY

The pessimism that has infected accounts of Polish workers' organisations is part of a wider dismalism about the role of trade unions. The arguments used in Poland are not that dissimilar to those advanced in the heartlands of capitalism, which point to the role of technology, the decline of traditional sectors and the rise of the 'new economy' as heralding the end of the working class and labour solidarity. However, these arguments are not new, and the notion of post-industrial society and claims that workers are uninterested in labour organisations have a legacy that stretches back several decades.[1]

Assessments of the current state of the Polish trade union movement suggest that its role is declining and peripheral (Pollert, 1999; Cox and Mason, 2000; Meardi, 2002 and 2004). Others have argued that workers' organisations have been further undermined by the main unions being ideologically driven, adversarial and mutually hostile, because of their political associations with either post-Solidarity or post-communist governments (Ost, 2001 and 2002). Further, it has been suggested that the possibility of solidarity has been reduced by fragmentation and the proliferation of small unions (Gardawski, 2003). Gloomy prognostications are compounded by claims that there is widespread scepticism about organisational participation in political parties and trade unions (Martin and Cristescu-Martin, 2004).

In this chapter I want to argue that this miserable picture does not reflect what is happening to Polish workers' organisations and to offer a different account from the one of decline, fragmentation and ongoing marginalisation. By 2005, existing trade unions (as well as new ones) had responded to the challenges of an increasingly liberalised and marketised economy, by a step change in attitudes to recruitment, organisation and industrial action, particularly in new sectors of the economy. In addition, the adoption of new discourses on issues such as 'mobbing' (bullying) and discrimination in the workplace offered the possibility of reinvigorated activity against managerial control, while accession to the EU consolidated relationships with other European trade unions through European Works' Councils. Many accounts have focused almost exclusively on organised workers in production, at the expense of paying attention to the large number of disputes and protests in the public sector, often led by women workers. The summer of 2007 saw the second wave of huge protests by nurses and health workers, with a camp set up for four weeks on the pavement next to Łazienki Park opposite the Prime Minister's office.

By 2008 there were marked changes in labour market conditions brought about by Poland's entry to the European Union in 2004. Migration and the subsequent fall in unemployment had led to an increase in strikes (or threatened strikes) on pay and union recognition rather than defensive strikes for back pay or the non-payment of wages. Further, the existence of long standing hostilities between the main trade unions has to be tempered by a recognition that relationships between them are much more complex and not as divisive and destructive as some accounts suggest. Relations between unions at a national level and the degree of solidarity or hostility vary from sector to sector. At a regional or workplace level there is much more evidence of solidarity than antipathy.

The debate about Polish labour organisations has to be seen against the backdrop of the huge challenges that workers' organisations faced as a result of deep restructuring and rapid integration with the global economy since 1990. Steel, shipyards, mining and heavy industry were the backbone of the economy before 1990 and were workplaces where workers were relatively privileged in terms of pay and the prestige they commanded. Changes that have taken place in more than three decades in advanced European economies have been condensed into a much shorter time period in Poland with profound impacts on the structure of employment. There has been a rapid growth in the service sector with an expansion of jobs in retailing and business services, as well as the growth of new types of flexible and casual contracts. These growing sectors had little tradition of workplace organisation and attempts to start unions from the mid-1990s met with enormous hostility, particularly from foreign investors. Furthermore, many SOEs, which had been at the centre of workers' struggles in the early 1990s, have been either closed, 'downsized' or fragmented.

Some foreign investments brought relatively good quality jobs, in term of wages and conditions, for example, in some of the new car plants. However, foreign owned supermarkets have brought a litany of complaints about poor pay and degrading treatment, of largely women workers. Exploitation is not simply about low pay or bad treatment at work. There is an inherent contradiction between capital and labour and therefore workers are exploited in an objective sense, whether they work in car factories or supermarkets. The intensification of competition has meant that those workers, even in relatively well paid workplaces, have been put under pressure to cut costs and increase productivity and this was clearly evident in the disputes about pay that dominated the car factories in Poland in 2007. Any discussion about the role of organised labour must take as its starting point the assumption that the conditions for exploitation always exist under capitalism. How this is manifested in terms of employers' offensives and the response and combativity of workers depends on the complex interplay of structural and institutional conditions, as well of course as the role played by labour organisations themselves.

Workers' Organisations from 1945 to 1990

The history of Polish workers' organisations was covered in detail in Chapter 2, and therefore only a very brief summary is given here. Migration to the cities, violent class conflict, unemployment, poverty and powerful labour organisations were all familiar experiences to pre-war Polish workers (Kenney, 1997).

When Stalinism was imposed in 1948, Poland's working-class communities drew on shared history to be a much more powerful force than the Communist Party expected. In the immediate post-war period there was a struggle over factories and the labour process as dozens of factories were taken over and run by workers. What began as a continuation of wartime workers' resistance, briefly promised to sprout into a foundation of workers democracy, but ended as a barely remembered forerunner of the workers' councils of 1956–57 and 1980–81.

The communist leaders' rhetoric of a 'workers' state' masked the way in which the terrain of the shop-floor was always a key area for conflict between workers and the state in general, and their immediate managers in particular. The Communist Party used a combination of coercion and cajoling to try and increase productivity and dominate the workforce, which included speedups, discipline and enthusiasm campaigns. Passive resistance from workers included absenteeism and general indiscipline and therefore SOEs were sites of permanent conflict (Burawoy, 1985).

The high spot of workers' struggles in Poland was in 1980, when Solidarity drew every oppressed, downtrodden and exploited section of society behind its banner. In only a few months 10 million people had joined Solidarity and there were factory occupations from one end of the country to the other. Although Solidarity united disparate elements who opposed the communist regime, it was essentially a workers' organisation formally founded by inter-workplace committees in September 1980 (Barker, 1986; Biezenski, 1996).

The defeat of Solidarity and the introduction of martial law in 1981 led to the imprisonment of thousands of the most militant workers and leaders. Solidarity's struggle was driven by the idea of a 'self limiting revolution',[2] and the rest of the decade witnessed the rout of any element of socialism within Solidarity's analysis. During the 1980s, the leadership of Solidarity moved to the right, to the extent that by 1989 it held a position that the introduction of unbridled market forces was the only way of reforming the system.

In the months leading up to the creation of the first post-war non-communist government, the National Executive Committee of Solidarity publicly stated its support for the market reforms. Lech Wałęsa called for a six-month strike moratorium and, fêted by the likes of Thatcher and Reagan, consistently played a role of calling off strikes and trying to deliver an acquiescent working class. Therefore the Solidarity leadership saw its role as providing a 'protective umbrella' for the new government, necessary because of the potential backlash of the effects of shock therapy.

From Survival to Revival: 1990–2004

No Blank Cheque for Neoliberalism

January 1990 saw a jump to the market through the implementation of draconian economic policies collectively known as shock therapy. Ost (2006) claims that Solidarity, as an organisation, smoothed the way for the implementation of neoliberalism by diverting labour onto the safe targets of 'red barons' and nationalism. In his earlier work he wrote extensively about the pro-market stance of workers and the blank cheque that Solidarity gave for the shock therapy measures, which he argues helped to negotiate the terms of labour's capitulation. This takes a very top-down view of Solidarity and does not give sufficient recognition to the tension between Solidarity as a political party and Solidarity as a trade union. It also fails to take account of the conflict evident within the national leadership and its workplace and regional organisations. This was reflected in the fact that the 'protective umbrella' did not stop strikes and workplace struggles.

In 1990 as the reality of shock therapy set in, there were strikes in transport, coal and copper mining. In 1991 teachers went on strike as their wages were held down by an incomes policy (the *popiwek*), which particularly punished public sector workers. From 305 strikes in 1991 the number of strikes rose to 6,322 in 1992 and 7,443 in 1993 in a huge upsurge of industrial action and protest. Two of the largest protests included a strike of 38,000 workers at the Polska Miedź copper mining and smelting plant in Lublin and a strike involving 3,000 workers at the FSM car plant in Tychy. In December 1992 an 18-day strike in the Silesian coal mines involved 300,000 workers at 65 of the region's 70 coal mines as they demanded higher pay and a slower pace of restructuring. This upsurge in industrial action culminated in a two-day strike in the capital, called by the Warsaw region of Solidarity in May 1993. One of the Solidarity miners' members of parliament called for a vote of no-confidence in the Prime Minister Hanna Suchocka, leading to the collapse of her government. The 'Solidarity' Prime Minister had been overthrown by the Solidarity union.

The belief that the new market model would quickly bring Western-style capitalism and rising living standards to all gave way to despair and disillusion as unemployment grew. In the early phase of transformation, some workers and Solidarity members had illusions in the market, but in workplaces there were big struggles against privatisation and job cuts. The leadership of Solidarity could not contain their angry members. The strikes in the early 1990s enabled the Network (*Siec*), an informal grouping of local Solidarity branches in the country's largest SOEs, to pose a direct challenge to the Solidarity leadership. Members of the Network argued for a much more radical approach and some branches, especially those affiliated to the August '80 trade union,[3] openly called for sympathy strikes and mass protests throughout the whole state industrial sector (Kramer, 1995).

From the high point of industrial action in 1993 there was a gradual decrease in the number of strikes. However, it should be noted that the data on strikes over this period are not compatible with those from previous years. This is because GUS (the Polish Statistical Office) applied new methods that understate the number of disputes. More importantly, strike statistics tell us nothing about struggles in workplaces that fell short of strike action. The labelling of workers as pro-market does not grasp the contradictory attitudes of Polish workers to transformation. It is not surprising that some workers supported the idea of the market; after all, this appeared to be the antithesis of the communist system, which had been repressive and had failed miserably to deliver any increase in standards of living. However, the realities of the market in the workplace were met with fierce struggles to maintain control and representation, as well as implacable opposition to redundancies. The account below tells the story of the struggle in one factory.

Polar: The Struggle for One Workplace

In 1990 Polar was Poland's largest producer of washing machines and refrigerators and employed 5,000, largely women workers. Polar was an archetypal SOE that owned buildings, transportation, warehousing facilities and railway sidings. In addition, in 1997 it continued to provide extensive social functions such as holiday homes, child care, cheap summer camps for children, and a health centre with a physiotherapist and gynaecologist. Aside from being a flagship enterprise and large employer, it was also politically significant. Polar was one of the main centres for Solidarity in the region and one of the first factories on strike in 1980.

Within the factory, the privatisation process was slow and contested at every stage. Between 1989 and 1996, Solidarity and the workers' council were a major force in negotiating and shaping the restructuring process. The reinvigoration of workers' councils in late 1989 enabled the employees of large SOEs to have a major influence on the disposal of their firms. They used their leverage to slow down the pace of large scale privatisation and prevent, or at least forestall, major layoffs. In Polar between 1989 and 1996, there were seven managing directors who were dismissed in turn by the workers' council as Solidarity tried to protect the long-term development of the firm. The company Prospectus (1996) reveals the frustration of Western consultants, who appeared to be completely taken aback when their 'restructuring package' was challenged by workers. They saw the workers' council as blocking change and preventing the emergence of a structure, which enabled management to reassert control over the workplace:

It should be pointed out that key members of the company's management were removed from their offices several times in the 1990s resulting from

> recurrent conflict with the trade unions. The lack of personal continuity and the above mentioned conflict made efficient management of the company difficult and diverted attention of individual teams from issues related to the company's development. (Prospectus for Polar company, 1996: 38)

Privatisation *per se* was not opposed by Solidarity, but the particular route to be followed was disputed. Any situation where there would be one (foreign) strategic investor such as Electrolux or Daewoo, both of whom had already shown an interest in the company, was strongly opposed. Solidarity's argument was that this would not be in the best long-term interests of the firm and its workers, because the new investor would not be interested in developing the firm, only gaining a foothold in the market. This was in line with aspirations for a distinctly Polish capitalism (see Hardy and Rainnie, 1996).

It was eventually agreed in December 1995 that Polar would be floated on the Warsaw Stock Exchange. Solidarity and the workers' council bargained hard for 9.6 million Polish złoty to be set aside from earnings retained by the enterprise for the purchase of shares by workers through the establishment of a company called EKO Polar. The Western consultants were clearly nonplussed by this arrangement, which ceded a significant proportion of shares to the workers collectively, with the workers' council as the guardian.

> the envisaged outflow of a part of the Company's equity (reserve privatisation capital) in the amount PLN 9,600,000 allocated for borrowings to the company's employees has to raise doubts of the auditors. (Prospectus, 1996: 13)

There was further conflict over redundancies. In May 1998, following the November 1997 privatisation, McKinsey consultants recommended 910 redundancies, 410 of which would be compulsory. Solidarity refused to accept these recommendations and commissioned a counter report, which suggested that the McKinsey figures were superficial and the financial arguments unconvincing. Management withdrew the 410 redundancies.

A further battle ensued over the proposed cuts in social provision, particularly getting rid of health care. The low wages of women workers in the factory and an underfunded and deteriorating state health service meant that the retention of on-site medical facilities was considered a huge benefit for workers. Despite threatening to sell off holiday homes in 1998, Solidarity managed to ensure that they retained part of these social assets. According to Solidarity, in 1998 an average of 1,300 children per year used the facilities. Workers paid 25 per cent of the cost of a holiday, and if they did not use the facilities and took a 'holiday under the pear tree' (stayed at home), they were entitled to a bonus of 600 złoty (approximately £140).

By 2008 a new dispute had erupted between the unions in Polar (OPZZ[4] and Solidarity) and the management over the poor conditions of work and pay of agency workers in comparison with permanent employees. Polar was not an exception in the battle over the control of work, jobs and welfare and many other SOEs resisted marketisation, to a greater or lesser degree. The scant coverage of these workplace struggles in accounts of transformation overestimates the degree of compliance with the market and neoliberalism.

Organising in the 'New Economy'

One general claim made in advanced economies is that restructuring has undermined the traditional bases of trade unions, and that the rise of the new economy has undermined workers' solidarity. Ost's research reported workers who were 'apologetic about their [union] allegiance', and who only 'grudgingly admitted to their status' (2002: 521). Further, he suggested that unions had an 'allergy against the notion of recruitment', because given the obligation of trade union membership in the communist period, it was 'seen as bad taste to try to convince others to join' (Ost, 2002: 521). The changing structure of the Polish economy has been discussed at some length in Chapter 5. This had profound implications for labour organisations, which faced falling membership in traditional bastions, and a growth in employment in the finance and retail sectors and other service sectors such as security guards and drivers, which had little tradition of trade union organisation. Whereas productive capacity had contracted in some industries other new areas were opening up, such as automobiles and vehicles, where most major transnational automotive producers had a presence in the country.

By 1998 Solidarity took stock of a dismal situation, where haemorrhaging membership threatened the existence of the union in workplaces, and adopted a strategy of active recruitment. In general, although not exclusively, this was aimed primarily at new sectors of employment and in particular focused on supermarkets, truck drivers and security guards. The head of Solidarity's Recruitment and Organisation Department in Gdańsk attended the AFL/CIO Solidarity Centre in the USA to gain experience of strategies for recruitment. By 2005 there were six full time organisers based in Gdańsk, each having responsibility for different sectors and another 24 organisers based in 14 Polish regions.

A fundamentally different strategy was demanded by this recruitment initiative. This had to be much more energetic in identifying workplaces, imaginative in establishing contact with workers and persuasive in recruiting employees in the face of a poor media image. This was a huge departure from the way that Solidarity had operated previously. In supermarkets, workers had been sacked for trying to start unions and organisers were ejected from the premises if they came on site. Solidarity's tactics included high profile stunts such as a group of organisers, dressed in union teeshirts, leafleting inside a supermarket to try and embarrass management to negotiate with them. In other supermarkets every shift from 5.00 in the morning was leafleted, in addition to holding meetings outside of the workplace. Innovative tactics had to be deployed. One union organiser reported recruiting off-duty security guards at the gym and transport workers at international borders.

This new strategy posed a number of challenges. The first step was to convince Solidarity's full-time employees of the need to 'quit their desks and get out to workplaces'. Some of them found this new way of working difficult, or objected to it as being evangelical and using scarce resources. Long standing members carried the memory of the 1980s, when people joined in their hundreds and thousands spontaneously. In some quarters this legacy reinforced passivity and widened the gap between 'old veterans' and 'new activists'.

In 1999 Gardawski wrote that unions barely existed in factories owned by foreign investors and Ost talks about his experience in the state-of-the-art General Motors factory in Gliwice, which was opened in 1998. Ost concludes that:

> Modern HRM practices came to Silesia with a sheen and a glitter that makes trade unions seem hopelessly retrograde. For its young and hopeful workforce, Opel offered a smarter and shinier community than any of the available unions could provide. And the unions seemed to agree. Far from developing innovative strategies to gain access to the site, local officials stayed away, seeing it as one of the hopes of the future where unions do not belong. (2002: 45)

By 2005, these comments had been overtaken by new developments as this very factory was cited as one of Solidarity's success stories. It had recruited 40 per cent of the workforce, established negotiating structures with management and spawned a new layer of young activists. The sheen of even the most dazzling of foreign investments can eventually wear thin. In an increasingly competitive global market, conditions will always exert continual pressure on management to drive down costs with implications for working conditions and salaries. Therefore despite firms in the automotive sector having handpicked young and eager workers, they have not succeeded in sidelining trade unions.

The discussion so far has centred on Solidarity and it is important to make a few comments about the second largest union OPZZ, about which much less has been written. OPZZ, founded in 1984, was the official union established by the Communist Party, which absorbed all existing trade unions into a federated organisation to try and counteract the influence of Solidarity, which had been banned in 1981. OPZZ is absent from many accounts of trade unions or dismissed as a moribund organisation that was simply a transmission belt for Communist Party policies in the workplace. After the fall of the communist government it was viewed as being politically allied with various left wing post-communist parties such as the SLD. However, some of its affiliated unions have long histories and especially since 1990 a large degree of autonomy. For example, the ZNP (Polish Teachers' Union),[5] had 300,000 members in 2007 and a strong sense of individual identity. It has been confident not only in opposing both post-Solidarity and SLD government on the wages and working conditions of teachers, but also has criticised both governments for sending (and keeping) troops to Iraq.[6] Although OPZZ has some continuities with the past, one of its affiliates has also had some success in recruiting workers in supermarkets and the finance sector.

Labour Solidarity

It is claimed that the fragmentation of labour organisations and mutual hostility between the main players has undermined solidarity and limited the influence and power of trade unions in the workplace, and in the movement as a whole. The formation of a plethora of small unions was the product of legislation, which allowed a minimum of ten people to form a union and protected its leaders from dismissal. This splintering into many small unions was often a defensive reaction to the threat of redundancy and seemed to be much more prevalent in former SOEs. For example, in 2005 there were 30 different unions in the railway sector.

The formation of the trade union federation FZZ goes against this trend, representing the consolidation of some of the previously fragmented unions. It was formed after discussions in the late 1990s between major independent unions (notably the nurses, steelworkers and railway workers), and held its inaugural conference in 2002. This new federated organisation gave a collective voice to a number of unions that had remained outside of Solidarity and OPZZ, and with a membership of 450,000 in 2007 it represented a significant third force among trade unions. Some of the participating unions had a long history, such as the railway workers' union founded in 1918, whereas the nurses' union was only formed in 1995. In contrast to OPZZ and Solidarity, which were viewed as having strong links with or allegiances to political parties, one of the aims of FZZ was to establish a trade union federation that was politically independent.

Another strand of pessimistic thinking about the Polish labour movement suggests that the potency of trade unions is undermined by 'controversial pluralism' or 'conflictual pluralism', which views the main unions, Solidarity and OPZZ, as 'adversarial and dependent on political conflict' (Meardi, 2002: 83). The hostilities between Solidarity and OPZZ have their roots in the 1980s, when many Solidarity activists were arrested and interned after the introduction of martial law in 1981. Solidarity's property, land and equipment were confiscated and given to OPZZ – this was a huge bone of contention and only resolved in 2005. Those that joined OPZZ were considered by Solidarity to have passively or actively collaborated with the regime, and in turn OPZZ regarded Solidarity as a right wing union that had actively condoned the introduction of unbridled market forces.

These ideological differences were exacerbated and entrenched by the direct participation of trade unions, or rather trade union leaders, in political parties. Solidarity was associated with post-Solidarity governments, while OPZZ worked closely with the post-communist SLD; in both cases union leaders had been elected as deputies. During the 1993–97 parliament, more than two thirds of the 169 SLD deputies were or had been members of OPZZ. In the 1997 elections Solidarity activists ran on an AWS ticket. These political connections at the top of trade unions, with either post-Solidarity or post-communist parties, meant that trade union leaders were much more ready to organise protests against those governments in which they were not represented. When the post-communists have been in power the Solidarity leaders have organised occasional big set-piece demonstrations. OPZZ leaders have done the same when the government is post-Solidarity, although pressure from below has made the leaders of both organise actions against their governments.

However, this notion of 'conflictual pluralism' is a simplification of what happens in individual workplaces, where, on the contrary, a remarkable degree of cooperation and coordination is evident. At national level, a dispute in the Post Office in 2005 is illustrative of the fluidity of the cooperation and coordination between major unions in responding to restructuring. Out of 100,000 workers in the Post Office, the 60,000 union members were distributed between 360 branches and represented by eleven national unions. OPZZ had the largest membership with 40,000 members, Solidarity had 15,000 members and the other nine unions had 5,000 members between them.

The initiative for a Joint Union Committee in 2004 came from proposals to restructure the Post Office in anticipation of (partial) privatisation, with rumours that there would be 20,000 to 30,000 redundancies. An initial demonstration was organised in October 2004 that involved all trade unions from the Post Office. The mandate of the joint committee was then extended from simply focusing on job cuts, to concerns regarding proposals to change the redundancy package, which resulted in an agreement to coordinate their campaign for salary increases. It was agreed that voting on the joint committee should be proportionate to membership size of the participating unions, although the aim was to reach a consensus. Cooperation was strongest at branch level. In one post office in a major Polish city, the union membership from a total of 1,400 employees was as follows: 500 (OPZZ), 350 (Solidarity); 100 (August '80); 80 in smaller unions. In the trade union branch in this post office there had been complete unity in participating in the national demonstration, and a ballot for further action had been jointly organised.

Relationships and cooperation between unions, however, could be fragile. In 2004, a national demonstration was supported by the main unions representing health workers protesting against reforms, but this cooperation evaporated at the level of the leadership at least, when according to Solidarity, OPZZ supported a bill that 'favoured employers'. In Spring 2005, telecommunications sector workers were faced with 4,000 job losses, and while Solidarity wanted to take immediate industrial action OPZZ wanted to wait for the legal 21 days. In 2005, the disputes about job losses and restructuring associated with the privatisation of the railways and telecommunications illustrated the fluidity of the situation. These unions had joint committees, but in all the disputes elected representatives argued that 'holding the line was difficult' when Solidarity wanted to take what OPZZ or FZZ thought was premature industrial action.

It is not being suggested that cooperation between unions is either uniform or automatic, rather it varies between localities and workplaces, and often depends on the attitudes of local leaders. Unity was most easily forged on issues relating to wages, redundancies and changes to the social package, and there were numerous examples of joint action in factories and in the health sector. Rather than being *ad hoc* and temporary, in some cases cooperation was more regular and structured. For example, OPZZ and Solidarity representatives met to coordinate their approach to negotiations with management at the headquarters of their transnational supermarket in Warsaw. The dichotomy of cooperation, or conflict and competition as the way of characterising the relationship between the unions, does not reflect the reality of disputes and workplace action and is pessimistic about the possibility of building solidarity between workers.

Workers on the Offensive in a Global Economy: 2004 Onwards

Poland's accession to the European Union in 2004 marked a decisive change in the challenges to, and opportunities for, the Polish labour movement. The migration of Polish workers in search of employment and better wages led to an estimated 2 million people leaving the country. They looked for work elsewhere in Europe, and particularly in the UK and Ireland, which fully opened their labour markets. This had a dramatic impact on labour markets in Poland, leading to shortages of labour in some regions and industries, which has given workers much more confidence in demanding higher wages. At the end of 2003, unemployment in Poland stood at an all time high of 20 per cent (GUS, 2007a: 30); in some regions and among young people this was even higher. As a result of mass migration, the unemployment rate had fallen to 12.4 per cent by 2007 (GUS, 2007a: 30). However, the large number of Poles in the UK and

Ireland working in the worst paid jobs has challenged Polish trade unions to try and forge cross-border links to mitigate exploitation. Further, unprecedented inward migration to Poland from Ukraine, Belarus, India and North Korea to fill labour market gaps has raised issues about the exploitation of workers from outside the European Union and the possibility that they can be used to undermine wages and working conditions in Poland.

Tight Labour Markets, New Opportunities

By 2007, the joke that 'you can't get a plumber in Poland', reflected severe labour shortages in the construction industry. I heard several stories where gangs of construction workers were simply poached on the job, and induced to go and work for another firm by the offer of higher wages. Meardi (2007) talks about the way that labour market conditions across Central and Eastern Europe have led to a resurgent 'voice' from workers, 'through strikes, organising campaigns, informal collective protests and collective bargaining innovations' (Meardi, 2007: 503). This is certainly evident in Poland. Table 8.1 is a very broad indicator of a change from defensive to more offensive industrial disputes. In 2003 disputes were largely about defending jobs and issues around privatisation or the non-payment of wages. By 2006 and 2007 the nature of disputes was very different, and centred on defending union organisation or getting recognition for new branches and, in particular, disputes focused on demands for higher wages.

Furthermore, this is reflected in a strong relationship between changing conditions in the labour market and the ability (or rather inability) of employers to drive down labour costs. Table 8.2 shows an inverse relationship between the rate of unemployment and the fall of real unit labour costs – a proxy for how much employers are able to raise the rate of exploitation.[7] As unemployment increased between 2000 and 2004, real unit labour costs were falling – the year after unemployment peaked in 2003, real unit labour costs fell by 6 per cent. As unemployment decreased and labour markets tightened, the decrease in real unit labour costs slowed down.

By 2007 there was a slight increase in real unit labour costs as workers became more confident in organising in the workplace.

Table 8.1   Disputes Involving Solidarity in 2003

Issues	2003	2006	2007
Non-payment of wages	8	1	0
Unfair dismissal of shop stewards or union members	1	5	3
Union recognition	1	5	0
Wages	1	4	5
Fair payment for agency workers	0	0	3
Restructuring, privatisation, redundancies	6	1	0
Other	1	1	0

Source: Author[8]

Table 8.2   Relationship Between Real Unit Labour Cost Growth and Unemployment

Year	Real unit labour cost growth	Unemployment
2000	−2.4	15.1
2001	−2.9	17.5
2002	−4.4	19.0
2003	−3.6	20.0
2004	−6.0	19.0
2005	−2.3	17.6
2006	−0.7	14.0
2007	+1.2	11.6

Source: Author adapted from GUS, 2008 and Eurostat

This picture was supported by interviews carried out in Wrocław in late 2007. With 5 per cent unemployment in the city (and its close surrounds), some firms were unable to recruit workers at the wages on offer. In 2006 and 2007 at the Korean LG factory, Solidarity were able to intervene, recruit, organise and win a wage increase of 30 per cent. Even then LG had to bus workers from a town 70 kilometres away as well as having to ask the local government's permission to bring in North Korean workers to fill labour shortages (which was refused). A member of the regional committee of Solidarity, who was also the union president of a large foreign owned automotive factory, confirmed this new confidence among workers. He told the story of how he had been into an ununionised brick making factory in the city ten times between 2002 and 2007 to try and persuade them to set up a union branch – but without success. In 2007 workers from the factory went on strike demanding higher wages, contacted him and set up a branch, which 80 per cent of the workers joined.

This anecdotal evidence is supported by the declaration of disputes and strike warnings for higher wages in car factories such as Opel, GM and Fiat. At the end of 2007, there were important strikes in the coal mining industry. Miners in the Kompania Węglowa (Coal Company) struck for 24 hours over their 14 per cent pay rise. The next day miners at another company, JSW, voted to strike and threatened to block the transport of all coal out of the mine. In both cases the employers conceded to the demands of the workers. The dispute in the Budryk coal mine, in early 2008, was much more bitter and protracted. A 46-day strike and occupation (with 25 days underground), led by August '80, eventually led to a 10 per cent pay rise and lump sum payment. These successes were despite the fact that the workforce had been cut from 450,000 to 120,000 workers, and the sector divided into separate companies to try to weaken the unions.

Therefore, by 2007, with growing shortages of skilled labour, employers were forced to improve pay levels in the private sector. In the public sector, however, the situation was different – wages had been continually held down, a situation exacerbated by new demands for cutting public spending after EU accession.[9] Teachers and nurses are among the lowest paid groups in Poland, and doctors' pay is far below their counterparts in Western Europe. In the summer of 2007, Poland witnessed one of the biggest social protests in health care in many years. Early in 2007, doctors demanded minimum wage levels and there were strikes in 200 out of 700 hospitals. In mid-June the nurses' union (OZZPiP) joined the protests. When the Prime Minister refused to talk to them the leaders of the nurses' union occupied his office for eight days. Meanwhile the large number of protesting nurses stayed on site, giving rise to the 'White village' protest by Łazienki Park opposite the occupied building. The camp lasted for four weeks and was supported by the public and joined by other trade unionists, most prominently miners from August '80. The protests ended in deadlock, but this is more likely to be a brief pause than an end to turmoil in the health service.

Organising Polish Migrant Workers

The exploitation of Polish migrant workers in other parts of Europe presented a challenge for trade unions in Poland. Legal status in the labour market in the UK and Ireland has not removed the threat of abuse by employers, which has included no written contracts, not being paid for hours worked, unauthorised deductions and in some cases reports of wages being withheld for months (Anderson et al., 2007). Often migrant workers were forced to work excessive hours, in some cases with no rest day being provided or inadequate breaks between shifts, often enforced by the threat of withdrawing tied accommodation (Anderson et al., 2006; Friberg and Tyldum, 2007).

The three main Polish trade unions federations (Solidarity, FZZ and OPZZ) were on record as being opposed to the labour market restrictions being placed on Polish nationals in most EU member states (EIRO, 1/2004) and advocated a free market in labour. Nevertheless, migration posed problems in further depleting members and potential members, and young people in particular. In the pre-accession period Solidarity ran a campaign to discourage their members from going abroad and taking 'low wage' jobs, and were adamant that they should not aim to play the role of a 'recruitment agency'. However, as legal migration has become a reality in the post-accession period, their policy has changed to one where they try to reduce the exploitation of Polish migrant workers. Aside from concerns regarding the welfare of their individual members, they argued that migration should not be allowed to divide and rule workers and accelerate a 'race to the bottom' in terms of low labour costs.

Initiatives by Solidarity included information points in their largest 16 regional offices. Essentially these provide information on countries to which workers are considering migrating, as well as specific information about particular sectors and jobs and any collective agreements that might exist. They provide information about unions with which they are cooperating in order that workers can access further help and information on arrival. In another initiative in 2005 the North-West TUC (Trade Union Congress) in Britain (based in Liverpool) hosted a three-month visit by a full time organiser from Solidarity who tried to raise the profile of trade unions with the Polish community and worked with UK trade unions in the region to recruit workers.

While 13 per cent of (mostly Polish) migrant workers surveyed were members of trade unions in their home country, only 3 per cent had joined a trade union in Britain (Anderson *et al.*, 2006). Despite claims by some that Polish migrant workers were suspicious of, and hostile to, unions, low membership did not represent antipathy to trade unions, and a clear majority were interested in joining. According to the report (Anderson *et al.*, 2006), even on the most pessimistic assumptions, the interest in trade union membership was significantly greater than actual membership. Of the workers who were not interested in joining, half gave practical reasons such as cost, lack of information and brevity of stay. Less than 10 per cent gave ideological reasons or bad experiences of unions as a reason for not joining. The responses to being asked why they might be interested in joining a union were varied, and by no means all associated with individual protection, services or 'insurance'. The need for a 'sword of justice' and a view of collectivism at work also motivated many of those responding.

Where Polish migrant workers were in organised workplaces they have been on strike alongside British workers. Some of the placards on the Iceland depot picket line in 2005 read *Strajk Oficjalny* (official strike), reflecting the large number of Polish workers in dispute alongside colleagues from the UK over pay and management bullying (Kimber, 2006). A dispute over pay and pensions with First Bus involved both British and Polish T&G[10] members in the Midlands (Hilditch, 2005). In the Post Office dispute over privatisation and pay in 2007, Polish agency workers were bused in to break the strike. However, at Watford pickets climbed onto the bus, explained the dispute and the Polish workers voted not to go into work.

The response of the GMB[11] trade union in Southampton to 'two angry young Polish women who were seeing their colleagues exploited' was to set up an all Polish branch. In August 2006, a meeting was held on a hot evening in a room for 90 workers – 112 turned up. The following October the branch was established with 50 workers joining – by 2008 the branch had grown to 500 members. The branch members were young, mostly with no previous experience of unions and half were women. They had a number of successes, one of which was forcing the management of an agriculture processing factory to recognise the union, negotiate and provide health and safety equipment. According to the GMB full-timer in another factory owned by the same firm: 'we went in [to the other factory] with no members and recruited forty people in one day – Latvians, Lithuanians, Russian as well as Poles'. Although Polish workers have been subject to exploitation, far from being passive victims they have joined unions and taken part in industrial action.

Conclusion

Labour organisations have faced serious challenges as a result of the large scale restructuring of the economy since 1990, and particularly since the deepening of integration with the global economy since 2004. This has had a profound impact on labour markets in terms of where and what types of job are available. In short, while jobs have haemorrhaged in areas of traditional trade union membership, employment has opened up in new sectors of the economy and foreign owned investments, which were characterised, until relatively recently, by an absence of trade union organisation. Further, by 2008 labour markets had opened up to one degree or another in several European Union economies offering the possibility of widespread migration.

A reluctance to recruit during most of the 1990s and lingering optimism that rising poverty and unemployment would be stemmed and reversed led to the organisational stagnation of both OPZZ and Solidarity. Workers had been told that the sacrifices and 'nasty medicine' of shock therapy would institute a Polish capitalism that would bring rising living standards and increased opportunities. In 2008, OPZZ and Solidarity continued to be involved in parliamentary politics, but from the late 1990s both of these unions have put more emphasis on, and resources into, the basics of workplace organisation. This has meant rebuilding the membership by recruiting aggressively in new sectors, private companies and foreign investments. Achievements have been modest and mixed, but represent a decisive turn in organisational thinking. The example of the Opel factory encapsulates the speed of change. Far from workers being seduced by the lure of working in a state-of-the-art foreign owned factory, this plant now has a large and active trade union branch, which threatened to strike in 2007. The role played by trade unions in the 1990s was defensive as they attempted to mitigate the worst effects of transformation, but by 2007 the fall in unemployment has given workers a new confidence in organising unions and demanding better wages.

There are the beginnings of links across national boundaries to defend Polish workers in other parts of Europe. However, defending migrant workers in Poland is uncharted territory and any strategies are at best embryonic. Although hostilities between Solidarity and OPZZ persist in some quarters, ideological differences are relegated to the sidelines in the face of redundancies, the non-payment of wages and underfunded public services, when workers have much more to gain through unity than division.

9

'NO MORE STOCKINGS AND RED CARNATIONS': WOMEN, TRANSFORMATION AND RESISTANCE

Celebrating Women's Day under communism involved presenting women with stockings and red carnations. Rather than being focused on women's rights and equality it was much more a celebration and confirmation of women's traditional social role. Before 1990, although equality was enshrined in legislation, this was not the experience of the vast majority of Polish women, either at home or in the workplace. Since 1990, Poland is the post-communist country where neoliberal policies have been pursued with the most zeal by successive governments. Under the tutorship (and sometimes coercion) of organisations such as the IMF, successive governments have instituted cuts in public spending and welfare provision that have both pushed women out of work and pulled them back into the home.

Women's experience of and resistance to neoliberalism in Poland has been different from that of other communist countries in the region. First, the dominant role of the Catholic church in Poland, supporting a view of women gaining fulfilment as wives and mothers rather than through work, has provided a discourse that has tried to justify the return of women to the home and their relegation in the workplace (Plakwicz, 1992; Pine, 1995; Millard, 1997; Knothe, 1999). Second, in stark contrast to the traditional ideas of women enshrined in Catholicism, is a longstanding history of labour activism from 1945 culminating in the birth of Solidarity in 1980, which brought together men and women, as workers and as citizens (Bivand, 1983; Touraine *et al.*, 1983; Barker, 1986; Laba, 1991).

The accounts of women's lives and their resistance in this chapter draws on research conducted over the last decade, much of it with Alison Stenning (Hardy and Stenning, 2002; Stenning and Hardy, 2005; Hardy *et al.*, 2008). We wanted to document the experiences of ordinary women under neoliberalism by looking at how working lives had changed in factories, which were exposed to international competition and the conditions that existed in new workplaces such as supermarkets. In the late 1990s we also conducted dozens of interviews with nurses and teachers who had felt the full brunt of the restructuring and commodification of welfare. However, our work does not simply characterise women as 'surviving' or victims of transformation, rather we have focused on the way that women, in very difficult circumstances and in the face of dramatic change, have organised and been involved in some of the biggest struggles against neoliberalism.

There has been considerable research that has explored women's activism in CEE (Graham and Regulska, 1997; Heinen, 1997; Gal and Kligman, 2000), the impacts of changing work on women (including unemployment and equal opportunities) (Einhorn, 1993; Lazreg, 1999; Rumińska-Zimny, 1999; van Hoven, 2001; Pollert, 2003 and 2005; Dunn, 2004; Fodor, 2005) and women's 'survival strategies' (Bridger and Pine, 1998; Ashwin, 2000; Smith and Stenning, 2006). However, there has been very little research that has focused explicitly on women's activism in work and labour politics, and even less on women and trade unions in post-communist economies. In this way, women's activism as workers has been all but ignored, yet, in parts of the region, recent years have seen a burst of activity.

The first part of the chapter looks at how women have borne the brunt of transformation since 1990 in terms of carrying an additional burden, because of neoliberal welfare policies that have exacerbated their position in the labour market. This has been buttressed by the emergence of a right wing ideology, which seeks to return women to the home and marginalise their role in the workforce. The second part of the chapter argues that the small proportion of women in the formal politics and in the higher echelons of union bureaucracies belies the way in which they have been at the forefront of resisting market driven policies in the workplace and the community.

Women Bear the Brunt

Increasing the Double Burden

As in all communist countries there were high female participation rates in the workforce, but barred from certain blue collar jobs, women were mainly employed in light industry and the service sector, occupying the lowest levels of employment hierarchies (Hübner *et al.*, 1993). There was a panoply of provision in large SOEs, which included child care, holiday homes and access to medical services. As the double burden of home and work was largely carried by women, where extensive welfare existed, this undoubtedly helped balance child care and domestic duties with employment. However, these welfare services were available differentially and were not so easy to access outside of large firms or in rural areas.

Women found themselves at the heart of the economic contradictions of the communist economy, which experienced regular and increasingly frequent crises from 1956 onwards. Heinen and Wator (2006) trace the changes in child care policies from 1945 onwards, and demonstrate how these were dictated in large part by the needs of the labour market and vagaries of the economy. Propaganda veered between emancipatory language and the notion of 'worker-mothers' between 1944 and 1955 to that of 'mother-workers' as the economy stagnated and female employment contracted between 1956 and 1970. Calls for child care were one of the demands of the various waves of protests. The extension of child care leave for one to three year olds was adopted under the pressure of the strikes in Gdańsk and Łódź in 1970/71 that led to the downfall of Gomułka.[1] In response to strikers' demands in 1970 Gierek expanded the number of child care centres. The subject of paid child care leave reappeared during the strikes that gave rise to Solidarity in 1980 and in the 21 points of the Gdańsk agreements.

Compared with conditions in other communist countries, collective child care in Poland was one of the worst and never achieved a satisfactory level of provision for children under the mandatory school age – this was not only in terms of the number of places, but also the quality of what was on offer. Child care centres never managed to accommodate more than 5 per cent of the children under the age of three, while nursery schools provided places for 50 per cent of three to six year olds at the most (Heinen and Wator, 2006). After transformation this already poor situation was exacerbated by the administrative reforms in the early 1990s, which transferred responsibility for the infrastructure to the smallest territory – *gminas*. Since then many non-profit child care centres have closed and by 2006, in a country of 38 million, the number of child care centres was only 371 in 2006, compared with 591 in 1995 and 1,553 (including those based in SOEs) in 1989 (GUS, 2006b: 394).

Between 1989 and 2003 three quarters of child care centres closed their doors, and the number of nurseries declined by one third. By 2006 only 2 per cent of Polish children had places at day care centres (compared with 10 per cent in Hungary) and 50 per cent of three to six year olds attended nursery schools (compared with 85 per cent in Hungary) (Glass and Fodor, 2007). This polarisation of provision is exacerbated by the fact that there are fewer educational or welfare institutions in poor regions. The network of private nursery schools is growing slowly, but most of them are unaffordable except for a small group of high income earners. This is reflected in the proportion of women relying on family help, which increased from 10 to 60 per cent in the decade between 1985 and 1995. The burden of this huge shortcoming in child care often falls on older women and in 23 per cent of families children under seven are cared for by grandmothers (Titkow *et al.*, 2004).

The withdrawal of the state from welfare policy in such spheres as education, health and social welfare has increased the 'double burden' of women. Previous SOEs have either outsourced or,

more often, discontinued firm-based welfare provision as they
have concentrated on their 'core' activities. Crucially a lack of
nursery provision or help with holidays increases the difficulties
of managing the balance between home and work (Hardy and
Stenning, 2002). These burdens have also been deepened through
increased male unemployment, rising poverty and the creation of a
'third burden', as the responsibility for household food production
and the maintenance of reciprocal relationships seems to fall disproportionately on the shoulders of women (Bridger and Pine,
1998; Smith and Stenning, 2006).

Despite this huge deterioration in the availability of child care
and higher costs for what is on offer, women still need and want
to work. However, although female participation rates continue
to be high, women face another tranche of problems in the labour
market, where they have disproportionately felt the impacts of
unemployment, poor wages and discrimination.

Work

The demands of industrialisation after the Second World War
led to a substantial increase of women in the workforce; after
the rural population, women constituted the only free accessible
labour resource and were called into service to help build the
new Poland (Malinowska, 1995). Legal regulations intended
to enable women to reconcile the role of mother with their
participation in the labour force were supported by expanded
access to education and an extensive welfare system – in theory
at least. Yet, extensive discrimination against women persisted.
Women's access to paid work was accompanied by processes of
gender-based labour market segmentation and stratification. This
was manifest in the concentration of women in lower priority
and badly paid sectors of the economy, a process sometimes
supported by trade unions seeking to protect women in the
workplace (Hübner et al., 1993).

The exposure of firms to international competition, privatisation
and the end of subsidies led to widespread factory closures and
redundancies in manufacturing and other sections of the 'old

economy'. However, women bore the brunt of job loss. While some sectors such as coal mining and steel production were the focus of domestic and European Union subsidies and other interventions, which eased and slowed the process of 'downsizing', sectors where women predominated, such as light industry and textiles, were exposed to the full rigours of competition (see Pine, 1998, on the fate of women workers in Łódź). The shedding of labour from SOEs has disproportionately affected women, while those who remain in jobs have experienced an intensification of work and deskilling (Hardy and Stenning, 2002).

The unemployment rate for women has been consistently higher than that of men and this was particularly true of the younger age groups (25–34) where the gap was even bigger (GUS, 2008). Women continue to account for a disproportionate number of the unemployed and in 2007 comprised 59 per cent of the total (GUS, 2008: 25). Further, women have faced greater difficulties in finding new employment (Einhorn, 1993; Rumińska-Zimny, 1999) and also suffer from long-term unemployment. For example, at the end of 2007 65 per cent of women had been looking for work for more than 12 months compared with 38 per cent of men (GUS, 2008: 27). Women face outright discrimination in the workplace, with employers demanding that female applicants present certificates proving that they are not pregnant and/or sign a written declaration that they will not take leave to care for sick children or become pregnant during a minimal period (Heinen and Wator, 2006).

The public sector is dominated by women; in the health sector in 2005 they comprised 74 per cent of the workforce and in education 72 per cent (GUS, 2006a). Therefore the so-called 'second wave' of reforms in 1999, focused on decentralisation, rationalisation and the introduction of market forces (Kolarska-Bobińska, 2000a and 2000b), disproportionately affected women to the detriment of their conditions of work and pay as well as their work–life balance (Stenning and Hardy, 2005). In the health sector particularly, chaotic reforms have resulted in bankruptcy, hospital closures and chronic low pay.

In the communist era most work was full-time and permanent, and part-time work and flexible labour were unknown. Flexibility has been the rallying call of neoliberalism and its introduction has been facilitated by the arrival of foreign firms, hypermarkets and supermarkets in particular, which account for the largest growth area of women's employment (Stenning and Hardy, 2005). Therefore one characteristic of the post-1990 labour market has been a slight growth in part-time work and a more significant increase in other atypical labour such as temporary, flexible, contract and tele-work (Cazes and Nesporova, 2003).

Women also continue to play an important part in manufacturing where they make up 33 per cent of the workforce (GUS, 2006a). Notwithstanding the lack of democracy and poor wages in the communist era, some women we interviewed in two large SOEs in Kraków (cigarette factory) and Wrocław (white goods factory) were nostalgic for their working lives before 1990. This was not so much true of the 1980s, which was a period of repression and economic chaos, but the 1970s were viewed as something of a golden age. Work was secure and benefits in terms of health care, holiday homes, nurseries, transport to work and predictable shifts made balancing home, work and children easier. Mushroom picking expeditions and other social events meant that there was a strong social aspect to work which engendered camaraderie. It should be noted that no such feelings of camaraderie were extended to bosses or the communist regime as both these workplaces were at the forefront of the 1980 Solidarity protests.

There has been an expansion in employment in other parts of the service economy, but it seems that men have benefited from these opportunities more than women (Pollert and Fodor, 2004). For many women, the promotion of self-employment has been less a choice than an enforced strategy as outsourcing work and the use of employment agencies has shifted the responsibility for pension provision and health insurance on to the employee. There has been much written on women entrepreneurs and exhortations to entrepreneurship, but for most women setting up a small business is a strategy for surviving in the face of unemployment rather than being emancipatory.

Since accession to the EU in 2004 made it possible to work legally in Britain and Ireland, a large proportion of Polish migrant workers have been women (44 per cent of those registering in UK) working in agriculture, food processing and 'hospitality'. Although women migrants from Poland face similar problems to migrant workers in general regarding pay and working conditions, they also face specific problems associated with harassment and accessing maternity rights. One trade union organiser reported how an agency had simply sacked a woman for being pregnant. A Polish migrant worker in a banana packing factory in the south-east of England claimed that she suffered a miscarriage because her employer would not put her on lighter duties (BBC News, 2007).

Ideological Backlash

Women's activism in Poland needs to be situated in the context of material changes in Poland's economy brought about by neoliberal reform, and understood in the ideological context of the powerful myth of the Polish Mother. *Matka Polka* places a duty on women to sacrifice themselves for the family, and in particular for the good of the children, in order to support the reproduction of the Polish nation. It is an icon that is overly exploited in the public discourse on masculinity and femininity in Polish culture (Kwiatkowska, 1999). This icon persisted throughout the communist era. It is argued that it continues to play a critical role in the socialisation of young Polish women (Firkowska-Mankiewicz, 1995; Janion, 1996; Siemieńska and Marody, 1996; Boski, 1999; Giza-Poleszczuk, 2004). The gender politics of the *Matka Polka* myth have been refreshed and reinforced by the post-communist revival of conservative Catholic and nationalist/patriotic politics and their dissemination through the radio station *Radio Maryja*, the political party the League of Polish Families (Liga Polskich Rodzin, LPR) and the revived nationalist youth movement, All-Polish Youth (Młodzież Wszechpolska). These organisations have together campaigned against women's rights, abortion, gay rights and promoted conservative family politics.

Their influence was strengthened when the right wing Law and Justice Party (Prawo i Sprawiedliwość, PiS) was in power between 2005 and 2007 (Day, 2005).

To give a flavour of this conservatism, it is worth quoting an excerpt from a legal debate in the *Sejm* over the equal status of women and men. The following is taken from a senator from the right wing party AWS:

> Women have always been treated very well in Poland. They have been given due respect and many honours. They can fulfil themselves in many fields of their lives. It is said proudly that 'we women are, as Mothers, to emphasise our significant role in both the family life and the nation's life'. The majority of Poles are Christian and Catholic. Our Christian culture and religion gives women a special role. God has created woman and man and has given them different roles in their lives. It is not up to us to change and mend what God intended. (Chowaniec, 2004: 2)

Women artists have also felt the sharp end of this conservatism in finding their work censored if it was deemed to be overtly sexual (Leszkowicz, 2005).[2] Dorota Nieznalska's piece *Passion*,[3] ignited huge controversy. Members of the right wing LPR lodged a complaint on religious grounds and mounted a campaign against the piece. Activists raided the gallery where her work was being shown and the All-Polish Youth – the LPR's skinhead militia – threatened to shave Nieznalska's head (as was done with women who were believed to have had relations with Nazis). In 2003 the LPR sued the artist, who was found guilty, given a six month restriction on her freedom, ordered to do community service work and pay all trial expenses.[4]

This ideological backlash has had an impact, not only in providing a justification for cuts in welfare and deteriorating position of women in the labour market, but has had a hugely detrimental impact on women's ability to control their fertility.

Reproduction

In 1993 abortion, which had been free on request under communism, was virtually made illegal. These highly restrictive regulations on access to abortion were introduced under strong pressure from the Roman Catholic Church, with the personal backing of Pope John Paul II. This restrictive law was initiated by the right wing element of Solidarity at the end of the 1980s, and efforts by the women's section to oppose this anti-abortion position resulted in the dissolution of their organisation (Tarasiewicz, 1993). The law was introduced even though 1.3 million people signed a petition demanding a national referendum on plans to restrict access to abortion. The referendum never took place. The law permits an abortion only under very restrictive circumstances, and anyone who assists in obtaining an illegal abortion can be sentenced to three years in prison.[5]

Even though these laws virtually outlaw abortion, in practice access is even more draconian as many women who are legally eligible to have an abortion are often refused it. Doctors may exercise their 'right not to perform an abortion on the grounds of conscientious objection' and may refuse to perform an abortion even on the grounds of severe health problems. In 2007 the European Court of Human Rights ruled that Poland was failing to guarantee access to legal abortions. The court awarded damages to Alicia Tysiac, a single mother of three from Warsaw who is nearly blind, when she sued the Polish government after being denied an abortion in 2000 despite medical testimony that pregnancy would seriously impair her eyesight (Traynor, 2007).[6] Therefore in a country with a population of around 10 million women of reproductive age, no more than 200 legal abortions per year are performed.

As elsewhere abortion is an issue of class. A secret code in newspapers advertises 'Gynaecologist: full service' or 'Bringing back your period'. For those who have sufficient funds obtaining an illegal abortion is not a problem, but with the cost of such an operation at between 370 and 1,000 euros it is the privilege of only a small minority. It is estimated that between 80,000 and 200,000 illegal abortions per year are performed – with no control over their quality or the conditions in which they are carried out, sometimes without anaesthetic, and usually by the most dangerous curettage method. Such facts, however, have rarely been brought up in public debates. The language in which abortion is discussed – if it is discussed at all – has been appropriated by the opponents of the right to choose. Calling themselves 'pro-life', they accuse women who have abortions of murdering 'conceived' or 'unborn' children, or simply 'children', and portray these women as criminals. Despite unbridled hostility from the church and right wing organisations, a national demonstration to legalise abortion took place at the beginning of November 2007. There had already been three public gatherings of women in front of the parliament building, who, facing hostility and accusations of being murderers, admitted that they had had an abortion.

While the fertility rate rose to 2.43 in 1982, it fell to roughly 1.3 in 2003, the lowest rate in the European Union (Eurostat) – this is in a country where abortion is illegal and the use of contraception not widespread. According to Heinen and Wator:

> Faced with backward policies and taking into account the difficulties and high costs of obtaining contraception women have responded more and more (according to accounts of activists in the scarce family planning centres) by carrying out what nineteenth century feminists called a 'womb strike'. (2006: 197)

Alarmed by the drop in the birth rate Polish governments set up two programmes: the 1997 *Programme of Family Policy* and the 1999 *Programme of Pro-family Policy*. The latter proposed a reduction in tax for the birth of a third child and denied support to one-parent families, which were considered pathological, while the role of fathers was completely omitted from the programme.

The strong rhetoric of motherhood, the lack of child care and difficulties in the labour market mean that many women are delaying having children, or deciding not to have them at all. An almost complete ban on abortion takes away a women's right to choose not to go ahead with a pregnancy, while poor welfare and labour market conditions reduce the possibility of a positive choice of motherhood.

Women and Resistance

Women and Formal Politics

The marginalisation of women in formal politics since 1990 does not appear to bode well for resisting the right wing backlash to women's rights. Pollert argues that 'women's absence at senior levels early in transition left the path clear for conservative policies that undermined women's protection' (2003: 343). However, this has not always been the case and women played a pivotal role in the emergence of an organised opposition (Kennedy, 1999). Indeed, the first wave of protests in 1980, which led to the creation of the independent Solidarity union movement, was sparked off by the dismissal of a respected woman worker in the Gdańsk shipyards – Anna Walentynowicz. It has long been recognised that women were Solidarity activists in the early 1980s, despite the fact that they were also managing households under conditions of severe shortages of basic commodities (and often absent spouses) (Siemieńska, 1986; Penn, 1994, 2005; Long, 1996). In these ways, the early success of Solidarity rested not just on the mass protests and factory occupations, but also relied on women playing a critical role in organising the underground press and producing and distributing illegal literature. In more formal structures, however, women's representation was limited; only 7 per cent of women were delegates at the First Congress of the union in 1981 and, of 19 members of Presidium of National Commission, only one was a woman.

The period from 1990 onwards has seen the removal of women from formal political office; in 1989 women comprised 20 per cent of parliamentary deputies, but by 1990 this had fallen to 12 per cent (Leven, 1994). In particular, the purging of the pro-abortion women's section in Solidarity facilitated the passage of reforms likely to limit women's independence, depriving the organisation of a critical voice that could have challenged the right wing drift of the organisation. Therefore, any attempts to strengthen women's rights and gender equality were hampered by the declining influence of women in national political life (World

Bank, 2004). That women have been decreasingly involved in party and parliamentary politics since 1989 has been well documented (Watson, 1993; Fuszara, 2000; Silovic, 2000).

The ratification of international treaties and the legislative demands of European Union accession have incorporated women's rights in national legislation. Indeed, the existing legal protection for working women, regarding recruitment, promotion, salaries, job protection, and the prevention of gender-based discrimination, fulfils the EU requirements. In reality, the implementation of these rights has been poor (Fuszara, 2002; Zalewska-Zemła and Zielińska, 2003). Labour legislation in Poland prohibits certain activities and forms of work for women, particularly for pregnant women, potentially disempowering them in their career decisions in certain occupations. Further, recent attempts to reinforce gender equality have fallen foul of Poland's conservative turn. A draft law on the equal status of men and women which would have: reaffirmed the equal right to education, work, social security and a family; required governmental and public organisations to have 50 per cent participation by women by 2012; prohibited questions concerning marital status or pregnancy during job interviews; asserted the equal right for men to raise families; and established a government office responsible for gender equality issues, was finally thrown out by the Senate on 17 June 2005.

Women and Trade Unions

The potential for women's rights in the workplace has to be set in the context of challenges to Polish trade unions in the face of the decline and closures of their traditional strongholds, as well as incoming foreign investors hostile to labour organisations (Rainnie and Hardy, 1995; Gardawski et al., 1999; Crowley and Ost, 2001; Ost, 2001). Yet, as unions in Poland struggle to revive, the recruitment and organisation of women in new sectors of the economy has become increasingly important.

While the three major trade union federations (Solidarity, OPZZ and FZZ[7]) have policies regarding equal opportunities and an end to discrimination, women remain under-represented, particularly in the higher echelons of these organisations. In Solidarity in 2005 there were eight women out of 106 members on the National Commission, and in the Presidium there are two women (out of 13 officers; one of them is Ewa Tomaszewska, widely recognised as a female leader of the union); among the chairs of the 16 sector secretariats, there are just two women (responsible for the health sector and for banking, trade and insurance respectively). In OPZZ, the second biggest union federation, women's participation in the executive committees is also very limited. In 2005, among 42 presidium officers there were three women, and among five union presidents there was only one woman, who had responsibility for social policy. There is a similar picture in the FZZ; there was only one woman out of six presidium officers, six women out of 33 members of the executive committee; and three out of the 16 commission presidents. Similar patterns of poor representation are evident across other post-communist economies, but the level of women's representation in Polish unions is particularly low (Petrović, 2001).

In 1995 Solidarity established a Plenipotentiary of the National Commission for Women's Affairs. Solidarity has been accused by some of being a 'right wing' union, however, aside from the taboo subject of abortion, the Catholic values in their statutes are not reflected in assumptions that women play a subordinate role in the workplace. For example, the concept of parental rather than only maternal responsibility is emphasised. Arguably, Solidarity may place a greater emphasis on the family, but this is manifest in women being supported in the workplace and also not being penalised for taking parental leave in terms of pensions and promotion. In this respect it would appear to be in line with demands raised by most unions, in Western Europe at least. In OPZZ, a Women's Commission has also been created, the main objective of which is to promote the equal status of women and men in the domains of work, politics, public and family life.

If this poor representation of women in the bureaucracy reflected the level of women's activism, then indeed the picture would be dismal. However, while there is an absence of women in the upper echelons of trade unions, this belies the way in which at regional and workplace level the reverse is true. There are numerous examples of women who have been elected as the head of their factory or workplace committees. In the Wrocław region in the 1990s, women were the leaders of the two biggest and most powerful factory branches of Solidarity in Jelcz and Polar[8] (Hardy, 2002). In particular, women have led protests in the public sector and are key activists in organising new sectors of the economy such as supermarkets. In addition to issues of working conditions and pay, women have been enthusiastically and actively engaged in workplace campaigns that have focused on issues new to Polish trade unionism, such as opposition to 'mobbing' (workplace bullying or emotional abuse), discrimination and sexual harassment.

Contesting Marketisation of the Public Sector: Nurses and Teachers

Teaching and nursing are the worst paid professions in Poland. Further, the decentralisation of finance has led to local wage setting, meaning that salaries can reflect local labour markets, the position of the individual hospital or the whim of the hospital director or head teacher. In the health sector younger nurses reported taking additional cleaning jobs for two to four hours daily to make ends meet. Older women nurses were dependent on spouses, or in the case of younger nurses on their parents. One nurse said, 'You can't divorce your husband and you have to hope he doesn't die, otherwise you can't survive'. Poor wages translate into poor pensions and many women who have retired take on different jobs, either in the informal sector or increasingly in supermarkets. Speaking of her low wages one nurse said that she was 'working for juice, coffee and cheap cosmetics'. In addition to struggling on poor wages, cuts in spending on health have brought about deteriorating working conditions and nurses are increasingly required to do administration and cleaning, in addition to their normal duties. Public sector reforms have transformed the nature of work, the shape of workplaces and possibility for organising. Against this background, the turbulence of the reforms has led to the emergence of new organisations (Stenning and Hardy, 2005).

Dissatisfaction with Solidarity, which had introduced reforms, and a feeling of being sidelined by doctors and other health workers led to the formation of the OZZPiP in 1996. This union was remarkable, not only because it grew from nothing to 100,000 members in five years, but also because the founders and main activists were women with no previous experience of or involvement in politics. This union was engaged in very militant action in December 2000 in support of higher pay. The occupation of the Ministry of Health, walkouts and blockades of international borders and railway lines were far from conforming to the stereotype of Polish women as long-suffering carers. Further, nationwide protests erupted in the health service in 2006 over the issue of wages. However, in many cases this was a rather empty gesture on the part of national government as there were no additional resources to finance it – and some hospitals went bankrupt. As we saw in the previous chapter, in the summer of 2007 nurses escalated protests that had started alongside those of doctors, resulting in an eight-day occupation of the Prime Minister's office where nurses tried to put their case directly. This escalated into the 'White village' protest, which was triggered by police violence against a large nurses' demonstration. Hundreds of nurses, with the support of other unions, the public and celebrities, camped in Łazienki Park for four weeks.

Women continue to dominate the teaching profession. In the communist period, the ZNP teachers' union had been affiliated to OPZZ, but its long history (founded 1905) and size gave it a degree of autonomy. Strikes took place in 1991 and 1992 and persistent low pay and profound changes to the curriculum sparked two further phases of industrial action in 1998 and 1999, which included the withholding of marks and one-day strikes. Further protests took place in 2007, which included a two-hour warning strike and demonstration in Warsaw. The demands were again for higher pay, extended pension rights and also for the sacking of the far right Minister for Education, Roman Giertych. Giertych was accused of increasing intolerance, because he proposed passing a law to sack openly gay teachers or anyone openly promoting homosexuality.

Organising in Supermarkets

One of the few expanding sectors for women's employment has been in hotels and restaurants, business and in retailing. In particular, the foreign-owned hypermarkets and supermarkets, which have expanded exponentially since 1989, have been at the centre of new forms of workplace activism. In Białystok, a large city in eastern Poland, a state-owned textiles enterprise closed in the mid-1990s with the loss of 5,000 (mainly women's) jobs. A government-sponsored agency, which retrained workers, told me that after teaching 'skills' and 'strategies' for the 'new economy', the reality of the local labour market was that the only jobs on offer were in supermarkets, where 40 per cent of the redundant women found employment.

Firms in the foreign-owned food retail sector compete fiercely in terms of cutting labour costs, and have tried to impose Western European working practices without the inconvenience of having to negotiate with unions or change established routines. As in their Western European counterparts, casualisation, flexibility and uncertainty in working patterns are the cornerstone of employment. The majority of women were on fractional contracts, even though many of them wanted to work full time (Hardy and Stenning, 2002). The demand by the supermarkets that women were 'on call' at short notice meant that they were unable to take on second jobs. Employment in this sector has been very controversial, with growing numbers of stories in the press about poor working conditions, abuses of the labour code and bullying managers who have simply sacked workers who join or organise unions.

The initiative for establishing unions in these retail outlets has come from new strategies employed by Solidarity and OPZZ to recruit in the new economy, but in addition, there have been campaigns from below, often led by women. A couple of stories are typical of the experience of women forming or joining unions. Women workers described how they were fed up with the disrespectful treatment they received from management whose power and control seemed to have no limits. In one example, five women started a union secretly, by forming a committee that met in homes rather than the workplace. When they had recruited the legally required number of members they registered the union and then informed management as a *fait accompli*. Another activist explained that it was women in their forties and fifties who took the initiative to establish a union because this was their only option in the job market, strengthening their resolve to better their working conditions.

The recognition of trade unions, however, was only the first step in what one activist described as a 'partisan war'. Although the management used the rhetoric of cooperation it was suggested that they were 'killing the union with white gloves'. Every concession had to be battled for; negotiations were always delayed and protracted, and this was viewed as an attempt to make the union look weak and unable to deliver concessions. Veiled threats were made to workers on temporary contracts suggesting that getting a permanent contract might be jeopardised by joining the union.

Similar to the nurses, the supermarket activists were by and large women with no previous political affiliation or union experience, who were playing a central role in the workplace negotiating with management locally and nationally and representing the grievances of their members. Despite threats and other obstacles, women activists in hypermarkets had had considerable successes. These included getting workers reinstated, changing the dress code, getting a manager sacked for sexual harassment and bullying, changing the rotas, mitigating health and safety risks, ensuring consultation on redundancies and on the disbursement of the social fund.[9]

Social Activism

Civil society activism has been dominated by women in Central and Eastern Europe (Einhorn, 2006: 141). Indeed in Poland women have also been at the centre of new forms of social activism in their communities, often associated with current or past membership of trade unions – and not primarily focused on traditionally defined 'women's concerns'. This activism is not always formalised in NGOs: in one small town outside Warsaw, a woman activist – a health worker and trade unionist – used her membership of the district (*powiat*) council and its housing, education and work committees to influence local issues. Through these channels and by building informal coalitions, she has successfully argued for a work experience programme to combat and alleviate youth unemployment in the town and mobilised the community against the bankruptcy and closure of a debt-ridden hospital, drawing in resources from the local government, local builders, farmers and other local businesses.

The founding president of OZB (Ogólnopolski Związek Bezrobotnych: All-Poland Union of the Unemployed), based in Ełk, is a woman social activist who combined local action with wider international and social movements. Ełk is a small city in north-east Poland with high regional unemployment as a result of the closure of the food processing and agriculture related industries in the 1990s, and the restructuring of the local hospital caused further job losses. In this context, the establishment of OZB based in premises secured from the city government has enabled a range of community and political activities in the town. While the centre developed initially as an information exchange for jobs in Poland and abroad, as a meeting place (with a crèche) and as a legal advice centre, the OZB president also led campaigns in the town on benefits, housing, community cohesion and anti-racism. Outside of the locality, she has developed a much wider perspective for the union through its participation in international events, such as the European Social Fora and the Euro March for Jobs (in Brussels in 2005). In addition, she has also spearheaded the expansion of the union beyond its Ełk headquarters – there are now eleven branches of the union across Poland, many of which are run by women, all involved in a variety of economic, social and political activism.

Polish Feminism

Polish women's groups were numerically small and politically isolated during the earliest years of transition, when they had been focused on trying to prevent the anti-abortion law passed in 1993. Despite much hostility, feminism is gaining increasing support, especially among younger generations. OSKa (Ośrodek Informacji Środowisk Kobiecych), the women's rights and information centre in Warsaw, and eFKa (Fundacja Kobieca), the Women's Foundation in Kraków, both founded in their current format in the late 1990s, draw together women's groups that are diverse in their interests and location. By 2007 the Polish women's movement was vibrant, comprising 300 organisations advocating women's interests, including abortion rights, the prevention of violence against women and the promotion of women in politics and at work. A series of women's rights abuses led to a renaissance of the women's movement reflected in the founding of the Women's Coalition of the 8th March. Since 2000, it has held annual demonstrations on International Women's Day campaigning for: equal pay and equal representation (2001); abortion rights (2002 and 2003); and against censorship in art (2004).

A core theme of this new activism has been the focus on women's rights at work, such that the 2005 march was jointly organised by feminist organisations and by the newly formed lesbian coalition and focused around the theme of economic discrimination on the grounds of both gender and sexuality. In its early stages, the feminist movement was mainly dominated by, and was the domain of, professional women, particularly those from academic backgrounds. More recently, there has been increasing participation by women from the labour movement and a broader diversification of feminist agendas. This was reflected in the participation of working-class women and women trade union activists (including, for example, LOT air stewards protesting against redundancies) in the Women's Day marches in 2004 and 2005.

Conclusion

It is easy to paint a pessimistic picture of the position of women in post-communist Poland, and to be less than sanguine about the possibility of resisting the profound impacts of neoliberal policies on work and welfare. The scope for organising around the concerns of working women looks even more dismal in view of the ascendancy of conservative organisations, which have peddled a reactionary agenda for women. However, accounts which focus on the poor representation of women in the upper echelons of the main trade unions have failed to recognise their significant activism in union organisation at a local level. The embryonic trade unions in new sectors of the economy are a considerable achievement given the unbridled hostility of some employers. Women have shown a capacity for challenging the marketisation of public services, with new forms of action and new forms of organisation. The ZNP teachers' union transformed itself into a much more campaigning organisation with grassroots participation, which has contested the reforms. At the same time, in OZZPiP nurses bypassed existing structures to form a new and completely independent organisation, which was at the forefront of militant and high profile action. While women workers in Poland face continuing threats to their workplaces and working conditions, and the challenge of conservative ideas, evidence from a range of sectors, regions and, indeed, generations suggests that women are often refusing passively to accept the restructuring of their working lives.

10

POLITICAL PARTIES AND NEW MOVEMENTS

The revival and reinvigoration of workers' organisations discussed in Chapter 8 has been paralleled by deep-seated disillusionment and discontent with political parties. This is reflected in the fluidity of the post-1989 Polish political scene, characterised by extraordinarily high levels of electoral volatility and party instability. This has led to regular voting out of the incumbent government, with participating parties vanishing from the scene to reappear shortly afterwards in another form with a new name.

Between 1990 and 2000, the main formal division in Polish politics was between politicians who had their roots in the Solidarity movement and those who had been in the ruling Communist Party. The PZPR, after going into voluntary liquidation in 1990, managed to reconstitute itself as Social Democracy of the Republic of Poland (Socjaldemokracja Rzeczypospolitej Polskiej, SdRP). With other groupings, including the OPZZ trade union federation, this formed an electoral bloc called the Democratic Left Alliance, which by the 2001 elections had become a political party – the SLD. During its eight years of illegality between 1981 and 1988 Solidarity had been moved from a mass movement to being dominated by a right wing leadership wedded to the market as a mechanism for reform. Since 2000 the main division has been between two right wing parties, which have their origins in the Solidarity camp.

Despite the rhetoric and the espoused differences between the post-Solidarity and post-communist parties, both have pursued neoliberal policies on welfare and work with zeal and enthusiasm. In short, this has produced widespread disillusionment among workers reflected in low turnouts in elections, vacillation between post-Solidarity and post-communist governments and the formation of new radical right and left wing parties.

This chapter provides a short commentary on the elections from 1991 to 2007 and the politics and policies of each government in order to explain the disillusionment and discontent as both post-communist and post-Solidarity parties have implemented more of the same market driven reforms. It is argued that although Poland has produced a particularly pernicious ideologically reactionary variant of neoliberalism, it does not follow that the vast majority of Poles are wedded to these ideas. The idea that so-called transition must be market driven has been challenged by the emergence of new parties and new movements, which have derived some of their inspiration from wider European and global social movements.

Political Parties and Elections

1991–93: Solidarity Governments

The defeat of Solidarity and introduction of martial law in 1981 led to the imprisonment of thousands of the most militant workers and leaders. From this illegal phase a new elite emerged which was transformed into 'a republic of buddies' (Modzelewski, 1993: 9) and the workers' Solidarity was in a sense 'decapitated' (Kowalik, 2001: 226). Solidarity's struggle was driven by the idea of a 'self limiting revolution',[1] and the rest of the decade witnessed the rout of any element of socialism within its analysis. During the 1980s the leadership of Solidarity moved to the right to the extent that by 1989 it held a position that the introduction of unbridled market forces was the only way of reforming the system.

The implementation of shock therapy and attendant rise in unemployment and pay freezes for public sector workers (*popiwek*), quickly destroyed any illusions in the market by sections of rank and file workers. Any vestiges of optimism gave way to disillusion and anger, which led to political crises and a quick turnover of prime ministers.[2] This was reflected at the third

Solidarity conference in February 1991, when delegates, instead of electing Lech Wałęsa's deputy as new leader, chose the relatively unknown Marian Krzaklewski. They wanted Solidarity 'to close the protective umbrella' over a government, which was instituting anti-working-class reforms.

The disillusionment with transformation intensified and an increasing level of public sector strikes forced the post-Solidarity Prime Minister Hanna Suchocka to appeal for calm on TV. The action culminated in a two-day strike in the capital called by the Warsaw region of Solidarity in May 1993. Only days later, one of the Solidarity miners' members of parliament called for a vote of no-confidence in Suchocka leading to the collapse of her government.

1993–97: Post-communist Government

Table 10.1 shows the complete collapse of the vote for Solidarity in 1993 when the post-communist SLD won the election. This was only two years after the first free parliamentary elections and had seemed unimaginable only a few months earlier, particularly when considered in the context of the massive vote for Solidarity in 1989.[3] The fact that many, if not most, working-class people had not benefited from the so-called transformation reforms, and in many cases were worse off, led to deep disillusionment with the leaders of Solidarity.

The leader of the post-communist SLD, Aleksander Kwaśniewski, very narrowly defeated Lech Wałęsa for the presidency in the 1995 elections. Wałęsa's fall from a great height symbolised the dashed hopes of millions of working-class people and Kwaśniewski drew votes from those living in poverty who had been at the sharp end of the post-Solidarity government's drive to the 'market'.

The new coalition was expected by its predecessors to signal a return to the communist past and to reverse the policies of the previous government bringing economic chaos. No such thing happened and the post-communists exerted huge efforts to gain acceptance from the West, and the US in particular, by continuing the economic policies focused on rapid privatisation

Table 10.1   Polish Election Results (number of seats)

	1993	1997	2001	2005	2007
Democratic Left Alliance (Sojusz Lewicy Demokratycznej: SLD)[a]	171	164	200	55	53
Civic Platform (Platforma Obywatelska: PO)[b]	–	–	65	133	209
Self Defence (Samoobrona)	–	–	53	56	0
Law and Justice (Prawo i Sprawiedliwość: PiS)[c]	–	–	44	155	166
Polish Peasant Party (Polskie Stronnictwo Ludowe: PSL)	131	27	42	25	31
League of Polish Families (Liga Polskich Rodzin: LPR)	–	–	38	34	0
Solidarity Electoral Action (Akcya Wyborcza Solidarność: AWS)[d]	–	201	0	–	–
Democratic Union-Freedom Union (Unia Demokratczna-Unia Wolności, UW)	74	60	0	–	–
Union of Labour (Unia Pracy: UP)	41	0	16	–	–
Others	43	8	2	2	1
Total	460	460	460	460	460

Source: Author (from various sources)

a The SLD and UP ran on a joint list in the September 2001 election, winning a combined total of 216 seats. In 2007 SLD, UP, SDPI (a breakaway from SLD) and the Democratic Party – Unia Wolności with a changed name ran as an alliance called the Left and the Democrats (Lewica i Demokraci: LiD).
b Formed January 2001 (formally registered as a party March 2002).
c Formed March 2001 (formally registered June 2001) following the popularity gained by Lech Kaczyński as Justice Minister (June 2000–July 2001). Most of PiS came from AWS.
d Formed summer 1996.

and restructuring started by the previous government. According to Stone (2002) Poland was very fortunate in its choice of communists who continued to be responsible actors and continued with market type reforms. The US Ambassador in Warsaw (Nicholas Rey) echoed this enthusiasm for the SLD post-government and said that they were 'bending over backwards to overcome their history, and were more cooperative with the US than some people on the right'. Kowalik (2001) points out that the SLD were 'more Catholic than the Pope' in their enthusiasm for neoliberalism, which included the ratification of exceptionally harsh tenancy regulations, which made many impoverished tenants homeless.

In 1997 the SLD was ousted. Its electoral base contracted as it continued to deliver more of the same neoliberal policies. Although it only lost seven seats the parties of the right were able to present a much more coherent and unified force.

1997–2001: Solidarity Electoral Action

The Solidarity leader Marian Krzaklewski successfully created the Solidarity Electoral Action alliance from 40 small Catholic and right wing organisations to fight and win the 1997 parliamentary elections. Apart from stressing the SLD's attacks on workers, he played on the 'traditional Polish values' of Catholicism, family and patriotism. In the run up to the elections Krzaklewski defused pressures in Solidarity for a general strike by arguing that 'the best general strike will be the elections in which we will vote for Solidarity'. He suggested that the 40 to 50 Solidarity parliamentary deputies that had been elected to parliament in 1997 as part of the AWS coalition meant that there was no need for the union to organise protest actions.

At the beginning of the 1997 parliament, the Polish electoral system seemed to be stabilising, with a previously highly fragmented and confusing party system giving way to a relatively consolidated one. This comprised four parties around two main axes. These were the post-Solidarity centre right Solidarity Electoral Action and the centre left Democratic Left Alliance. At the same time there were two medium sized parties: the liberal post-Solidarity Freedom Party (Unia Wolności, UW) and the agrarian populist Polish Peasant Party (Polskie Stronnictwo Ludowe, PSL). The UW was concentrated among young, urban and well-educated transition winners and the professional and public sector intelligentsia, while the PSL's electorate was predominantly rural based.

The AWS governed in coalition with the UW, the biggest neoliberal party, of which most of the well-known Solidarity leaders and advisors were members. The UW's leader, Balcerowicz, who had introduced shock therapy in 1990, became Deputy Prime Minister and Finance Minister. Workers had protested against the austerity they faced as a result of neoliberalism with strikes, protests, votes and abstaining from elections and now Krzaklewski, the most important union leader in the country, was again foisting the architect of neoliberalism on them.

The AWS introduced a second wave of reforms in local government, health, pensions and education (Kolarska-Bobińska, 2000a and 2000b), and by 1999 they faced a wave of protests and labour disputes, which began with a series of illegal farmers' blockades in January. The protests against the reforms in health and education by nurses and teachers, and their unpopularity with other workers, increased and worsened tensions within the coalition. Further, Krzaklewski made his closest ally, Łódź region Solidarity leader Janusz Tomaszewski, Interior Minister. In 1999 during Tomaszewski's time in office, police used rubber bullets against protesting workers and farmers five times and anti-terrorist police were used to evict nurses occupying a local government office in Gorzów Wielkopolski. These kinds of experiences of 'their' government attacking them led to complete disillusionment with political parties by many Solidarity activists.

Krzaklewski's project to create a Christian Democratic Party out of AWS could not stand the strain of its own contradictions. This was reflected in the fact that the AWS could not even rely on its own parliamentary deputies to support government sponsored legislation. One major problem was that Solidarity was the trade union whose members had organised the most strikes. Szczerbiak argued that, 'This, in turn, made an already fractious and ideologically political grouping even more unstable, and inevitably led to gridlock, immobilism and political cronyism' (2002: 44).

In 1997 the SLD was still a somewhat amorphous 33 member coalition clustered around the direct successor to the Communist Party, the SdRP, and the former pro-regime OPZZ. In June 1999, it had transformed itself into a single unitary party with a much clearer decision making structure and this allowed it a degree of success in distancing itself from its communist past. A survey by the Centre for the Research of Social Opinion (Centrum Badania Opinii Społecznej, CBOS) in January 2000 found that 43 per cent of voters considered the SLD to be primarily a West European type social democratic party compared with 31 per cent who saw it as a Communist Party successor. It also formed an alliance with weaker left parties such as the UP, which included former communists as well as leading Solidarity activists.

The widening gap in support between the AWS and the SLD was reflected in the landslide victory of the SLD backed Aleksander Kwaśniewski, who got 50 per cent of the vote in the October 2000 presidential election, while the AWS backed Krzaklewski got only 16 per cent of the vote. The AWS was plunged further into trouble when two new groupings broke away. First, the Civic Platform (Platforma Obywatelska, PO) was formed by Andrzej Olechowski, from the AWS, *Sejm* marshal Macieja Płażyński and the UW senate deputy marshal Donald Tusk. They wanted a more overtly liberal party building on the 'transition winners': young people, the better educated and entrepreneurs. The second grouping was the formation of the Law and Justice Party led by the twins Lech and Jarosław Kaczyński. Lech Kaczyński had portrayed himself as a tough enemy of corruption and crime, which had gained him huge popularity – this was the kiss of death for the AWS and sealed its fate.

The 2001 Parliamentary Election

In the 2001 election the Democratic Left Alliance-Freedom Party (SLD-UP) won 41 per cent of the vote and 216 seats, which represented the best result achieved by any political grouping in the four free parliamentary elections since 1989. Nevertheless, the turnout was below 50 per cent and they fell short of obtaining a parliamentary majority. The SLD coalition won support from every group and even persuaded a large number of former AWS (12.5 per cent) and UW (16.5 per cent) voters to cross the historical divide and support a formation led by former communists. However, the SLD-UP did not win on the basis of differentiating itself from the neoliberal policies of the previous AWS government and they avoided making any policy pledges. They were able to make great political capital from the deep unpopularity of the welfare reforms, even though they had no intention of reversing them. Instead they resorted to presenting a picture of pragmatism and stability with their slogan, 'Let's Return to Normality, Win the Future'. The SLD led by Leszek Miller was able to be an effective opposition, because it was much more internally coherent and disciplined than any of the post-Solidarity formations.

The September 2001 parliamentary election represented another huge earthquake and major reshuffling of the party system. Four new parties got over 40 per cent of the vote and it saw the consolidation of the PO and PiS, although the biggest surprise was the emergence and success of two new parties: Self Defence (Samoobrona) and the League of Polish Families (Liga Polskich Rodzin).

Civic Platform

With 12.7 per cent of the vote and 65 seats the PO emerged as the second force in Polish politics and the main opposition. During the campaign it had espoused its commitment to economic liberalism through reducing the role of the state, deregulating the labour market and the imposition of a unitary 15 per cent tax rate. It managed to tap into the widespread anti-establishment, anti-party sentiment evident in Polish society. A survey by CBOS found that 58 per cent of Poles were unable to name a single party with which they identified. By blending economic liberalism with calls for political reforms, the Civic Platform 'tried to present itself as a new kind of political movement based on the American model: an election machine and parliamentary caucus with a minimal party bureaucracy' (Szczerbiak, 2007: 54). This struck a chord as many Poles felt that public life was excessively partified and felt alienated from distant, oligarchic party elites. However, this rhetoric was extremely disingenuous as all the PO leaders were deeply enmeshed in the Polish political establishment.

The Law and Justice Party

With 44 seats and 9.5 per cent of the votes, the PiS were the second largest right wing party in parliament (PO being the first). They had run a campaign that focused on the twin themes of law and order and crime, proposing to establish an elite central anti-corruption office with sweeping powers of inspection and audit. There was much less focus on ideological issues compared with previous right wing campaigns such as the one run by AWS in 1997.

Self Defence

The biggest shock of the 2001 election was the unexpected success of Andrzej Lepper's radical populist agrarian Samoobrona grouping. Both a political party and a farmers' union, it won 10 per cent of the votes and 53 seats to emerge as the third largest grouping in parliament. Lepper had first come to prominence during the early 1990s as leader of radical farmers' protests against debt foreclosure and returned to front line politics during the January 1999 farmers' road blockades. Self Defence drew its support from a very eclectic base. Although it had originated as a farmers' union it picked up support from less well off voters in small towns and the losers of transition such as the unemployed. Basically it provided a focus for dissatisfied voters who were prepared to accept radical forms of action, as well as picking up a segment of potential SLD-UP voters disillusioned with the coalition's neoliberal economic policies. Therefore Lepper emerged as the most credible radical defender of the interests of the losers of transformation.

League of Polish Families

If Samoobrona is hard to place on the political spectrum then the LPR, a coalition of right wing catholic and extremist nationalist groupings, is an unambiguously right wing populist party. Only having registered as a party four months before the election, it won 8 per cent of the vote and 38 seats. It did not appear to appeal to any one group as its base was much more ideological than economic. The LPR harnessed the religious right electorate clustered around the anti-Semitic radio station Radio Maryja led by Father Tadeusz Rydzyk, which has disseminated a set of ideas so extreme and unpleasant that it was often at odds with the hierarchy of the Catholic Church. The LPR was dominated by extreme rightist Roman Giertych, a politician who was proud to continue the politics of the Endeks, whose violent anti-socialist and anti-Semitic past goes back to the 1905 revolution and pre-war Poland.

Solidarity Electoral Action's Catastrophic Defeat

One of the most striking aspects of the election was the stunning defeat of the former AWS parties by the huge anti-establishment and anti-incumbent backlash. It won only 5.5 per cent of the vote compared with 33.8 in 1997. One of the major reasons was the four flagship social reforms that contributed to making Buzek's government the most unpopular since 1989. Internal squabbling and the recurring theme of these politicians placing their own interests ahead of those of the country were also major factors in the opinion polls. Far from leading to the hoped-for 'departification' of the state and 'depoliticisation' of the economy the AWS placed its own, often unqualified, partisan appointees in key positions at every level. This was seen as perpetuating nepotism and recycling the gains of transition among a small group – hard to stomach from a party whose constant refrain had been criticisms of the old communist networks.

The Demise of the Freedom Party

The election was also a crushing defeat for the UW (AWS's former partner) who got 3 per cent of the votes compared with 13.8 per cent in 1997. Their catastrophic plunge in favour can be attributed to a vote against neoliberalism, personified in Leszek Balcerowicz as Finance Minister. 'Balcerowicz Must Go' was probably the most popular slogan on workers' and farmers' demonstrations for 15 years after 1990. Moreover, the PO were able to steal their pragmatic free market rhetoric and appeal to the transition winners, without the disadvantage of having been sullied in office and tainted with the unpopularity of the AWS.

Therefore the September 2001 parliamentary elections shattered what appeared to be the new emerging order and stability in the Polish party political system.

2001–05: The Democratic Left Alliance Back in Power

The Democratic Left Alliance was heralded as one of the big success stories in how to morph a former Communist Party into a modern, electoral social democratic one. It won the 2001 election in coalition with the UP falling just short of an overall majority in the *Sejm*. It went on to form a government under Leszek Miller, a former communist official. In its politics it was Blairite (neoliberal and pro-US) having enthusiastically sent Polish troops to assist the attack on, and occupation of, Iraq.

The SLD does not have the working-class roots and history of the British Labour Party or German Social Democratic Party, in fact its leaders had headed a police state. Nevertheless, people were prepared to vote for them after the experience of AWS, which had attacked welfare provision and presided over even higher increases in unemployment, and clung to some hope that the SLD would govern in the interests of ordinary people. However, the honeymoon period was very shortlived and the government quickly became mired in problems, which produced plunging ratings in approval.

The economy had stagnated and the much vaunted Polish economic progress was more of a mirage than a miracle, and as we have seen, any meagre economic gains were extremely unevenly distributed. High unemployment and increased insecurity meant that for the vast majority of people the 'feel good' factor was notably absent. Unemployment continued to rise and the unpopular neoliberal welfare reforms were continued rather than revoked.

Sleaze and corruption changed general discontent into much more open criticism. There were allegations that individuals linked to the SLD, including media mogul and film producer Lew Rywin, demanded payment from the newspaper publisher Agora in return for favourable changes to the government's media regulation law. Two years later this was followed by the Orlen affair, where allegations were made that Miller had used the security services to arrest the president of PKN Orlen (Poland's largest energy company) to block an oil deal supply concerning Russian oil. To compound the situation, while the government was seen to be embroiled in corruption and sleaze, Jerzy Hausner, Deputy Prime Minister responsible for economic affairs, introduced a series of tough and unpopular austerity measures, which attacked the already scant provision for health insurance and social benefits.

By the start of 2004 the SLD was in deep crisis and the most unpopular administration since 1989. Despite having won 41 per cent of the vote in the 2001 election its approval ratings were only between 5 and 10 per cent. Fears of electoral meltdown precipitated the first major split in the Polish centre left since 1989, when 33 SLD and UP deputies led by the *Sejm* speaker Marek Borowski broke away to form a new party – Social Democracy of the Republic of Poland (Socjaldemokracja Polska, SdPl). Having lost his majority Miller stepped down the day after EU accession and was replaced by Marek Belka. However, even the new Prime Minister Marek Belka left the SLD and joined a neoliberal post-Solidarity party.

The 2005 Election: Another Post-Solidarity Government

The result of the 2005 election was another major turnover for the Polish ruling classes. The PiS and its presidential candidate Lech Kaczyński came from behind to emerge as the narrow and unexpected winners with 27 per cent of the vote (155 seats out of 460) ahead of the PO with 24 per cent and 133 seats. The radical parties, Samoobrona (11 per cent and 56 seats) and the

LPR (8 per cent and 34 seats) retained the level of support they had had in 2001. The SLD lost three quarters of its 2001 share of the vote, winning only 11 per cent of the vote and 55 seats, doing just well enough to hang on to the party's hard-core ex-communist electorate.

Szczerbiak (2007) claims that the success of the Law and Justice Party was its ability to reframe the election as a choice between the Civic Platform's vision of a liberal Poland, which they argued would benefit the better off and winners, in contrast to their focus on the have-nots as being more 'social' or 'solidaristic':

> In other words, Law and Justice argued that it was the state's responsibility to build more solidarity between those that had succeeded in the new capitalist Poland and those who felt that they had lost out; in order to capitalize on the fact that most Poles were broadly sympathetic to state intervention in the economy and economic redistribution. This was exemplified by the party's extremely effective TV advertisement, purporting to demonstrate the effects of the Civic Platform's flagship policy to introduce a unitary 15 per cent 'flat tax', that showed the contents of a child's bedroom, a fridge and a pharmacy disappearing. (Szczerbiak, 2007: 16)

The PiS was founded primarily as an anti-corruption and law and order party. Its slogan of building a 'Fourth Republic' proposed a conservative project based on a critique of Poland as corrupt and needing deep moral and political renewal, reflected in their promise to establish a powerful, new anti-corruption office and special truth and justice commission. The Law and Justice Party attempted to link this renewal agenda to the familiar refrain of de-communisation, arguing that many ex-communist politicians and sections of the business community connected to the former regime formed a corrupt nexus with communist-era security service functionaries and organised crime.

Civic Platform voters were clearly the most liberal in terms of their attitudes towards socio-economic issues (privatisation, tax, agricultural subsidies and welfare benefits), while the views of Law and Justice voters were generally more socially oriented. However, behind the rhetoric and mutual hostility, the two parties had common historical roots and similar conservative views on social and moral issues and simply represented different hues of neoliberalism rather than polar opposites. Therefore this apparent conflict between a 'social-solidaristic' vision of Poland represented by the Law and Justice/Kaczyński platform and a 'liberal' vision represented by the Civic Platform/Tusk platform had much more to do with the packaging than the substance of their policies.

After the PiS won the largest number of seats it was assumed that they would form a coalition with the PO, particularly as many people saw them as almost indistinguishable. However, a failure to agree on the conditions of such an alliance led to the PiS entering a coalition with the extreme right wing LPR under Roman Giertych and the populist Samoobrona. From this time onwards the PiS and the PO have been implacable enemies.

The main thrust of policy during its short term in office was directed at perceived corruption and lustration. Lustration, a word not found in any English dictionary, describes the practice in post-communist countries of exposing those who supposedly collaborated with the former regime and barring them from public office. This was a useful device for diverting attention and blame from the government to small invisible groups of conspirators. For example, at the same time that the health service was in deep crisis and some hospitals were going bankrupt the Office of Anti-Corruption singled out a doctor for negligence in a high profile court case (he was remanded without trial and subsequently released). Bribery and corruption were given as reasons for the poor state of the health service rather than poor wages and low levels of spending.

While most efforts and energy went into so-called anti-corruption campaigns there were some very modest policies introduced to placate voters who had been promised social justice. These included the *becikowe*, which was a 1,000 złoty grant for new born babies, which amounted to little more than the cost of buying a new pushchair. In order to reward the (unofficial) support of some sections of Solidarity, there was an increase in the activity of the inspectors of working conditions to ensure compliance with labour regulations. The level of social insurance (Zakład

Ubezpieczeń Społecznych, ZUS) was reduced, but this benefited those with higher wages rather than lower income earners.

The economic circumstances could hardly have been more propitious for the Law and Justice Party. After the 2004 EU accession, Poland was the beneficiary of substantial structural funds and there was also a marked fall in unemployment as the result of mass outward migration to other parts of Europe. Despite these favourable conditions this fragile coalition broke down when Andrzej Lepper, the leader of Samoobrona, was accused of corruption. Samoobrona and the League of Polish Families withdrew from the coalition and left the minority government with no option but to call an election when it had been in power for less than two years.

2007 Election: A Civic Platform Victory and More Neoliberalism

Although the Law and Justice Party won a higher number of votes than last time the Civic Platform won the largest number of seats. The 2007 election saw a turnout of 55 per cent, the highest participation rate since 1989, with much of the support for the PO seen as an attempt to get rid of the PiS. Their anti-corruption crusade was seen by many as disproportionate, intimidating and a diversion from the real issues, to others they made the Polish government look ridiculous and lack credibility in a wider Europe. One PiS *Sejm* deputy, Mrs Sowińska (children's rights ombudsman at the time), argued that children should not watch Teletubbies, because the fact that Tinky Winky carried a bag cast doubts on his sexuality and was therefore a corrosive influence. In general the PiS appealed to the losers of transformation, particularly older people, while the PO tended to appeal to the winners of transformation and younger people. This was reflected in the voting patterns of migrants with the established community in the US voting for Law and Justice, while 62 per cent of migrants in Europe/UK, who tend to be much younger, voting for the Civic Platform.[4]

In order to appeal to the electorate, Donald Tusk (leader of the Civic Platform) had to play down the market reforms on which he was intent and to soften his language on neoliberalism, clearly unpopular with the electorate. The huge protests by health workers in the preceding summer (2007) against poor pay ruled out talking overtly about privatisation, instead the euphemisms of modernisation and rationalisation were used. Since their election the Civic Platform have floated proposals in the health service that amount to a sort of creeping privatisation. A basket of services (*koszyk świadczeń*) would comprise a minimum of health provision and additional services could only be accessed through extra health insurance or direct payment as hospitals are subject to commercial legislation. Tusk was much more overt and bold in his enthusiasm for neoliberal policies outside of Poland. In an interview with the *Financial Times* after the election, he invoked the slow return of socialism to justify 'the third phase of freedom', which is economic liberalism (Cienski and Wagstyl, 2007). In addition to getting rid of regulation, to which, 'You have to take a machete and cut, cut, cut', he referred to his intention to accelerate privatisation.

The Demonisation of the Polish Public as 'Far Right'

Some people have argued that discontent with unemployment, low wages, deteriorating welfare and corruption in Poland has manifested itself in nationalism, xenophobia and homophobia. This view that castigates the Polish electorate as being ideologically right wing and xenophobic needs to be contested, and a closer examination of voting behaviour and support for the new parties suggests a very different picture (McManus-Czubinska *et al.*, 2003). There is nothing new in the phenomenon that disillusionment with mainstream parties opens up a space for the ideas of the extreme right as well as those of the left – this has been clearly evident in the UK with local electoral success of the fascist British National Party and Jean-Marie Le Pen's Front National Party in France.

Groups that are overtly fascist exist in Poland, as they do elsewhere in the European Union, but these are small, on the fringes and play no role in electoral politics. On the other hand right wing groups such as the LPR invoke anti-Semitism in a way that would be completely unacceptable in other European countries. The leader Roman Giertych was honorary chairman of the All-Polish Youth (Młodzież Wszechpolska), a group whose members have been photographed giving the Nazi salute. Its origins can be traced to the inter-war period and in the 1930s it spearheaded attacks on Jewish university students (and led boycotts against Jewish businesses). Their violent and intolerant traditions have been continued and one of their targets has been Women's Day marches where participants have had eggs and tomatoes thrown at them. One particularly shameful episode was their violent physical attack on the Kraków March for Tolerance (in support of gay rights) in 2004. Giertych has now severed his links with this group, formally at least.

However, the idea that right wing and illiberal ideas are endemic and widespread in the Polish electorate is simply not the case. The biggest winner of elections has been abstentionism with turnouts at a very low level. The average turnout in parliamentary elections in the last 17 years has been 48 per cent in contrast to the 63 per cent turnout in the first election in 1989 (McManus-Czubinska *et al.*, 2004a: 407). A low point was the 20 per cent turnout in the first elections to the European parliament in 2004. Even the 2007 election, which was hailed as a success in terms of participation rates, only managed to get 55 per cent of the electorate to vote. Surveys confirm that people are highly sceptical of politicians, suggesting that they 'promise more than they deliver', that they 'lose touch' with voters and 'put their self interest first' (McManus-Czubinska *et al.*, 2004a: 407).

The rise and fall of populist parties such as Samoobrona are highly ambiguous. Its success came from its ability to be a focus for and articulate popular disenchantment with the whole post-1989 political order, which it portrayed as corrupt and out of touch with the concerns of ordinary Poles (McManus-Czubinska *et al.*, 2004b: 18). Samoobrona claimed to be committed to the true interests of Poland and Poles, and in terms of the background and income of their voters it had solid working-class support. To describe this support as being far right is to misrepresent both its attractions and dangers. Although Samoobrona has built on direct action to protect defaulting farmers from their creditors, and organised protests against EU imports, overridingly the most salient issues it talked about were unemployment and corruption among political elites.

The role of the church has been assigned a privileged role in many analyses of Polish politics, although it is contended here that its influence is overstated. For example, the landslide electoral victory of the SLD-UP in 2001 was despite intervention by the Catholic Church. Individual bishops and the Permanent Council of the Polish Episcopate issued a letter to be read out in all parishes on Sunday. This cautioned Catholics against voting for a party linked to an ideological continuity with the Communist Party and 'which straightforwardly declares its desire to introduce laws which undermines the right to life' (in other words to legalise abortion) (Szczerbiak, 2002). An article in *The Economist* puts the role of the church in perspective:

> The church in Poland is divided between Vatican loyalists, who often oppose close involvement in politics, and energetic dissidents linked to Radio Maryja, a hardline broadcaster. This once had huge clout, articulating the feelings of Poles alienated by the country's brisk, materialist business culture and the decay in moral norms. But Radio Maryja's audience has shrunk in the past decade to no more than 2% of all current listeners. (2007: 70)

This pessimistic view, which sees the rise of right wing ideas as a response to and refuge from transition, fails to engage with the growth of organisations, movements and intellectual alternatives that have developed as part of a wider critique of global capitalism.

New Parties and New Movements

Elections and the New Radical Left

A significant barrier to the formation of a radical left in politics has been the identification of socialism with the Stalinist pre-1989 political system. However, this identification is something of a double-edged sword. Although no one is arguing for a return to the old times, the neoliberal policies driving down living standards for the vast majority mean that the old system does not look so bad to many people. A layer of people, especially the young, has identified with the global anti-capitalist and anti-war movements or the newly emerging women's movement discussed in the previous chapter. For example, unemployed workers' organisations in Ełk, a town in the east of Poland (with 40 per cent unemployment) and Miastko in the north-west (with 30 per cent unemployment) regularly sent coaches to anti-war demonstrations, European Social Forums and demonstrations against unemployment in Brussels. Workers from Ożarów who had fought the closure of their factory for over a year in the face of brutal attacks from the police and security guards went to the Paris European Social Forum in 2003. A year later a group of nurses from the OZZPiP nurses' union went to the London European Social Forum. Some of these activists have been co-opted by the post-communist social democrats, and in the 2005 election campaign leading members of left wing and green organisations were persuaded to join the electoral lists of the SLD and SdPl.

The most vociferous and visible left wing electoral organisation is the Polish Labour Party (Polska Partia Pracy, PPP), which was founded by the trade union August '80 (Sierpień '80).[5] This is a radical offshoot from Solidarity and has its strongest base and support in Silesia. Its programme is overtly and unapologetically left wing including demands for a minimum wage of 68 per cent of the average wage and a 35 hour week; progressive taxation with 50 per cent for the wealthiest and 10 per cent for the poor; and guaranteed benefits for the unemployed.[6] The PPP's policies go beyond economic demands; they have been consistently against Poland's invasion and occupation of Iraq, regularly supporting demonstrations against the war, as well as protests in defence of a woman's right to choose and gay rights. Outside of Poland they identify with movements for global justice and the negative effects of neoliberal globalisation: 'What unites us are demands for social justice, real democracy and the primacy of labour over capital' (Ostrowska, 2005). However, their high profile has not been matched by electoral success as they gained only around 1 per cent of the votes in the 2005 and 2007 elections. Nevertheless they are an embryonic party and face the usual problems of small parties in gaining media coverage and profile. The PPP would be an obvious candidate for the basis of a left alternative grouping, but its top-down organisation without structures has made it difficult for other groupings and individuals to join.

Among other groupings on the radical left are New Left (Nowa Lewica), which lost members following its leader Piotr Ikonwicz's decision to fight the 2007 *Sejm* elections on the Samoobrona list. There is a weekly paper *Trybuna Robotnicza* (Workers Tribune) published by the union Sierpień '80 and a Marxist monthly and agitational paper *Pracownicza Demokracja* (Workers Democracy). In addition, there are also intellectual challenges to neoliberalism and US imperialism such as the Polish edition of *Le Monde Diplomatique*. Further, a left wing think tank based in Warsaw, Krytyka Polityczna, publishes a range of books and articles and provides a forum for radical critiques of neoliberalism. The public face of this group is Sławomir Sierakowski who has become prominent on TV discussion programmes.

The Anti-discrimination, Anti-capitalist and Anti-war Movement

The most hopeful prospect for creating a radical alternative is around the opposition to neoliberalism, war and discrimination. It is a journalistic commonplace in Poland that most people have left wing views that are not reflected in the character of the parties in parliament. Polls show that opinions on privatisation, free education and health, the war in Iraq, the installation of US bases[7] and abortion are left wing. In a poll taken in 1999, weeks before the momentous Seattle demonstration that launched the anti-capitalist movement, 50 per cent of those polled had a negative attitude to the word 'capitalism' (Hardy and Zebrowski, 2005). This is a huge shift if you consider that in November 1988 Margaret Thatcher was cheered by thousands of workers on the streets of Gdańsk.

In the Polish context the use of the terms right wing and left wing are confusing and do not reflect the way they are used in 'old Europe'. Some working-class people call themselves right wing as a way of showing their hatred and opposition to the communists. However, in terms of their attitudes, which support unions and the welfare state and oppose privatisation, they would be considered to be left wing. But it is equally true to say that the word 'Solidarity', when it is used as a political justification for the market reforms, evokes as much or even more hostility from other groups of workers.

When it comes to street demonstrations the biggest protests remain those organised by trade unions, on which some of the slogans of the anti-capitalist movement have been in evidence. However, outside of these trade union demonstrations, between 2003 and 2005 there were four significant demonstrations of up to 10,000 people. Some 70 to 80 per cent of the population oppose the occupation of Iraq and this was reflected in the first two demonstrations just before and just after the US-led attack on 20 March 2003. While the anti-war movement does not exist on the same scale as the UK, but there have been regular demonstrations of hundreds or thousands of people which have taken place in Warsaw, as well as smaller protests in dozens of smaller cities and towns.

A third demonstration took place in 2004 when 10,000 people demanded the shutting down of the Warsaw summit organised by the World Economic Forum. Initially the authorities tried to ban the march, but gave up the idea when they were told it would go ahead anyway. There were two months of hysterical attacks in the media about the oncoming hordes of alterglobalist[8] hooligans with pictures of violent confrontations on some of the previous anti-capitalist demonstrations. Shop windows were boarded up for miles and hopeful glaziers offered their services leafleting worried shop owners. In the event the march was non-violent and was joined by large numbers of ordinary people.

This demonstration showed that the anti-globalisation, anti-capitalist movements could organise a significant march in Poland. Importantly the Warsaw region of Solidarity advertised the march twice on its website and included articles arguing for attendance. The media witch hunt backfired and the combination of extensive coverage and a highly successful demonstration meant that millions of people for the first time heard that there was an alterglobalist movement in Poland.

The fourth march took place in June 2005 around the issue of gay pride. The president of Warsaw, right wing populist Lech Kaczyński, had stressed that he would not allow 'the public propagation of homosexuality' and banned the Equality Parade for the second year running. The organisers withstood his threats and the march took place anyway. The protest was joined by diverse individuals and groups of people, as it became a rallying call for those protesting about homophobia, illiberality and threats to freedom of association and speech. This was a significant victory for activists arguing that mass protest was the way to defeat bans on demonstrations.

Conclusion

Although divisions between post-Solidarity and post-communist parties are alive and kicking in some quarters, particularly in the higher echelons of parties and unions, this division now has much less resonance among workers. It is noticeable on trade union protests and demonstrations that workers who are in Solidarity or OPZZ or some other union have similar views. Us and them is no longer 'Us – Solidarity' and them the 'Communist Party' but 'Us – ordinary people' and them 'corrupt government and thieving privatisers'. The widespread disillusionment with mainstream political parties has been reflected in low turnouts in elections. However, this has been paralleled by a growing critique of neoliberal policies and opposition to the war. Although the existence of radical groups should not be overstated, workers' organisations, new political parties and social movements are laying the foundations of an alternative to the neoliberal policies of the mainstream parties.

11

PROSPECTS FOR THE FUTURE

Neoliberalism, Happiness and Freedom

The idea of happiness and wellbeing has attracted a new wave of interest in both popular culture and academic circles (Ferguson, 2007). At a European level the Deutsche Bank recently commissioned research into happiness within OECD countries with a view to establishing the factors that contribute to the 'happy variety of capitalism' (Bergheim, 2007). In my last book *Restructuring Krakow: Desperately Seeking Capitalism* (1996 with Al Rainnie) we reported that the much promised 'feel good' factor of transformation was elusive for many people. In 1996 the memory of a repressive, police state was very much alive, but the fear of surveillance and imprisonment had been replaced by a different kind of fear. There was a much greater feeling of insecurity about work, about being paid, about accessing good quality health care and about meeting the rising costs of necessities. By 2008 these insecurities had intensified.

The collapse of the communist regime in 1990 was hailed as bringing freedom to the people of Poland. However, the concept of freedom has been debased by advocating the market and free enterprise as the solution to organising the economy and society. Freedom is not an absolute concept, but relative to people's material conditions. Harvey argues that there is

> the fullness of freedom for those whose income, leisure and security needs no enhancing and a mere pittance of liberty for the people who may in vain attempt to make use of their democratic rights to gain shelter from the power of the owners of property. (2005: 183 quoting Polanyi, 1957 [1944]: 257)

This has been reflected in the Polish electoral system since 1990, which shows that having fought for 'democracy', people's enthusiasm for exercising it through the ballot box has been tepid. Disillusionment and disappointment have also been evident in support (or lack of it) for political parties, which has been manifest in the swings between post-Solidarity and post-communist governments since 1990. In 1990 it would have seemed simply inconceivable that the refashioned Communist Party in the form of the Democratic Left Alliance could have won a decisive victory in 1993 and then again in 2001. The collapse, disintegration, fragmentation and regrouping of political parties seems bewildering as people search for representation that defends their employment and welfare and represents the aspirations they have for themselves and their families.

There have been winners of transformation; this is clearly evident in a high average growth rate over the last five years, as well as being manifest in the new housing estates and expensive shops that have sprung up in the big cities. The large number of losers of restructuring Polish capitalism, the people cast aside and increasingly deprived of social protection are much less visible. In as much as poverty is regarded as a social issue, in Poland as elsewhere, the solution by the ruling class is not to increase spending on welfare or to consider a more substantial redistribution of wealth, rather it is to promote flexible labour markets designed to make people take any job on offer. For some the only hope is to eke a living in the informal or illegal economy as petty traders or street vendors. However, there is no distinction between capitalist and non-capitalist sectors of the economy; the reach of capital is overarching and its tendrils stretch into all aspects of people's work or lives. Capital includes workers in differentiated ways in the labour market and determines their access to welfare and as such shapes the nature of exclusion.

Whither the Polish Economy?

Despite the celebratory language about the growth of the Polish economy and its attractiveness as a site for foreign capital, I have presented a much more sober analysis as to where Poland fits in the international division of labour. There have been two competing claims – one is that Poland is moving into higher technology and knowledge economy activities, which explains the arrival of some foreign investors. A more pessimistic view is that low wages in Poland, in the context of Europe at least, have made it attractive as an outpost of the relatively low skilled activities of foreign capital, in the automobile industry for example. However, this dichotomy is too simplistic to understand the uneven way in which Poland is integrating with the global economy.

We should avoid the trap of assuming that TNCs are footloose, stateless and able to close production in one area and open it up elsewhere – this would be a crude characterisation of the strategies of capital. However, in a situation where capital is constantly reviewing its options, the politics of entering new countries and imposing discipline in the workplace has had implications for work and workers. Ultimately it has brought Polish workers into a new arena of competition not only between firms, but also within their own firms as each workplace becomes a 'profit centre'. In those parts of production that are not mobile, Polish workers have been used to fill labour shortages in other parts of the European Union.

Undeniably there are opportunities in Poland, particularly in the big cities, for well paid, relatively secure jobs with promotion prospects. However, this is not the experience of the vast majority of Polish people; working in the public sector for most remains poorly paid and stressful. The availability and quality of work on offer in the private sector is highly variable and has much more to do with where you live, your age or gender than skills and abilities. The unevenness of Polish capitalism means that living in certain regions, often small towns and rural areas, or being older, younger or female means that you will be disproportionately excluded from the gains of transformation. An analysis and understanding of this combined and uneven development is not an esoteric exercise, but can inform activists as to how this unevenness can be reversed. This needs to be linked to eviscerating production and social relationships that are driven by the logic of capital and replacing them with those which are the outcome of debate, collective and individual choice (Bond, 1999).

The Limits of Neoliberalism

By 2008 Poland was the forerunner among the post-communist countries of Europe in pursing neoliberal policies. The path for this was smoothed from 1990 when the political conditions were possible for the introduction of shock therapy. This was something akin to 'neoliberalism in a bullet' as draconian economic policies, liberalisation and privatisation were imposed overnight, setting the tone of policies for successive governments, both from the post-Solidarity and the post-communist camps.

The doublespeak of neoliberalism has been exposed, as claims of the withdrawal of the state and unfettered markets have much more to do with rhetoric than practice (Chang, 2002). The state remains critical in securing the conditions for capital accumulation, by providing physical infrastructure and the conditions for reproducing labour such as education and guaranteeing a minimum of social provision. In the wider global economy this has rarely been more clearly illustrated than when the US and major European governments pumped billions of dollars, euros and sterling into the financial system to bail out the banks, in effect taking them into government ownership thereby (re)nationalising vast swathes of the financial system.

Further, it is not the case that neoliberal policies have been foisted on an acquiescent or demoralised working class. The Polish state is aware of the objective nature of labour, in that there is a limit to how far social capital can be degraded in a competitive economy, where there is a premium placed on skills and knowledge. Even if trade union leaders are sometimes unconfident about their ability to lead disputes, the ruling class is fully aware of the subjective and oppositional nature of labour and the potential for confrontation. Since 1990 successive governments have had to compromise or even shelve policies and initiatives in the face of protests, or potential protests. The government had to make concessions to labour on the question of privatisation by allowing so-called management buyouts and allocating shares to workers as part of the *Mass Privatisation Programme*. Successive governments have also had to temper their draconian proposals for welfare, such as the Hausner Plan in 2003. Further, the massive protests by health workers in 2007 forced the main opposition party, the Civic Platform, to temper its neoliberal languages and gloss over market-led reforms that were on its agenda.

By 2008 mass migration to other parts of Europe had brought substantial changes to Polish labour markets. Whereas jobs in foreign owned firms had been coveted and subject to intense competition, after 2004 unemployment fell and significant labour shortages started developing. The Korean LG factory had to bus workers from a distance of 70 kilometres, and even applied for permission (which was refused by the regional government) to import North Korean workers. These new labour market conditions have led to a new confidence for workers and whereas labour struggles up to 2004 were defensive, by 2007 there was a decisive turn to more offensive disputes that focused on demands for higher pay and union recognition.

The situation of a tight labour market looks to be shattered by the spiralling economic crisis and deepening recession. Since October 2008 there have been daily reports of redundancies and short time working across all sectors from hotels to construction. The biggest sectors that have been affected are automotives – including some of the flagship factories of the Polish economy, and textiles and furniture.

The Polish Working Class

One of the popular myths of capitalism in the twenty-first century is that class is dead. The declining importance of traditional industries as major workplaces in many advanced economies and the rise of new forms of employment have led to declarations that labour organisations are marginal and solidarity a thing of the past. Very often these new forms of work have been given an emancipatory gloss, with references to the 'weightless economy' or the 'knowledge economy', which suggests that work is more interesting and fulfilling. Whether workers are employed in shipyards or supermarkets, steel factories or call centres they are all subject to the pressures of competition and anarchy of the market. In the case of the Polish working class it is too easy to look back to the high point of workers' struggles in 1980 or the explosion of strikes in the early 1990s and make assumptions about a dissipated and complacent working class. Strike statistics or union membership are certainly one proxy of the health of labour organisations, but they can fail to take account of rebelliousness from below.

Ost (2006) provides a rich and fascinating account of labour and class in post-1990 Poland. However, the title of the book *The Defeat of Solidarity* reflects a deep pessimism about the prospects of the Polish working class. Ost argues that there is something exceptional about Poland and that emerging class differences are the result of 'structural legacies' and 'ideological fashions', the product of which is 'a weak labour movement' unable to defend it own interests. The reason for this is the view that class allegiances have been clouded by Solidarity's preferred targets of 'communists', 'atheists' and 'liberals'.

This paints a gloomy one-dimensional picture of working-class consciousness and activity. The demand that workers must be secular, internationalist and have a set of politically correct ideas before they can engage in struggle is to misunderstand the complex and contradictory ideas that are in people's heads. In a country that has been dominated by foreign powers for much of its history it is understandable that a strong vein of nationalism runs through the Polish consciousness. This in part explains the desire, in some quarters, for a Polish capitalism (see Hardy and Rainnie, 1996). It is assumed by some workers and sections of the ruling class that Polish capital can be harnessed to the development of firms and the national economy as a whole, whereas foreign capital would have no allegiance to Polish workers and their employment. However misguided this might be, the experience of foreign investors cherry picking the most profitable firms, asset stripping and paying low wages coupled with the exploitation of Polish migrant workers elsewhere in Europe has done little to dispel these ideas. Neither can we make any assumptions about religion being a barrier to class consciousness; after all in 1980–81 the church was a place for Solidarity activists to meet. A more recent example is the long and bitter fight (including clashes with the police and security guards) against the closure of the Ożarów cable factory near Warsaw, which was conducted by workers who set up an altar outside the factory gates so that a priest could say mass on Sundays.

Ost cannot be accused of having done insufficient research, as he has done extensive interviews in dozens of workplaces since the 1980s – however, the interviews that I have conducted with activists and trade union officials from 1993 onwards paint a very different picture from his. This argument was developed at length in Chapter 7, but the main threads are worth restating. The protests and disputes, which have involved largely women workers, do not accord with a picture of defeat. ZNP, which represents the majority of teachers, for example, has been in dispute with both post-Solidarity and post-communist governments on pay, conditions and reforms and has gone beyond this in challenging foreign policy on Iraq as well as the right wing ideas of Education Minister Roman Giertych – whose resignation they called for. OZZPiP, the nurses' union, formed in the mid-1990s, comprising women who had not been involved in trade unions or politics before, has been at the forefront of the most militant and high profile protests.

Class consciousness is not always the product of a 'long discursive struggle', but can emerge quickly when engagement in protests and disputes challenges pre-conceived ideas about the natural order of things and power. Ost (2006) is quite right to argue that workers do not always see themselves as anti-capitalist, and this is true of many, if not the majority, of trade unionists I know in the UK. Yet some trade unions and trade unionists in Poland have been inspired by and participated in the anti-globalisation and anti-capitalist events and demonstrations in Europe and beyond. This has been a link between organised workers and the wider social movements and underpins common cause with trade unions in other countries.

Finally, gloomy accounts of the Polish working class seem to ignore the fact that there is now a new generation of Poles, many of whom with no experience of living under communism and less likely to have baggage from the past. Exhortations of lustration by right wing government to purge those with a communist past are lost on many young people. Further, in the UK young migrant Polish workers have not shown themselves to be allergic to joining labour organisations, and this has been reflected in the formation of an all Polish branch of the GMB trade union in the UK, for example. While we should not overstate the level of cross-border collaboration between trade unions, there have been initiatives at both the national and rank and file level to build solidarity between Polish trade unions and those in other parts of Europe to defend migrant workers.

Another World Is Possible

At the time of finishing this book, the global economy is being plunged into recession after the spiralling and unprecedented banking crisis that started in the US, and that is now infecting and enveloping the entire global economy. Events are unravelling so quickly that it would be unwise to make predictions about the length or depth of the current crisis, or about its specific impacts on the Polish economy. It is clear that the events of the autumn and winter of 2008 have punctured the confidence of the global ruling class in their ability to deal with the flaws of the system. Keynes has been resurrected in some quarters as a 'prophet reborn', whose ideas may be able to rescue capitalism from itself. However, the arena is now wide open for more radical critiques of capitalism, as a system where crises are endemic and cannot simply be regulated by sound management.

To believe that there is an alternative to neoliberalism, and indeed capitalism itself, does not mean that some blueprint of a future society is appropriate. However, there are a number of simple tenets and propositions that could form a base line as to the guiding principles of a better society. In the face of commodification, exclusion and highly differential provision we should reassert the importance of universal welfare, health provision and education. Further, pensions should be guaranteed, predictable and not left to the vagaries of global financial markets – a situation that leaves millions of old people in poverty. We should constantly raise the demand for secure jobs for all, with minimum wages and conditions and the right to be treated with dignity, as well as workplace representation by independent labour organisations. This checklist is by no means exhaustive. These are not radical expectations, but even these very modest demands are a long way removed from the reality of people's lives under neoliberalism in Poland.

I remain pessimistic about the ability of Polish capitalism to deliver a decent standard of living for the majority of people. If anything, this is even more unlikely than when I wrote my last book in 1996. Instability in the global economy, heightened competitive pressures and the neoliberal discipline of the European Union, threaten public spending as inflation and competitiveness are prioritised over welfare. At the time of finishing this book there is huge uncertainty about the prospects for the global economy. The debate is not about whether there will be a recession, but only about how deep and severe its impacts will be.

Capitalism has a resilience and propensity for surviving, although often at a high human cost – so what of its gravediggers? The hundreds of interviews that I have done in workplaces and with activists leave me optimistic about the possibilities for resistance to commodification and marketisation through both social movements and organised labour. From supermarkets to coal mines, to hospitals, schools and factories the empty promises of neoliberalism have provoked ordinary people to fight against inequities in their workplaces, their communities and wider societies. Political alternatives are rooted in a different critique of consumerism, the starting point of which is a rejection of the notion that our lives, relationships and our world are simply commodities for sale. There is a theoretical and political alternative that argues that human happiness, wellbeing and individuality can only be realised in a society that is free from exploitation and oppression.

NOTES

Chapter 1

1. The intellectual traditions of neoliberalism can be traced back as far as Adam Smith (1776) (see also Viner, 1927) who argued that the invisible hand of the market was a superior mechanism for producing and allocating goods. More recently the heritage of neoliberalism comes from neoclassical economics, which purports to demonstrate mathematically the superiority of the market, combined with the political liberalism of Friedrich Hayek (1944 and 1960).

2. A project on gender aspects of transformation, particularly on women in the public sector, was carried out with Alison Stenning in 1999 (Nuffield Foundation Social Science Small Grant – SGS/LB/0317). In 2005 interviews were carried out on women's activism with funding from the British Academy in collaboration with Professor Wiesia Kozek and Alison Stenning. The book also draws on some material gathered as part of an ESRC funded project *Cross Border Trade Union Collaboration and Polish Migrant Workers in Britain* (RES-000-22-2034) with Ian Fitzgerald during 2006/2007.

Chapter 2

1. The number of Poles who died during the Second World War is estimated at 5.6 million, which includes 2.36 million civilians and the 3 million Polish Jews who perished in the holocaust. For a full discussion see Gniazdowski (2007).

2. Spheres of influence were agreed at the end-of-war conferences held at Yalta in the Crimea (January 1945) and Potsdam (July 1945). However, Stalin and Churchill had already come to some agreement about their respective empires in October 1944. Birchall (1974: 26) quotes the following:

    I wrote out on half a sheet of paper:
    Romania: Russia 90% – the others 10%
    Greece: Great Britain (in accord with the USA) 90% – Russia 10%
    Yugoslavia: 50–50%
    Hungary: 50–50%
    Bulgaria: Russia 75% – the others 25%

I pushed this across to Stalin, who had by then heard the translation. There was a slight pause. Then he took his blue pencil and made a large tick upon it, and passed it back to us. It was all done in no more time than it takes to set down. (Churchill, 1954: 198)

3. The Polish Workers' Party (*Polska Partia Robotnicza*, PPR) was a communist party in Poland from 1942 to 1948.

4. The Polish United Workers' Party (*Polska Zjednoczona Partia Robotnicza*, PZPR) was the Communist Party in the People's Republic of Poland founded in 1948 from a merger of the PPR (see note 3) and the Polish Socialist Party (Polska Partia Socjalistyczna, PPS).

5. See www.nowahuta.info (last accessed 12 February 2009).

6. According to Landau and Tomaszewski (1985) the Polish Central Statistical office reported that in 1980 real per capita income decreased, as compared with the previous year, in 69 per cent of pensioner households, 54.5 per cent of peasant households and in 45.5 per cent of households with employees in the socialised economy.

7. The Fiat Licence and equipment for the production of cars was bought from Italy, the Berliet bus licence from France and Massey Ferguson tractors from Great Britain.

8. Between 1971 and 1980 Poland bought 452 licences, 416 of which were from the USA, France and Germany. In 1976 only 238 out of 385 licences were applied in practice.

9. Kuroń and Modzelewski's (1982) 'Open Letter to the Party' was not a criticism of communism *per se*, but an indictment of the way it was manifest in the Soviet bloc and Poland, in particular. They argued that these were class societies, where the ruling class imposed 'production for production's sake' on the working class. They argued that the system could not be reformed, but that a revolution was necessary to bring about real socialism. Later they disowned these ideas and Jacek Kuroń was a supporter of shock therapy as the only way to reform the system. He became a minister in Solidarity's first government. However, Kuroń came to be a strong critic of neoliberalism, which he saw as deepening social divisions and alienating ordinary people. His last public speech from April 2004 was addressed to alterglobalists (anti-globalists), who were protesting against the World Economic Forum held in Warsaw. He said, 'It is you, my dear friends, who have to perform the actions which contemporary political elites cannot perform: who have to create new concepts of social cooperation, implement ideals of freedom, equality, and social justice.'

Chapter 3

1. Neoliberalism is an alliance between neoclassical economics and the political and moral philosophy of the Austrian libertarian tradition. See Chang (2002) for a good critique.
2. Some schools of thought would see evolutionary thinking as a subset of institutionalist thinking. Indeed one of Veblen's (1898) major contributions was an essay entitled 'Why Is Economics Not an Evolutionary Science'. As Hodgson (2004) points out, evolutionary economics is a vague and ill-defined term, which does not necessarily imply drawing directly on biology. Evolutionary theory in this section should be understood as those theorists who lean more heavily on the use of biological metaphors.
3. A detailed history of institutionalist thought and a taxonomy of the various strands have been done extensively elsewhere (see for example, Mayhew, 1988; Hall and Taylor, 1996; DiMaggio, 1998; Hodgson, 2001 and 2004; Nielsen, 2001).
4. The old institutionalism (Veblen, 1899) belongs to that social science tradition based on a strategy of seeing people as a product of culture, whereas the new institutionalism (Williamson, 1975; North, 1990) favours a view of people as 'rational choosers' (Mayhew, 1988).
5. For a further discussion and critique of combined and uneven development see Elster (1986).
6. In the first two decades of the twentieth century the question of 'catching up' with the British economy by US and Germany was addressed by Marxists such as Gramsci (Hoare and Nowell-Smith, 1971).
7. Modern versions of this argument have been made with reference to the tiger economies of South-East Asia.
8. See Aglietta (1979) for the fullest and original synthesis of regulation theory and Glick and Brenner (1991) for a critique.

Chapter 4

1. There is a long lineage of those who have tried to explain the way in which those with power and wealth have convinced those that have not, that this state of affairs is part of the natural order of things. Every established order tends to reproduce, in different ways and to different degrees, the naturalisation of 'its own arbitrariness' (Bourdieu, 2003 [1977]: 164). It was Gramsci (in Hoare and Nowell-Smith, 1971) who elaborated this idea by suggesting that the ruling class achieved hegemony through their control of the ideological

apparatus of the state, and pointed to the existence of 'organic intellectuals' whose role was to justify the status quo.

2. Except Serbia and Turkmenistan.
3. The last agreement between Poland and the IMF was signed in 1994. This programme was conditional on structural and systematic reform such as the mass privatisation of 444 large state enterprises and changes in the pensions indexation rule.
4. SLD (Sojusz Lewicy Demokratycznej, Democratic Left Alliance).
5. BOC, the British Oxygen Company, is a supplier of industrial gases and logistics services, and a major supplier to other TNCs.
6. Derivatives are extremely complex financial instruments. They are an individual bet on some combination of changes in interest rates and exchange rates.
7. Regional government is organised in three tiers. The first tier is sixteen *voivode*, equivalent to EU NUTS (Nomenclature of Territorial Units for Statistics) regions. Below that are *powiats* and the *gmina* is the lowest territorial division. A *gmina* could be a town or city, or a town and surrounding villages or a set of villages. As of 2004 there were 2,478 in Poland.
8. The American Federation of Labor and Congress of Industrial Organizations, commonly AFL-CIO, is a national trade union centre, the largest federation of unions in the United States, made up of 56 national and international unions (including Canadian), together representing more than 10 million workers. It is contended that the AFL-CIO has always played a reactionary role in international politics (Scipes, 2005).
9. In the 2004 accession Poland, Hungary, the Czech Republic, Slovakia and Slovenia, Estonia, Latvia and Lithuania were admitted to the EU. Romania and Bulgaria were admitted in 2007. Other countries, particularly those in the south-east, still remain outside the EU.
10. In 2006 there were 60 owners, including governments, pan-European institutions such as the European Investment Bank and the European Commission.

Chapter 5

1. The Committee for Mutual Economic Assistance (CMEA) was the trading bloc of Soviet bloc economies. These arrangements collapsed in 1991.
2. The World Bank Pension model has been foisted on countries as part of the neoliberal package. It means that workers are forced to save for their retirement with private pension companies who then gamble this money on financial markets.

3. See www.poland.gov.pl/index.php?document+1631.
4. Established research centres include Delphi Automotive, Siemens AG, Motorola Inc, Samsung Electronics, ABB and GE Aircraft Engines. New research units include TRW Automotive, Lincoln Electric, WABCO.
5. This was on the basis on an interview in June 2005. Further information can be found on www.aviationvalley.pl (last accessed 12 February 2009).
6. See Note 8 in Chapter 8.

Chapter 6

1. See Chapter 2 for a full discussion.
2. There was a long tradition of workers' councils in Poland. The revival of these with increased powers was one of the reforms that were conceded to workers in the aftermath of the imposition of martial law in 1981.
3. The decision to relocate bus production to Poland was related to changes in the market that had undergone concentration. By 1992, the number of bus producers was one third of the number in 1962, and between 1992 and 1998 that number had fallen by a further 40 per cent.
4. Lodmel, along with Pafawag, was a centre for Solidarity in the region in 1981 and the site of running battles with the army who used tanks to break the occupation of the factory.

Chapter 7

1. The welfare and social provision of SOEs was extensive including housing, sports facilities and hospitals. See Alison Stenning's accounts of Nowa Huta.
2. By definition the number of Poles migrating is notoriously hard to measure. First, because there is free movement to a number of European countries, and second, because it is not possible to know whether migration comprises short or longer stays abroad. One estimate is that since 1 May 2004, up to 2 million of the 39 million Poles have migrated to the EU-15 countries for at least a period of work, with most headed to Germany, Ireland and the UK (by some estimates, four Poles a minute leave, although many return, see http://migration.ucdavis.edu/mn (last accessed 12 February 2009).
3. After harmonisation with other EU unemployment rates.
4. Alison Stenning has done rich research on Nowa Huta, Kraków. For further details see www.nowahuta.info (last accessed 12 February 2009).

5. In the UK the main measurement of workers from Poland and other A8 countries is the Worker Registration Scheme. However, this has limitations as it does not measure the self-employed or migrants who return to Poland.
6. Poland received 7.4 billion USD in recorded remittances in 2005, up from 2.6 billion USD in 2002, see http://migration.ucdavis.edu/mn (last accessed 12 February 2009).
7. The reforms were named after Jerzy Hausner, the SLD government Minister for Labour and Social Policy, who proposed the reforms.
8. In 2005 only 15 per cent of the unemployed, equivalent to just over half a million people, received unemployment benefits. The compensation rate is around 20 per cent of the average wage. Instead many people receive social benefits, especially disability pension, where the compensation rate is 75 per cent of the average wage.
9. These health funds in turn signed renewable contracts with service providers (i.e. hospitals, clinics and doctors), which were then under pressure to compete for contracts by offering high quality, low cost health services.
10. Ogólnopolski Związek Zawodowy Pielęgniarek i Położnych (Polish Union of Nurses and Midwives).

Chapter 8

1. See Goldthorpe et al. (1968) and Gorz (1982).
2. The notion of the 'self limiting revolution' was that it was possible to organise from below, but not to take power. It meant that the demands were aimed at reforms within the system, rather than a challenge to the system itself.
3. The August '80 Free Trade Union (Wolny Związek Zawodowy 'Sierpień '80', WZZ Sierpień '80) is a split from Solidarity, which claims to have its radical roots in the ideals of the 1980 strikes. It is particularly militant in terms of supporting other groups of workers and campaigns (see Ostrowska, 2005).
4. Ogólnopolskie Porozumienie Związków Zawodowych (All-Poland Alliance of Trade Unions).
5. The ZNP (Związek Nauczycielstwa Polskiego) was formed in 1905 and in 2008 represented between 40 and 50 per cent of all teachers in comparison to Solidarity's 15,000.
6. The ZNP support the Stop the War Initiative (Inicjatywa STOP Wojnie) and hosted a conference in their building in March 2006. The Vice President represented the union by speaking on the platform at several meetings.

7. Real unit labour costs are the compensation per employee in current price divided by GDP in current prices per total employment.
8. This table was derived from an analysis of the industrial disputes reported on the Solidarity website www.solidarnosc.org.pl/en from the beginning of 2003 until the end of 2006.
9. Reforms are aimed at reducing public debt in line with the Maastricht criteria, which is a precondition for the introduction of the euro.
10. Transport and General Workers' Union is a general British trade union that has merged with Amicus to form the Unite union.
11. The GMB is a British trade union (originally General Municipal Boilermakers; now known simply as GMB) and represents workers in a variety of industries.

Chapter 9

1. See Chapter 2.
2. The first major case of Feminist Art being censored was Alicja Zebrowska's video installation *Original Sin* 1993. The second major case deals with artist Katarzyna Kozyra's photo-piece called *Blood Ties* in 1999.
3. According to Leszkowicz (2005) this work is an exploration of masculinity and suffering, and consists of a video close-up of the face of an exercising bodybuilder, together with a cross on which a photograph of male genitalia has been placed.
4. They asserted that article 196 of the criminal code had been violated which stated that offending religious feelings through public mis-representation of an object or place of worship was liable to a fine or maximum prison sentence.
5. Legal abortion is only permissible if pregnancy constitutes a threat to the woman's life or health; or if there is a high probability that the foetus is severely damaged; or if pregnancy is the result of a criminal act.
6. After giving birth Ms Tysiac suffered a retinal haemorrhage, making her eyesight so poor she needed daily treatment.
7. See Chapter 10.
8. Jelcz was Poland's main producer of buses and had been a huge employer at the beginning of the 1990s. Polar is discussed at length in the previous chapter. The woman president of Solidarity from 1990 (at least) to 2008 (at least) led continuous struggles against closing welfare facilities, redundancies and reducing the participation of unions in the factory.
9. This is a compulsory fund, stipulated in Polish law: social funds are administered jointly by the unions and management and oriented to

the provision of social services such as funds for housing, cultural facilities, holidays and other forms of material and financial help.

Chapter 10

1. *Gazeta Wyborcza*, 4 November 1999.
2. After Wałęsa took the President's office and Mazowiecki resigned as Prime Minister there were governments headed by Bielecki, Olszewski, Pawlak (33 days) and Suchocka.
3. The huge Solidarity vote was in the 1989, semi-free elections – the 1991 election produced a parliament with 29 parties – eleven of which had just one MP. Most were post-Solidarity, but some were neither post-communist nor post-Solidarity, for example the Polish Friends of Beer Party won 16 seats. In 1991 the Solidarity to non-Solidarity vote was approximately 2 to 1. At 43 per cent it was the lowest turnout until 2005.
4. Donald Tusk went to London on Saturday 3 November 2004, mainly to say thank you to thousands of Polish immigrants who helped his party win in the recent parliamentary election. According to the Polish Consulate in London, 62 per cent of Polish voters in Britain voted for Tusk's party, the Civic Platform, with only 11 per cent voting for Kaczyński's Law and Justice Party. Available on www.aniaspoland.com/?p=Polish%20Election%202007 (last accessed 28 April 2008).
5. August '80 split away from Solidarity '80 in late 1992 and was legally registered in 1993. Led by Marian Jurczyk, the Szczecin shipyard workers leader, Solidarity '80 broke away from Wałęsa's Solidarity in 1990, but was not legally registered until 1991.
6. The PPP had been involved with the extreme right and then did a sharp turn about; it is worth making this point in order to underline the confused and confusing nature of the Polish political scene.
7. The US, with the support of the Polish government, is planning a missile base in the north of Poland (just outside Słupsk) to house interceptor missiles, which could be used for offensive purposes. 60 per cent and half of all Poles are strongly against this base.
8. Alterglobalisation is the most common term for anti-globalisation/anti-capitalism in Poland, which is derived from the French movement (alter-mondialistes), which implies that we should globalise but in a different way.

REFERENCES

Aglietta, M. (1979) *A Theory of Capitalist Regulation*, London: New Left Books.

Akai, L. (2006) 'Halemba mine tragedy: the high costs of greed and outsourcing'. Available on: http://libcom.org/news/halemba-mine-tragedy-the-high-costs-of-greed-and-outsourcing-24112006 (last accessed 20 April 2008).

Altvater, E. (1998) 'Theoretical deliberations on time and space of post socialist transformation', *Regional Studies*, Vol. 32, No. 7: 591–605.

Amin, A. and Cohendet, P. (1998) 'Learning adaptation in decentralised business networks', *Environment and Planning D*, Vol. 17, No. 1: 87–104.

Amin, A., Bradley, D., Howells, J., Tomaney, J. and Gentle, C. (1994) 'Regional incentives and the quality of mobile investment in the less favoured regions of the EC', *Progress in Planning*, Vol. 41: 1–112.

Amsden, A., Kochanwicz, J. and Taylor, L. (1994) *The Market Meets Its Match*, Cambridge, MA: Harvard University Press.

Anderson, B., Clark, N. and Parutis, V. (2007) *New EU Members? Migrant Workers' Challenges and Opportunities to UK Trades Unions: A Polish and Lithuanian Case Study*, TUC Report, London.

Anderson, B., Ruhs, M., Rogaly, B. and Spencer, S. (2006) 'Fair enough? Central and east European migrants in low-wage employment in the UK', Oxford: COMPAS. Available on: www.compas.ox.ac.uk/changingstatus (last accessed 10 February 2009).

Antonelli, C. (1999) 'The evolution of the industrial organization of the production of knowledge', *Cambridge Journal of Economics*, Vol. 23: 243–260.

Appel, H. (2004) *A New Capitalist Order: Privatization and Ideology in Russia and Eastern Europe*, Pittsburgh: University of Pittsburgh Press.

Asheim, B.T. (1997) 'Learning regions in a globalised world economy: towards a new competitive advantage of industrial districts', in M. Taylor and S. Conti (eds), *Interdependent and Uneven Development: Global-Local Perspectives*, Aldershot: Ashgate: 143–176.

Ashwin, S. (ed.) (2000) *Gender, State and Society in Soviet and Post-Soviet Russia*, London: Routledge.

Baker, S. and Welsh, I. (1999) 'Differentiating western influences on transition societies in eastern Europe: a preliminary exploration', *Journal of European Area Studies*, Vol. 8, No. 1: 79–103.

Bakowski, A. (2004) 'Innovation transfer in Poland: present status and future developments'. Available on: www.techpark.ir/Parks/English/Articles/bakowski.htm (last accessed 20 March 2007).

Barker, C. (1986) *Festival of the Oppressed: Solidarity, Reform and Revolution 1980–81*, London: Bookmarks.

Barker, C. (1987) 'Poland, 1980–81: the self-limited revolution', in C. Barker (ed.), *Revolutionary Rehearsals*, London: Bookmarks: 169–216.

Barker, C. (2006) 'Beyond Trotsky: extending combined and uneven development', in B. Dunn and H. Radice, *100 Years of Permanent Revolution: Results and Prospects*, Pluto Press: London: 72–87.

Batchelor, C. (1997) 'Global forces put rail groups on the line', *Financial Times*, 12 March.

BBC News (2007) 'Banana firm "exploits migrants"', 23 May. Available on http://news.bbc.co.uk/1/hi/uk/6682689.stm (last accessed 10 February 2009).

Bergheim, S. (2007) *The Happy Variety of Research*, Deutsche Bank, April, Frankfurt-am-Main.

Bieler, A. (2002) 'The struggle over EU enlargement: a historical materialist analysis of European integration', *Journal of European Public Policy*, Vol. 9, No. 4: 575–597.

Biezenski, R. (1996) 'The struggle for Solidarity 1980–81: two waves of leadership in conflict', *Europe-Asia Studies*, Vol. 48, No. 2: 261–284.

Birchall, I. (1974) *Workers Against the Monolith: The Communist Parties Since 1943*, London: Pluto Press.

Bivand, R. (1983) 'Towards a geography of "Solidarność"', *Environment and Planning D: Society and Space*, Vol. 1, No. 4: 397–404.

Blanchard, O., Dornbusch, R., Krugman, P., Layard., R. and Summers, L. (1991) *Reform in Eastern Europe*, Cambridge, Mass. and London: MIT Press.

Bohle, D. (2005) 'The EU and Eastern Europe: failing the test as a better world power' in L. Panitch and C. Leys, *Socialist Register 2005*, London: Merlin Press: 301–312.

Bohle, D. (2006) 'Neoliberal hegemony, transnational capital and the terms of the EU's eastward expansion', *Capital and Class*, Vol. 88: 57–86.

Bohle, D. and Neunhöffer, G. (2006) 'Why is there no third way?' in D. Plehwe, B. Walpen and G. Neunhoffer (eds), *Neoliberal Hegemony: A Global Critique*, London: Routledge: 89–104.

Bond, P. (1999) 'What is uneven development?', in P. O'Hara (ed.), *The Encyclopaedia of Political Economy*, London: Routledge: 1198–1200.

Bornschier, V. (2000) *State Building in Europe: The Revitalisation of Western European Integration*, Cambridge: Cambridge University Press.

Boski, P. (1999) 'Meskość – kobiecość jako wymiar kultury: Przegląd koncepcji i badań' [Masculinity – femininity at cultural level: a review of concepts and research], in J. Miluska and P. Boski (eds), *Meskość - Kobiecość w Perspektywie Indywidualnej i Kulturowej* [Feminity and masculinity in Polish culture], Warsaw: PAN.

Bourdieu, P. (2003) [1977] *Outline of a Theory of Practice*, Cambridge: Cambridge University Press.

Bowles, S. and Gintis, H. (1981) 'Structure and practice in the labour theory of value', *Review of Radical Political Economy*, Vol. 12: 1–26.

Boyer, R. (1995) 'The great transformation of eastern Europe: a regulationists perspective', *EMERGO*, Vol. 2, No. 4: 25–31.

Brada, J.C. (1993) 'The transformation from communism to capitalism: how far? how fast?', *Post-Soviet Affairs*, Vol. 9, No. 2: 87–110.

Bridger, S. and Pine, F. (eds) (1998) *Surviving Post-Socialism: Local Strategies and Regional Responses in Eastern Europe and the Former Soviet Union*, London: Routledge.

Broomby, R. (2008) 'Poles head home as UK dream fades', *BBC News*, 6 March. Available on: http://news.bbc.co.uk/1/hi/world/europe/7281608 (last accessed 30 April 2008).

Burawoy, M. (1985) *The Politics of Production: Factory Regimes Under Capitalism and Socialism*, London: Verso.

Business News from Poland (1993) 'Consulting services in Poland', 102, 29 October.

Callinicos, A. (2001) 'The contradictions of European monetary union', in W. Bonefeld (ed.), *The Politics of Europe: Monetary Union and Class*, Basingstoke: Palgrave: 10–35.

Capital Market Research (2004) 'The emerging market road map: Poland', Calyon Corporate and Investment Bank, May.

Carchedi, G. (2001) *For Another Europe: A Class Analysis of European Integration*, London: Verso.

Cazes, S. and Nesporova, A. (2003) *Labour Markets in Transition*, Geneva: ILO.

Chang, H.-J. (1995) 'Return to Europe? Is there anything for Eastern Europe to learn from East Asia', in H.-J. Chang and P. Nolan, *The Transformation of Communist Economies*, Basingstoke: St Martin's Press: 82–399.

Chang, H.-J. (2002) 'Breaking the mould: an institutionalist political economy alternative to the neo-liberal theory of the market and the state', *Cambridge Journal of Economics*, Vol. 26: 539–550.

Chavance, B. and Magnin, E. (1997) 'Emergence of path-dependent and mixed economies in Central Europe', in A. Amin and J. Hausner (eds), *Beyond Market and Hierarchy*, Cheltenham: Edward Elgar: 196–232.

Chowaniec, U.M. (2004) 'Polish women in literature, art and political debate of the 1990s', *Femina Post-sovietica*. Available on: www.stfx.ca/pinstitutes/cpcs/perspectives/vol3no1/feminapostsovietica.pdf (last accessed 9 January 2008).

Chowaniec, J. and Harbinson, D.K. (1994) 'An alternative approach to American foreign aid: regional partnership in Poland', *East European Quarterly*, Vol. 28, No. 1: 131–151.

Chrzan, M. and Kowalski, M. (2006) 'Slaves from North Korea work in Gdansk shipyard', *Gazeta Wyborcza*, 24 March.

Churchill, W.S. (1954) *The Second World War*, Vol. 7, London: 198.

Cienski, J. and Wagstyl, S. (2007) 'Polish PM promises "machete" approach', *Financial Times*, 30 November.

Cieochinska, M. (1992) 'The development of the private sector in Poland, 1989–1990', *Communist Economies in Transition*, Vol. 4, No. 2: 213–239.

Clarke, S., Fairbrother, P., Burawoy, M. and Krotov, P. (1993) *What About the Workers? Workers and the Transition to Capitalism in Russia*, London: Verso.

Coe, N.M., Johns, J.L. and Ward, K. (2007) 'Flexibility in action: the temporary staffing industry in the Czech Republic and Poland', *Environment and Planning A*, Vol. 59, No. 4: 503–520.

Cox, R. (1993) 'Gramsci, hegemony and international relations: an essay in method', in S. Gill (ed.), *Gramsci, Historical Materialism and International Relations*, Cambridge: Cambridge University Press: 93–124.

Cox, T. and Mason, B. (2000) 'Trends and developments in east central European industrial relations', *Industrial Relations Journal*, Vol. 31, No. 2: 97–114.

Coyle, D. and Quah, D. (2002) *Getting the Measure of the New Economy*, The Work Foundation. Available on: www.theworkfoundation.com.pdf/New_Economy.pdf (last accessed 10 February 2009).

Crowley, S. and Ost, D. (2001) *Workers After Workers' States: Labor and Politics in Postcommunist Eastern Europe*, Oxford: Rowman and Littlefield.

Czaban, L. and Henderson, J. (1998) 'Globalization, institutional legacies and industrial transformation in Eastern Europe', *Economy and Society*, Vol. 27, No. 4: 585–613.

Czarzasty, J. (2003) 'Waves of strikes anticipated', EIROnline, 12 November. Available on: www.eurofound.europa.ie/2003/11/inbrief/p10311102n.html (last accessed 9 February 2009).

Czarzasty, J. (2006) 'Doctors clash with the National Health Fund over healthcare agreement to be', EIROnline, 12 April. Available on: www.eurofound.europa.eu.eiro/2006/02/feature/p10602103f.htm (last accessed 9 February 2009).

Czarzasty, J. (2007) 'Pay disputes in public sector escalate', EIROnline, 20 August. Available on: www.eurofound.europa.eu.eiro/2007/07/articles/p10707019i.htm (last accessed 3 January 2008).

Czbanski, K. (1983) 'Privileges', in A. Brumberg (ed.), *Poland: Genesis of a Revolution*, New York: Vintage Books: 156–163.

Czerwieński, A. (2007) 'Dzieci chore z biedy' [Children sick of poverty], *Gazeta Wyborcza*, No. 276, Warsaw edition, 26 November: 4. Available on: www.gazetawyborcza.pl, under the following address: http://szukaj.wyborcza.pl/archiwum/1,0,4986368.html?kdl=2007112 6GW&wyr=dzieci%2Bchore%2Bz%2Bbiedy%2B%2B (last accessed 8 February 2009).

Danmarks National Bank (2005) 'Poland – the EU's large new member state', *Monetary Review*, Fourth Quarter.

Davidson, N. (2006) 'From uneven to combined development', in B. Dunn and H. Radice, *100 Years of Permanent Revolution: Results and Prospects*, London: Pluto Press: 10–26.

Day, M. (2005) 'Conservative twins set to dominate politics in Poland', *The Telegraph*, 24 October 2005.

DiMaggio, P.J. (1998) 'The new institutionalism: avenues of collaboration', *Journal of Institutional and Theoretical Economics*, Vol. 154, No. 4: 696–705.

Dobbs, M. (2001) 'Aid abroad is business back home', *Washington Post*, 26 January.

Dobosiewicz, Z. (1992) *Foreign Investment in Eastern Europe*, London: Routledge.

Doherty, A. and Hoedeman, O. (1994) 'Misshaping Europe – the European Round Table of Industrialists, *The Ecologist*, July/August, 24. Available on: www.itk.ntnu.no/ansatte/Andresen_Trond/finans/others/EU-ecologist-24-4 (last accessed 18 March 2008).

Domanski, B. (1997) *Industrial Control Over the Socialist Town: Benevolence or Exploitation?* London: Praeger.

Donaghey, J. and Teague, P. (2006) 'The freedom of workers and social Europe: maintaining the European ideal', *Industrial Relations Journal*, Vol. 37, No. 6: 652–666.

Donges, J.B. (1992) 'Foreign investment in Eastern Europe', paper presented at the *International Economics Study Group Conference on International Investment*, University of Nottingham.

Dugger, W.M. (1989) 'Radical institutionalism: basic concepts', in W.M. Dugger (ed.) *Radical Institutionalism: Contemporary Voices*, Connecticut: Greenwood Press: 1–20.

Dugger, W.M. (2000) 'Deception and inequality: the enabling myth concept', in R. Pollin (ed.), *Capitalism, Socialism and Radical Political Economy*, Cheltenham: Edward Elgar: 66–80.

Duménil, G. and Lévy, D. (2005) 'The neoliberal (counter)revolution', in A. Saad-Filho and D. Johnston (eds), *Neoliberalism: A Critical Reader*, London and Ann Arbor: Pluto Press: 9–19.

Dundon, T., Gonzalez-Perez, M. and McDonough, T. (2007), 'Bitten by the Celtic Tiger: immigrant workers and industrial relations in the new "Glocalised" Ireland', *Economic and Industrial Democracy*, Vol. 28, No. 4: 501–522.

Dunn, B. and Radice, H. (eds) (2006) *100 Years of Permanent Revolution: Results and Prospects*, London: Pluto Press.

Dunn, E. (2004) *Privatizing Poland: Baby Food, Big Business, and the Remaking of Labor*, Ithaca: Cornell University Press.

Dunning, J.H. (1997) *Alliance Capitalism and Global Business*, London: Routledge.

Dyszel, A. (2006) 'Bieda zostanie z nami', *Przegląd Tygodniowy*, 20, 15 May.

Easton, A. (2006) 'Accidents dog improved Polish mines', *BBC News*, 22 November. Available on: http://news.bbc.co.uk/2/hi/europe/6174138. stm (last accessed 20 April 2008).

The Economist (2007) 'Religion in Central and Eastern Europe is waning and plagued by scandal', 15 March: 70.

Einhorn, B. (1993) *Cinderella Goes To Market: Citizenship, Gender and Women's Movements on East Central Europe*, London: Verso.

Einhorn, B. (2006) 'Gender(ed) politics in central and eastern Europe', *Journal of Global Ethics*, Vol. 2, No. 2: 39–162.

Ellerman, D. (2001) 'Lessons from Eastern Europe's voucher privatization', *Challenge*, Vol. 44, No. 4: 14–37.

Ellingstad, M. (1997) 'The Maquiladora Syndrome: Central European prospects', *Europe-Asia Studies*, Vol. 49, No. 1: 7–21.

Elster, J. (1986) 'The theory of combined and uneven development: a critique', in J. Roemer (ed.), *Analytical Marxism*, Cambridge and Paris: Cambridge University Press: 202–220.

Epstein, R. (2005) 'Diverging effects of social learning and external incentives in Polish central banking and agriculture', in F. Schimmelfennig and U. Sedelmeier, *The Europeanization of Central and Eastern Europe*, New York: Cornell University Press: 178–198.

ERT (1993) 'Beating the crisis', Brussels (ERT publications are available free from ERT, Avenue Henri Jaspar 113, B-1060 Brussels, Belgium).

EuroInvestor (2008) 'Volvo: Volvo Buses plans to close plant', 5 March. Available on: www.euroinvestor.co.uk/News/ShowNewsStory. aspx?StoryID=9756377 (last accessed 29 April 2008).

European Industrial Relations (2004) 'The Polish Labour Market and EU Membership'. http://www.ciro.eurofound.eu.int//2004/01/feature/ p10401105f.html (last accessed 13 April 2009).

Eyal, G., Szelenyi, I. and Townsley, E.R. (1998) *Making Capitalism Without Capitalists: Class Formation and Elite Struggles in Post-Communist Central Europe*, London: Verso.

Ferguson, I. (2007) 'Neoliberalism, happiness and wellbeing', *International Socialism*, Winter, Vol. 117: 123–142.

Financial Times (1993) 'Pioneer looks east for profit', 16 April.

Financial Times (1997) 'ABB to cut jobs in western Europe', 9 June.

Firkowska-Mankiewicz, A. (1995) 'Czy tak samo wychowujemy dziewczęta i chłopcow?' [Do we bring up girls and boys in the same way?], in A. Titkow and H. Domański (eds), *Co to Znaczy Być Kobieta w Polsce?* [What does it mean to be a woman in Poland?], Warsaw: Wydawnictwo IFiS PAN: 41–64.

Florio, M. (2002) 'Economists privatization in Russia and the waning of the "Washington consensus"', *Review of International Political Economy*, Vol. 9, No. 2: 359–400.

Fodor, É. (2005) *Women at Work: The Status of Women in the Labour Markets of the Czech Republic, Hungary and Poland*, Occasional Paper 3, Geneva: United Nations Research Institute for Social Development.

Friberg, J.H. and G. Tyldum (eds) (2007) *Polonia i Oslo – En studie av arbeids – og levekår blant polakker i hoveds.tadsområdet* [Polonia on Oslo – a survey of working and living conditions among Polish migrants], Fafo Report 27, Oslo: Fafo.

Froebel, F., Heinrichs, J. and Kreye, D. (1980) *The New International Division of Labour*, Cambridge: Cambridge University Press.

Fukuyama, F. (1992) *The End of History and the Last Man*, London and New York: Penguin Books.

Fuszara, M. (2000) 'Women's share of power', in Women's Rights Centre (ed.) *Polish Women in the 90s*, Warsaw: Women's Rights Centre: 19–37.

Fuszara, M. (ed.) (2002) *Kobiety w Polsce na Przełomie Wieków: Nowy Kontrakt Płci?* [Women in Poland at the turn of the century: a new gender contract?], Warsaw: ISP.

Fynes, B. and Ennis, E. (eds) (1997) *Competing from the Periphery: Core Issues in International Business*, London: Dryden Press.

Gal, S. and Kligman, G. (eds) (2000) *Reproducing Gender: Politics, Publics, and Everyday Life After Socialism*, Princeton: Princeton University Press.

Gardawski, J. (2003) *Konfliktowy pluralism Polskich Związków Zowodowych* [Controversial Pluralism of Polish Trade Unions], Warsaw: Freidrich Ebert Stiftung.

Gardawski, J., Gąciarz, B., Mokrzyszewski, A. and Pańków, W. (1999) *Rozpad Bastionu? Związek Zawadowe w Gospardarce Przywatyzowanej* [The Fall of a Bastion? Trade Unions in a Privatised Economy], Warsaw: Instytut Spraw Publicznych.

General Motors, Michigan (1996) Available on: http://media.gm.com/corpscom/releases/m960307a.htm (last accessed 9 June 2006).

Gill, S. (2001) 'Constitutionalising capital: EMU and disciplinary neoliberalism', in A. Bieler and A.D. Morton, *Social Forces in the Making of the New Europe*, Basingstoke: Palgrave: 47–69.

Giza-Poleszczuk, A. (2004) 'W poszukiwaniu nowego przymierza: Wzajemne oczekiwania mężczyzn i kobiet w Polsce' [The search for a new entente: mutual expectations of men and women in Poland], in M. Marody (ed.), *Zmiana czy Stagnacja? Społeczeństwo polskie po czternastu latach transformacji* [Change or stagnation? Polish society after 14 years of transformation], Warsaw: Wydawnictwo Naukowe Scholar: 49–68.

Glass, C. and Fodor, E. (2007) 'From public to private maternalism? Gender and welfare in Poland and Hungary after 1989', *Social Politics: International Studies in Gender, State and Society*, Vol. 14, No. 3: 323–350.

Glick, M. and Brenner, R. (1991) 'The regulation approach: theory and history', *New Left Review*, Vol. 188, July/August: 45–119.

Główny Urząd Statystyczny (GUS) [Central Statistical Office] (2004) *Rocznik Statystyczny Rzeczpospolitej Polski j* [Statistical Yearbook of the Republic of Poland], Warsaw.

Główny Urząd Statystyczny (GUS) [Central Statistical Office] (2006a) Yearbook of Labour Statistics, Warsaw.

Główny Urząd Statystyczny (GUS) [Central Statistical Office] (2006b) *Rocznik Statystyczny Rzeczpospolitej Polski j* [Statistical Yearbook of the Republic of Poland], Warsaw.

Główny Urząd Statystyczny (GUS) [Central Statistical Office] (2007a) [Central Statistical Office] *Aktywnosc Ekonomiczna Ludnosci Polski, III Kwartal* [Labour Force Survey in Poland, III Quarter], Warsaw.

Główny Urząd Statystyczny (GUS) [Central Statistical Office] (2007b) *Rocznik Statstyczny Wojewodztw* [Statistical Yearbook of the Regions], Warsaw.

Główny Urząd Statystyczny (GUS) [Central Statistical Office] (2008) *Bezrobocie Rejestrowane I–IV Kwartal 2007* [Registered Unemployment I–IV Quarter 2007], Warsaw.

Gniazdowski, M. (2007) 'Losses inflicted on Poland by Germany during World War Two: Assessments and estimates – an outline', *The Polish Quarterly of International Affairs*, Vol. 1: 95–126.

Goldthorpe, J.H., Lockwood, D., Bechofer, F. and Platt, J. (1968) *The Affluent Worker: Industrial Attitudes and Behaviour*, London: Cambridge University Press.

Golinowska, S. (2000) 'Bieda w swiecie, w Europe i w Polsce. Miary i tendencje' [Poverty in the world, in Europe and in Poland. Measures and trends], *Kronika, Instytut Lecha Walesy*, Vol. 5: 62–67.

Gomulka, S. (1993) 'Poland: glass half full', in R. Portes (ed.), *Economic Transformation in Central Europe: A Progress Report*, London: Centre for Economic Performance and Research: 187–273.

Gorz, A. (1982) *Farewell to the Working Class*, London: Pluto.

Gorzelak, G. and Jalowiecki, B. (2000) 'Territorial government reform', in Kolarska-Bobinska, L. (ed.) *The Second Wave of Polish Reforms*, Warsaw: Instytut Spraw Publicznych: 9–18.

Gowan, P. (1995) 'Neo-liberal theory and practice for eastern Europe', *New Left Review*, Vol. 213: 3–60.

Grabel, I. (2002) 'Ideology and power in monetary reform: explaining the rise of independent central banks and currency boards in emerging economies', in J. Kirshner, *Monetary Orders: Ambiguous Economics, Ubiquitous Politics*, New York: Cornell University Press: 25–52.

Grabher, G. and Stark, D. (1997) 'Organizing diversity: evolutionary theory, network analysis and postsocialism', *Regional Studies*, Vol. 31, No. 5: 533–44.

Graham, A. and Regulska, J. (1997) 'Expanding political space for women in Poland: an analysis of three communities', *Communist and Post-Communist Studies*, Vol. 30, No.1: 65–82.

Grahl, J. (2005) 'The European Union and Europe', in L. Panitch and C. Leys, *Socialist Register 2005*, London: Merlin Press: 284–300.

Granovetter, M. (1985) 'Economic action and social structures: the problem of embeddedness', *American Journal of Sociology*, Vol. 91, No. 3: 481–510.

Grodeland, A., Koshechkina, T. and Miller, W. (1998) 'Foolish to give and yet more foolish not to take: in-depth interviews with postcommunist citizens on their everyday use of bribes', *Europe-Asia Studies*, Vol. 50, No. 4: 649–675.

Grycuk, A. (2005) 'Investment conditions in Poland: highlights, trends and recent developments', Polish Agency for Foreign Investment. Available on: www.paiz.gov.pl (last accessed 12 February 2009).

Hall, D., Lobina, E. and de la Motte, R. (2005) 'Public resistance to privatization in water and energy', *Development in Practice*, Vol. 15, No. 3 & 4: 286–316.

Hall, P. and Taylor, C.R. (1996) 'Political science and the three new institutionalisms', *Political Studies*, Vol. 44, No. 44: 936–957.

Hardy, J. (1998) 'Cathedrals in the desert: transnationals, corporate strategy and locality in Wroclaw', *Regional Studies*, Vol. 32, No. 7: 639–652.

Hardy, J. (2002) 'An institutionalist analysis of foreign investment in Poland: Wroclaw's second great transformation', unpublished PhD, University of Durham.

Hardy J. and Clark, N. (2007) 'EU enlargement, workers and migration: implications for trade unions in the UK', *Trade Unions, Globalization and Development*, Geneva: International Labour Organization.

Hardy, J. and Rainnie, A. (1996) *Restructuring Krakow: Desperately Seeking Capitalism*, London: Cassell-Mansell.

Hardy, J. and Stenning, A. (2002) 'Out with the old, in with the new? The changing experience of work for Polish women', in A. Rainnie, A. Smith and A. Swain (eds), *Work, Employment and Transition: Restructuring Livelihoods in Post-Communism*, London: Routledge: 98–116.

Hardy, J. and Zebrowski, A. (2005) 'Poland and the New Europe', *International Socialism*, Autumn, Vol. 108: 39–51.

Hardy, J., Stenning, A. and Kozek, W. (2008) 'In the front line: women, work and new spaces of labour politics in Poland', *Gender, Place and Culture*, Vol. 15, No. 2: 99–116.

Harman, C. (1988) *Class Struggles in Eastern Europe 1945–83*, 3rd edn, Guildford: Bookmarks Publishing Cooperative.

Harman, C. (2008) 'Theorising neoliberalism', *International Socialism*, 117: 87–121

Harvey, D. (1996) *Justice, Nature and the Geography of Distance*, Oxford: Basil Blackwell.

Harvey, D. (2005) *A Brief History of Neoliberalism*, Oxford: Oxford University Press.

Hayek, F.A. (1944) *The Road to Serfdom* (reprinted 2001), Oxford and New York: Routledge.

Hayek, F.A. (1960) *The Constitution of Liberty*, Oxford and New York: Oxford University Press.

Haynes, M. (1987) 'Understanding the Soviet crisis', *International Socialism*, Vol. 54: 45–104.

Haynes, M. (1992a) 'Class and crisis: the transition in Eastern Europe', *International Socialism*, Vol. 54: 45–104.

Haynes, M. (1992b) 'State and market and the transition crisis in Eastern Europe', paper given at *Realism and Human Science Conference*, St Catherine's College, Oxford.

Haynes, M. and Hasan, R. (2002a) 'Whether the visible or invisible hand: the intractable problem of Russian and East European catch up', *Competition and Change*, Vol. 6, No. 3: 269–287.

Haynes, M. and Hasan, R. (2002b) '"Somewhere over the rainbow": the post-Soviet transition, the market and the mythical process of convergence', *Post-Communist Economies*, Vol. 14, No. 3: 381–398.

Hedlund, G. (1991) 'Managing international business: a Swedish model', in M. Maccoby (ed.), *Sweden at the Edge*, Philadelphia: University of Pennsylvania.

Heinen, J. (1997) 'Public/private: gender – social and political citizenship in Eastern Europe', *Theory and Society*, Vol. 26: 577–597.

Heinen, J. and Wator, M. (2006) 'Childcare in Poland before, during and after transition: still a women's business', *Social Politics: International Studies in Gender, State and Society*, Vol. 13, No. 2: 189–216.

Henderson, J. (ed.) (1998) *Industrial Transformation in Eastern Europe in the Light of the Eastern Asian Experience*, Basingstoke: Macmillan Press.

Hilditch, K. (2005) 'Bus drivers: "Bosses treat us all the same – badly"', *Socialist Worker*, 29 October, Issue 1874. Available on: www.socialistworker.co.uk (last accessed 7 April 2008).

Hoare, Q. and Nowell-Smith G. (1971) *Selections from the Prison Notebooks of Antonio Gramsci*, London: Lawrence and Wishart.

Hodgson, G.M. (1996) 'Varieties of capitalism and varieties of economic theory', *Review of International Political Economy*, Vol. 3, No. 3: 380–433.

Hodgson, G.M. (2001) *How Economics Forgot History? The Problem of Institutional Specificity in Social Science*, London: Routledge.

Hodgson, G.M. (2004) *The Evolution of Institutional Economics: Agency, Structure and Darwinism in American Institutionalism*, London: Routledge.

Hollingsworth, J.R and Boyer, R. (1997) *Contemporary Capitalism: The Embeddedness of Institutions*, Cambridge: Cambridge University Press.

Holman, O. (2004) 'Integrating peripheral Europe: the different roads to "security and stability" in Southern and Central Europe', *Journal of International Relations and Development*, Vol. 7, No. 2: 208–236.

HSBC (2006) Poland Report. Available on: www.hsbcnet.com/transaction/attachments/pcm/pdf/poland.pdf (last accessed 14 April 2008).

Hübner, S., Maier, F. and Rudolph, H. (1993) 'Women's employment in Central and Eastern Europe: status and prospects', in G. Fischer and G. Standing (eds), *Structural Change in Central and Eastern Europe*, Paris: OECD: 213–240.

Hudson, R. (1995) 'Regional futures: industrial restructuring new high volume production concepts and spatial development strategies in the new Europe', *Regional Studies*, Vol. 31: 467–478.

Hunya, G. (1992) 'Foreign direct investment and privatisation in Central and Eastern Europe', *Communist Economies in Transformation*, Vol. 4, No. 4: 501–511.

Hutton, W. (2004) 'Don't weep for our lost factories', *The Observer*, 19 December.

Ilinitch, A.Y., Lewin, A.Y., and D'Aveni, R. (eds) (1998) *Managing in Times of Disorder: Hypercompetitive Organizational Responses*, California: SAGE Publications.

Infobus (2008) 'Polish buses'. Available on: www.infobus.pl/text.php?id=14582 (last accessed on 20 March 2008).

Jackson, M. (1992) 'Constraints on systematic transformation and their policy implications', *Oxford Review of Economic Policy*, Vol. 7, No. 4: 16–25.

Janion, M. (1996) *Kobiety i Duch Inności* [Women and the spirit of otherness], Warsaw: Sic.

Jessop, B. (2001) 'Institutional (re)turns and the strategic-relational approach', *Environment and Planning A*, Vol. 33: 1213–1235.

Johnston, A.I. (2001) 'Treating international institutions as social environments', *International Quarterly Studies*, Vol. 45: 487–515.

Jordan, B. and Düvell, F. (2002) *Irregular Migration, the Dilemmas of Transnational Mobility*, Cheltenham: Edward Elgar.

Kaminski, B. and Smarzynska, B. (2001) 'Integration into global production and distribution networks through FDI: the case of Poland', *Post-Communist Economies*, Vol. 13, No. 3: 265–288.

Kennedy, P. (1999) The gender of resistance in communist Poland, *The American Historical Review*, Vol. 104, No. 2: 399–425.

Kenney, P. (1997) *Rebuilding Poland: Workers and Communists 1945–1950*, Ithaca and London: Cornell University Press.

Kimber, C. (2006) 'Chilling anti-strike tactics at Iceland', *Socialist Worker*, 16 December, Issue 2031. Available on: www.socialistworker.co.uk (last accessed 7 April 2008).

Knothe, M. (1999) 'Poland's economy in transition: a gender perspective', in UNCTAD, *Trade, Sustainable Development and Gender*: 149–162. Available on: www.unctad.org.en/docs/poedm_m78.en.pdf (last accessed 10 February 2009).

Kolarska-Bobińska, L. (ed.) (2000a) *The Second Wave of Polish Reforms*, Warsaw: Instytut Spraw Publicznych.

Kolarska-Bobińska, L. (ed.) (2000b) *Czetery Reformy: Od Koncepcji do Realizacji* [Four reforms: from conception to realisation], Warsaw: Instytut Spraw Publicznych.

Komorovsky, C. (2006) 'Polish mining disaster claims 23 lives'. Available on: www.wsws.org/articles/2006/nov2006/mine-n25shtml (last accessed 24 September 2008).

Kondratowicz, A. and Okolski, M. (1993) 'The Polish economy on the eve of the Solidarity take-over', in J. Kierzkowski, M. Okolski and S. Wellisz (eds), *Stabilisation and Structural Adjustment in Poland*, London: Routledge: 7–28.

Kowalik, T. (2001) 'Why the social democratic option failed: Poland's experience of systemic change', in A. Glyn (ed.), *Social Democracy in Neoliberal Times*, Oxford: Oxford University Press: 223–253.

Kozek, W. (2006) 'Liberalisation, privatisation and regulation in the Polish healthcare sector/hospitals', *Privatisation of Public Services and the Impact on Quality, Employment and Productivity*, PIQUE, Project (CIT5-2006-028478) funded by European Commission's Sixth Framework Programme.

Kozul-Wright, R. and Rayment, P. (1997) 'The institutional hiatus in economies in transition and its policy consequences', *Cambridge Journal of Economics*, Vol. 21: 641–661.

Kramer, M. (1995) 'Polish workers and the post-communist transition, 1989–93', *Europe-Asia Studies*, Vol. 47, No. 4: 669–684.

Kropiwiec, K. and King-O'Riain, R.C. (2006) *Polish Migrant Workers in Ireland: Polscy Migranci Pracujacy w Irlandil*, Community Profiles Series. Dublin: National Consultative Committee on Racism and Interculturalism.

Krugman, P. (2003) *The Great Unravelling*, London: Allen Lane.

Kruk, M. (2007) 'Poland struggles to keep indebted hospitals afloat'. Available on: www.alertnet.org.thenews/newsdesk/L02204509.htm (last accessed 2 January 2007).

Ksiezopolski, M. (1991) 'The labour market in transition and the growth of poverty in Poland', *Labour and Society*, Vol. 16, No. 2: 175–192.

Ksiezopolski, M. (1992) 'The prospects for social policy development in Poland', in B. Deacon (ed.), *Social Policy and Social Justice and Citizenship in Eastern Europe*, London: Sage: 228–244.

Kuroń, J. and Modzelewski, K. (1982) *Solidarnosc: The Missing Link – The Classic Open Letter to the Party* (reprinted), London: Bookmarks.

Kwiatkowska, A. (1999) 'Siła tradycji i pokusa zmiany, czyli o stereotypach płciowych' [Strength of tradition and temptation to change: gender stereotypes], in J. Miluska and P. Boski (eds), *Meskość – Kobiecość w Perspektywie Indywidualnej i Kulturowej* [Femininity and masculinity in Polish culture], Warsaw: IP PAN: 143–172.

Laba, R. (1991) *The Roots of Solidarity: A Political Sociology of Poland's Working Class Democratization*, Princeton: Princeton University Press.

Landau, Z. and Tomaszewski, J. (1985) *The Polish Economy in the Twentieth Century*, Kent: Croom Helm.

Lazreg, M. (ed.) (1999) *Making the Transition Work for Women in Europe and Central Asia*, Washington: World Bank.

Leszkowicz, P. (2005) 'Feminist revolt: censorship of women's art in Poland'. Available on: http://bad.eserver.org/reviews/2005/leskowicz. html (last accessed 12 April 2008).

Leven, B. (1994) 'The status of women and Poland's transition to the market', in N. Aslanbeigi, S. Pressman and G. Summerfield (eds), *Women in the Age of Economic Transformation*, London and New York, Routledge: 27–42.

Lewis, P. (1994) *Eastern Europe Since 1945*, Harlow: Longman.

Lewis, P. (2000) *Who Is Paying for Health Care in Eastern Europe and Central Asia*, Washington: World Bank.

Lipton, D. and Sachs, J. (1990) 'Creating a market economy in Poland', *Brooking Papers on Economic Activity*, Vol. 1, Brookings Institution, Washington: 75–147.

Lo, D. (1995) 'Economic theory and transformation of the soviet-type system: the challenge of the late industrialization perspective', in H.-J. Chang and P. Nolan, *The Transformation of Communist Economies*, Basingstoke: St Martin's Press: 78–109.

Long, K. (1996) *We All Fought for Freedom: Women in Poland's Solidarity Movement*, Boulder: Westview Press.

Lowy, M. (1981) *The Politics of Combined and Uneven Development*, London: Verso and NLB.

Mach, B.M. (2001) 'Przemiany w struktura I stratyfinacji spolecznej w pierwsza dekada niepodleglosci; proba sociologicznej syntezy' [Transformation in the social structure and stratification in the first decade of independence; a trial of sociological synthesis', Wnuk-Lipinski, E., Ziolkowski, Warsaw: ISP, PAN.

Maddison, A. (1991) *Dynamic Forces in Capitalist Development: A Long Run Comparative View*, Oxford: Oxford University Press.

Maddison, A. (2001) 'The world economy in the second half of the twentieth century' in *The World Economy: A Millennial Perspective*, Paris: OECD.

Malinowska, E. (1995) 'Socio-political changes in Poland and the problem of sex discrimination', *Women's Studies International Forum*, Vol. 18, No. 1: 35–43.

Mandel, E. (1970) 'The laws of uneven development', *New Left Review*, Vol. 59: 19–38.

Martin, R. (1998) 'Central and Eastern Europe and the international economy: the limits of globalisation', *Europe-Asia Studies*, Vol. 50, No. 1: 7–26.

Martin, R. and Cristescu-Martin, A. (2004) 'Consolidating segmentation: post-socialist employment relations in Central and Eastern Europe, *Industrial Relations Journal*, Vol. 35, No. 6: 629–645.

Maskell, P. and Malmberg, A. (1999a) 'The competitiveness of firms and regions: ubiquitification and the importance of localized learning', *European Urban and Regional Studies*, Vol. 6, No. 1: 9–25.

Maskell, P. and Malmberg, A. (1999b) 'Local learning and industrial competitiveness', *Cambridge Journal of Economics*, Vol. 23: 167–185.

Mayhew, A. (1988) 'Contrasting the origins of the two institutionalisms', *Review of Political Economy*, Vol. 1: 319–333.

McManus-Czubinska, C., Miller, M.L., Markowski, R. and Wasilewski, J. (2003) 'The new Polish right', *Journal of Communist and Transition Politics*, Vol. 19, No. 2: 1–23.

McManus-Czubinska, C., Miller, M.L., Markowski, R. and Wasilewski, J. (2004a) 'What does turnout matter? The case of Poland', *Europe-Asia Studies*, Vol. 5, No. 3: 401–420.

McManus-Czubinska, C., Miller, M.L., Markowski, R. and Wasilewski, J. (2004b) 'Why is corruption in Poland a serious cause for concern?', *Crime, Law and Social Change*, Vol. 41: 107–132.

Meardi, G. (2002) 'The Trojan Horse for the Americanization of Europe? Polish industrial relations toward the EU', *European Journal of Industrial Relations*, Vol. 8, No. 1: 77–99.

Meardi, G. (2004) 'Short circuits in multinational plants: the extension of European Works Councils to Poland, *European Journal of Industrial Relations*, Vol. 10: 161–178.

Meardi, G. (2007) 'More voice after more exit? Unstable industrial relations in Central Eastern Europe', *Industrial Relations Journal*, Vol. 38, No. 6: 503–523.

Meiksins Wood, E. (1997) 'Modernity, postmodernity of capitalism?', *Review of International Political Economy*, Vol. 4, No. 3: 539–560.

Messerlin, P. (1992) 'The Association Agreement between the EC and Central Europe: trade liberalization or constitutional failure', in

J. Flemming, and J.M.C. Rollo (eds), *Trade, Payment and Adjustment in Central and Eastern Europe*, London: The Royal Institute of Economics Affairs: 111–143.

Micek, G. (2005) 'Spatial clustering in the Polish IT sector', mimeo, Department of Regional Studies, Jagiellonian University, Krakow, Poland.

Millard, F. (1997) 'The influence of the Catholic hierarchy in Poland, 1989–96', *Journal of European Social Policy*, Vol. 7, No. 2: 83–100.

Miller, W., Grodeland, A. and Koshechkina, T. (2000) 'If you pay, we'll operate', *Journal of Medical Ethics*, Vol. 26: 305–11.

Modzelewski, K. (1993) *Dokąd od komunizmu?* [Whither from communism?], Warsaw: Oficyna Wydawnicza BGW.

Morris, N. (2008) 'Tide of migration turns as Polish workers return', *The Independent*, 27 February. Available on: www.independent.co.uk/news/uk/home-news/tide-of-migration-turns-as-polish-workers-return-787914.html (last accessed 16 April 2008).

Murrell, P. (1993) 'What is shock therapy? What did it do in Poland and Russia?', *Post Soviet Affairs*, Vol. 9, No. 2: 111–140.

Myant, M. (1993) *Transforming Socialist Economies*, Aldershot: Edward Elgar.

Myrdal, G. (1957) *Economic Theory and Under-developed Regions*, London: Duckworth.

Nielsen, K. (2001) 'Institutional approaches in social science: typology, dialogue and future challenges', *Journal of Economic Issues*, Vol. 35, No. 2: 505–516.

North, D. (1990) *Institutions, Institutional Change and Economic Performance*, Cambridge: Cambridge University Press.

Novack, G. (1972a) *Understanding History: Marxist Essays*, New York: Pathfinder Press.

Novack, G. (1972b) 'Uneven and combined development in history'. Available on www.marxists.org/archive/novack/works/history/ch06.htm (last accessed 20 February 2009).

Nuti, D.M. (1982) 'The Polish crisis: economic factors and constraints', in Drewnowski, J. (ed.) *Crisis in the East European Economy*, London: Croom Helm: 18–64.

Obloj, K. and Thomas, H. (1998) 'Transforming former state-owned companies into market competitors in Poland: the ABB experience', *European Management Journal*, Vol. 16, No. 4: 390–399.

Office for National Statistics (2005) *The Official Yearbook of the United Kingdom of Great Britain and Northern Ireland*, London.

Ost, D. (1989) 'The transformation of Solidarity', *Telos*, 79.

Ost, D. (1992) 'Shock therapy and its discontents', *Telos*, 92.

Ost, D. (2001) 'The weakness of symbolic strength: labor and union identity in Poland, 1989–2000', in S. Crowley and D. Ost (eds), *Workers After Workers' States: Labor and Politics in Postcommunist Eastern Europe*, Oxford: Rowman and Littlefield: 79–96.

Ost, D. (2002) 'The weakness of strong social movements: models of unionism in the East European context', *European Journal of Industrial Relations*, Vol. 8, No. 1: 33–51.

Ost, D. (2006) *The Defeat of Solidarity*, London and Ithaca: Cornell University Press.

Ostrowska, M. (2005) 'Interview, Impuls, Trybuna', 1 December. Available on: www.internationalviewpoint.org/spip.php?article949 (last accessed 29 December 2007).

Paci, P., Sasin, M.J. and Verbeek, J. (2004) 'Economic growth, income distribution and poverty in Poland during transition', *World Bank Policy Research Working Paper 3467*, December.

Palloix, C. (1977) 'The self-expansion of capital on a world scale', *Review of Radical Political Economy*, Vol. 9, No. 2: 3–28.

Peck, J. and Theodore, N. (2007) 'Flexible recession: the temporary staffing industry and mediated work in the US', *Cambridge Journal of Economics*, Vol. 31: 171–192.

Peck, J., Theodore, N. and Ward, K. (2005) 'Constructing markets for temporary labour: employment liberalization and the internationalization of the staffing industry', *Global Networks*, Vol. 5, No. 1: 3–26.

Penn, S. (1994) 'The national secret', *Journal of Women's History*, Vol. 5: 54–69.

Penn, S. (2005) *Solidarity's Secret: The Women Who Defeated Communism in Poland*, Ann Arbor: University of Michigan Press.

Peterson, C.L. and Burton, R. (2007) *US Health Care Spending: Comparison With Other OECD Countries*, CRS Report for Congress, Washington.

Petrović, J. (2001) *The Male Face of Trade Unions in Central and Eastern Europe: The Secret of Invisible Women*, Brussels/Zagreb: ICFTU/FNV Gender Project.

Phelps, N. (2000) 'The locally embedded multinational and institutional capture', *Area*, Vol. 32, No. 2: 169–178.

Phelps, N.A. and Fuller, C. (2000) 'Multinationals, intracorporate competition and regional development', *Economic Geography*, Vol. 76, No. 3: 224–243.

Phelps, N.A., Lovering, J. and Morgan K. (1998) 'Tying the firm to the region or tying the region to the firm? Early observations of LG in South Wales', *European Urban and Regional Studies*, Vol. 5, No. 2: 119–137.

Pickel, A. (1992) 'Jump starting a market economy: a critique of the radical strategy for economic reform in the light of the east German experience', *Studies in Comparative Communism*, Vol. 25, No. 2: 177–191.

Pine, F. (1995) 'Kinship, work and the state in post-socialist Poland', *Cambridge Journal of Anthropology*, Vol. 18, No. 2: 47–58.

Pine, F. (1998) 'Dealing with fragmentation: The consequences of privatisation for rural women in central and southern Poland', in S. Bridger and F. Pine, *Surviving Post-Socialism: Local Strategies and Regional Responses in Eastern Europe and the Former Soviet Union*, London: Routledge: 106–123.

Piotrowski, T. (1998) *Poland's Holocaust: Ethnic Strife, Collaboration With Occupying Forces and Genocide in the Second Republic, 1918–1947*, Jefferson, NC: McFarland.

Plakwicz, J. (1992) 'Between church and state: Polish women's experience', in C. Corrin (ed.), *Superwomen and the Double Burden*, London: Scarlet Press: 75–96.

Podemski, K. (2007) 'Social inequality and why it matters for the economic and democratic development of Europe and its citizens: post-communist Central and Eastern Europe in comparative perspective', *EUREQUAL Project Report*. Available on: http://eurequal.politics.ox.ac.uk/papers/eurequal%20desk%20research%20poland.pdf (last accessed 7 December 2007).

Poland Economic Newsletter (2004), 5 November. Available on: www.forum-polonia-houston.com/pub/econ/penews110504 (last accessed 2 June 2005).

Polanyi, K. (1957) [1944] *The Great Transformation: The Political and Economic Origins of Our Time*, United States: Beacon Press.

Pollert, A. (1999) *Transformation at Work in the New Market Economies of Central Eastern Europe*, London: Sage.

Pollert, A. (2003) 'Women, work and equal opportunities in post-communist transition', *Work, Employment and Society*, Vol. 17, No. 2: 331–357.

Pollert, A. (2005) 'Gender, transformation and employment in Central Eastern Europe', *European Journal of Industrial Relations*, Vol. 11, No. 2: 213–230.

Pollert, A. and Fodor, É. (2004) *Final Report: Gender, Work and Employment in Ten Accession Countries of Central Eastern Europe to the EU*, Dublin: European Foundation for Improvement of Working and Living Conditions.

Powell, W.W. and DiMaggio, P.J. (1991) *New Institutionalism in Organisational Analysis*, Chicago: The University of Chicago Press.

Rainnie, A. and Hardy, J. (1995) 'Desperately seeking capitalism: Solidarity and Polish industrial relations', *Industrial Relations Journal*, Vol. 26, No. 4: 267–279.

Rainnie, A., Smith, A. and Swain, A. (2002) 'Employment and work restructuring in "transition"', in A. Smith, A. Rainnie and A. Swain (eds), *Work, Employment and Transition*, London: Sage: 7–34.

Rashid, M., Rutkowski, J. and Fretwell, D. (2005) 'Labor markets', in N. Barr (ed.), *Labor Markets and Social Policy in Central and Eastern Europe*, Washington DC: The World Bank: 59–87.

Rugman, A. and D'Cruz, J. (1997) 'Strategies of multinational enterprises and governments: the theory of the flagship firms', in G. Boyd and A. Rugman (eds), *Euro-Pacific Investment and Trade: Strategies and Structural Interdependencies*, Cheltenham: Edward Elgar: 37–68.

Rumińska-Zimny, E. (1999) 'Globalization and gender in transition economies', in UNCTAD, *Trade, Sustainable Development and Gender*, Geneva and New York: UNCTAD: 149–162. Available on www.unctad.org.en/docs/poedm_m78.en.pdf (last accessed 10 February 2009).

Saad-Filho, A. and Johnston, D. (2005) *Neoliberalism: A Critical Reader*, London and Ann Arbor: Pluto Press.

Sapir, A. (2006) 'Globalization and the reform of European social models', *Journal of Common Market Studies*, Vol. 44, No. 2: 369–390.

Sapir, A., Aghion, P., Bertola, G., Hellwig, M., Pisani-Ferry, J., Vinais, J. and Wallace, H. (2003) *An Agenda for a Growing Europe: Making the EU Economic System Deliver: Report for the President of the European Commission*, Brussels: European Commission.

Sapir Group (2005) 'An agenda for a growing Europe – the Sapir Report', *Regional Studies*, Vol. 39, No. 7: 958–965.

Schaffer, M. (1992) 'The economy of Poland', London School of Economics, Centre for Economic Performance, Discussion Paper.

Schoenman, R. (2005) 'Captains or pirates? State-business relations in post-socialist Poland', *East European Politics and Society*, Vol. 19, No. 1: 40–75.

Scipes, K. (2005) 'Labor imperialism redux? The AFL-CIO's foreign policy since 1995', *Monthly Review*, Vol. 57, No. 1, May.

Screpanti, E. (1999) 'Capitalist forms and the essence of capitalism', *Review of International Political Economy*, Vol. 6, No. 2: 1–26.

Shields, S. (2003) 'The "charge of the right brigade": transnational social forces and the neoliberal configuration in Poland's transition', *New Political Economy*, Vol. 8, No. 2: 225–243.

Shields, S. (2004) 'Global restructuring and the Polish state: transition, transformation, or transnationalization', *Review of International Political Economy*, Vol. 11, No. 1: 132–154.

Siemieńska, R. (1986) 'Women and social movements in Poland', *Women and Politics*, Vol. 6, No. 4: 5–35.

Siemieńska, R. and Marody, M. (1996) 'Miejsce i rola kobiet w nowym ładzie ekonomicznym' [Women's place and role in the new economic order], in M. Marody (ed.), *Oswajanie Rzeczywistości: Między Realnym Socjalizmem a Realna Demokracja* [Taming the reality: between the real socialism and real democracy], Warsaw: Instytut Studiow Spolecznych: 41–58.

Silovic, D. (2000) 'EU accession – chance for gender equality in CEEC', *ETUC Transfer*, Vol. 3, 468–485. Available on: www.renner-institut. at/download/texte/frau_eu.pdf (last accessed 9 February 2009).

Simatupang, B. (1994) *The Polish Economic Crisis: Background, Causes and Aftermath*, London and New York: Routledge.

Sklair, L. (1997) 'Social movements for global capitalism: the transnational capitalist class in action', *Review of International Political Economy*, Vol. 4, No. 3: 514–538.

Slay, B. (1994) *The Polish Economy: Crisis, Reform and Transformation*, New Jersey, NJ: Princeton University Press.

Smelser, N.J. and Swedburg, R. (eds) (1994) *The Handbook of Economic Sociology*, Princeton, NJ: Princeton University Press.

Smith, A. (1776) *An Inquiry into the Nature and Causes of the Wealth of Nations* (reprinted 1998), Oxford and New York: Oxford University Press.

Smith, A. (2002) 'Imagining geographies of the "new Europe": geo-economic power and the new European architecture of integration', *Political Geography*, Vol. 21: 647–670.

Smith, A. and Hardy, J. (2004) 'Governing regions, governing transition: firms, institutions and regional change in east-central Europe', in A. Wood and D. Valler (eds), *Placing Institutions: Theorising the Governance of Local Economies*, Pearson: London: 147–176.

Smith, A. and Stenning, A. (2006) 'Beyond household economies: spaces and articulations of economic practice in post-socialism', *Progress in Human Geography*, Vol. 30, No. 2: 190–213.

Smith, A. and Swain, A. (1998) 'Regulating and institutionalizing capitalisms: the micro-foundations of transformation in Central and Eastern Europe', in J. Pickles and A. Smith (eds), *Theorising Transition: The Political Economy of Post Communist Transformation*, London: Routledge: 25–33.

Smith, A., Stenning, A., Rochovska, A. and Świątek, D. (2008) 'The emergence of a working poor: labour markets, neoliberalisation and diverse economies in post-socialist cities', *Antipode*, Vol. 40, No. 2: 283–311.

Smolar, A. (1983) 'The rich and the powerful', in A. Brumberg (ed.), *Poland: Genesis of a Revolution*, New York: Vintage Books: 42–53.

Solidarity (2006a) 'Roczny Przegląd Naruszania Praw Zwiazkowych w Polsce w roku 2006' [Annual survey of violations of trade unions rights in Poland in 2006]. Available on: www.solidarnosc.org.pl/obrona/pliki/rap2006.pdf (last accessed 15 April 2008).

Solidarity (2006b) 'Report on violations of trade union rights in Poland'. Available on: www.solidarnosc.org.pl/en/docs/others/viol2006.pdf (last accessed 12 February 2009).

Solidarity (2007) 'Union busting actions in supermarkets'. Available on: www.solidarnosc.org.pl/english/newsletter/news/2007/jan/jan_11.htm (last accessed 12 February 2009).

Stark, D. (1990) 'Path dependence and privatisation strategy', *East European Politics and Society*, Vol. 6, No. 1: 17–54.

Stark, D. (1995) 'Not by design: the myth of designer capitalism in Eastern Europe', in J. Hausner, B. Jessop and K. Nielsen (eds), *Strategic Choice and Path Dependency in Post-Socialism*, Aldershot: Edward Elgar: 67–83.

Stark, D. (1996) 'Recombinant property in East European capitalism', *American Journal of Sociology*, January, Vol. 4: 993–1027.

Stenning, A. (2000) 'Placing (post) socialism: the making and remaking of Nowa Huta, Poland', *European Journal of Urban and Regional Studies*, Vol. 7, No. 2: 99–118.

Stenning, A. and Hardy, J. (2005) 'Public sector reform, women and work in Poland: "Working for juice, coffee and cheap cosmetics"', *Gender, Work and Employment*, Vol. 11, No. 6: 503–526.

Stiglitz, J.E (2002) *Globalisation and its Discontents*, London: Allen Lane.

Stiglitz, J.E. (2006) *Making Globalisation Work*, London and New York: Penguin Books.

Stirewalt, B. and Horner, J. (2000) *Poland-National Bank of Poland: Final Report (for USAID)* 1 March, United States: KPMG Peat, Marwick and Barents Group.

Stone, R.W. (2002) *Lending Credibility: The International Monetary Fund and Post-Communist Transition*, Princeton and Oxford: Princeton University Press.

Stroinski, K. (1998) 'Poland: the reform of the pension system', *Economic Affairs*, Vol. 18, No. 1: 29–33.

Sula, P. (2006) 'Self employment trends in Poland'. Available on: www.eurofound.europa.ie/2006/08/articles/pl0608019i.html (last accessed 15 January 2008).

Swaan, W. (1996) 'Behavioural constraints and the creation of markets in post-socialist economies', in B. Dallago and L. Mittone (eds),

Economics, Institutions, Markets and Competition, Aldershot: Edward Elgar: 221–241.

Swaan, W. and Lissowska, M. (1996) 'Capabilities, routines and East European economic reform: Hungary and Poland before the 1989 revolutions', *Journal of Economic Issues*, Vol. 30, No. 4: 1031–1056.

Szczerbiak, A. (2002) 'Poland's unexpected political earthquake: the September 2001 parliamentary election', *Journal of Communist Studies and Transformation Politics*, Vol. 18, No. 3: 41–76.

Szczerbiak, A. (2007) '"Social Poland" defeats "Liberal Poland"? The September-October 2005 Polish parliamentary and presidential elections', *Journal of Communist Studies and Transition Politics*, Vol. 23, No. 2: 203–232.

Tagliabue, J.T. (1998) 'Volvo to cut 5,300 workers by mid-1998', *New York Times*, 21 March. Available on: http://query.nytimes.com/gst/fullpage.html?res=9A05E7DE163BF932A35751C1A96E958260 (last accessed 21 March 2008).

Tarasiewicz, M. (1993) 'Kobiety i związek zawodowy "Solidarność"' [Women in 'Solidarity'], *Pełnym Głosem*, Summer, Vol. 1.

Taylor, W. (1991) 'The logic of global business: an interview with ABB's Percy Barnevik', *Harvard Business Review*, March/April: 91–105.

Tewdwr-Jones, M. and Phelps, N.A. (2000) 'Levelling the uneven playing field: inward investment, inter-regional rivalry and the planning system', *Regional Studies*, Vol. 34, No. 5: 429–440.

Thirkell, J., Scase, R. and Vickerstaff, S. (1995) *Labour Relations and Political Change in Eastern Europe*, London: UCL Press.

Thrift, N. (1998) 'The rise of soft capitalism', in A. Herod, G. O'Tuathail and S.M. Roberts (eds), *Unruly World: Globalization, Governance and Geography*, London: Routledge: 25–71.

Thrift, N. (2001) '"It's the romance, not the finance, that makes the business worth pursuing": disclosing a new market culture', *Economy and Society*, Vol. 40, No. 4: 412–432.

Titkow, A., Duch-Krzystosek, D. and Budrowska, B. (2004) *Nieodpłatna Praca Kobiet: Mity, Realia, Perspektywy* [Women's unpaid work: myths, reality, perspectives], Warsaw: Wydawnictwo IFiS PAN.

Tittenbrun, J. (1993) *The Collapse of Real Socialism in Poland*, London: Janus Publishing.

Tittenbrun, J. (2005) 'Divide and rule: privatization in Poland and the working class', paper given at the 37th congress of the International Institute of Sociology, Stockholm, Sweden, 5–9 July. Available on: http://mainold.amu.edu.pl/~jacek/stockholm.doc (last accessed 15 April 2008).

Touraine, A., Dubet, F., Wieviorka, M. and Strzelecki, J. (1983) *Solidarity: The Analysis of a Social Movement, Poland 1980–81*, Cambridge: Cambridge University Press.

Toyota (2006) 'Toyota in the World and Europe'. Available on: www.toyota.eu/images/04ToyotaInTheWorldAndEurope.pdf (last accessed 29 April 2008).

Trade Union Congress (TUC) (2003) *Overworked, Underpaid and Over Here – Migrant Workers in Britain*, July, London.

Trade Union Congress (2004) *Propping Up Rural and Small Town Britain – Migrant Workers from the New Europe*, November, London.

Traynor, I. (2007) 'Court censures Poland for denying abortion rights', *The Guardian*, 21 March. Available on: http://guardian.co.uk/international/story/0,,2038739,00.html (last accessed 8 January 2008).

Treanor, P. (2005) 'Neoliberalism: origins, theory, definition'. Available on: http://web.inter.nl.net/users/Paul.Treanor/neoliberalism.html (last accessed 10 February 2009).

Trotsky, L. (1977) [1934] *The History of the Russian Revolution* (translated by Max Eastman), London: Pluto Press.

Tsang, S.-K. (1996) 'Against "big bang" in economic transition: normative and positive arguments', *Cambridge Journal of Economics*, Vol. 20: 183–193.

TVP1 (2007) *Chichot historii* [*Documentary: History's Snigger*], 15 March.

Tymowska, K. (2001) 'Health care under transformation in Poland', *Health Policy*, Vol. 56, No. 2: 85–98.

UNCTAD (2005) *World Investment Report: Transnational Corporations and the Internationalization of R&D*, New York and Geneva: United Nations.

UNCTAD (2007) *World Investment Report: Transnational Corporations, Extractive, Industries and Development*, New York and Geneva: United Nations.

USAID (2002a) 'USAID and the Polish decade'. Available on www.usaid.gov/pl/decadeof.htm (last accessed 12 February 2009).

USAID (2002b) 'USAID Mission to Poland: List of Projects'. Available on: www.usaid.gov/pl/listof1.htm (last accessed 12 February 2009).

Van Apeldoorn, B. (2000) 'Transnational class agency and European governance: the case of the European Round Table of Industrialists, *New Political Economy*, Vol. 5, No. 2: 157–181.

Van Apeldoorn, B. (2003) 'The struggle over European order: transnational class agency in the making of "embedded neoliberalism"', in N. Brenner, B. Jessop, M. Jones and G. MacLeod, *State/Space: A Reader*, London: Blackwell: 147–164.

Van Ees, H. and Garretsen, H. (1994) 'The theoretical foundations of the reforms in eastern Europe: big bang versus gradualism and the limitations of neo-classical theory', *Economics Systems*, Vol. 18, No. 1: 1–13.

Van Hoven, B. (2001) 'Women at work: experiences and identity in rural east Germany', *Area*, Vol. 33, No. 1: 38–46.

Van der Linden, M. (2007) 'The "law" of uneven and combined development: some underdeveloped thoughts', *Historical Materialism*, Vol. 15, No. 1: 145–165.

Van Zon, H. (1998) 'The mismanaged integration of Zaporizhzhya with the world economy: implications for regional development in peripheral regions', *Regional Studies*, Vol. 32, No. 7: 607–618.

Veblen, T. (1898) 'Why is economics not an evolutionary science', *Quarterly Journal of Economics*, Vol. 12: 373–397.

Veblen, T. (1899) *The Theory of the Leisure Class*, New York: Macmillan (reprinted, New York: Dover Publications, Inc., 1994).

Viner, J. (1927) 'Adam Smith and laisser faire', *Journal of Political Economy*, Vol. 35, No. 2: 198–232.

Watson, P. (1993) 'Eastern Europe's silent revolution: gender', *Sociology*, Vol. 27, No. 3: 471–487.

Wedel, J.R (2000) 'US assistance for market reforms', *Independent Review*, Vol. 4, No. 3: 393–417.

Wedel, J.R. (2001) *Collision and Collusion: The Strange Case of Western Aid to Eastern Europe*, New York: Palgrave.

Whitley, R. (1997) 'The social regulation of work systems: institutions, interest, groups, and varieties of work organization in capitalist societies', in R. Whitley and P.H. Kristensen, *Governance at Work: The Social Regulation of Economic Relations*, Oxford: Oxford University Press: 227–260.

Whitley, R. (1998) 'Internationalisation and varieties of capitalism: the limited effects of cross national coordination of economic activities on the nature of business systems', *Review of International Political Economy*, Vol. 5, No. 3: 445–481.

Whitley, R. and Czaban, L. (1999) 'Continuity amidst change: Hungarian enterprises in the mid-1990s', in A. Lorentzen, B. Widmaier and M. Laski (eds), *Institutional Change and Industrial Development in Central and Eastern Europe*, Aldershot: Ashgate Publishing: 61–88.

Williamson, O.E. (1975) *Markets and Hierarchies, Analysis and Anti Trust Implications: A Study in the Economics of Internal Organization*, New York: Free Press.

World Bank Report (1996) 'Social capital', unpublished manuscript of the Satellite Group on Social Capital, Washington: World Bank.

World Bank Report (2002) *Building Institutions for Markets*, New York and Oxford: Oxford University Press.

World Bank (2004) *Gender and Opportunities in Poland: Has Transition Left Women Behind?* Report No. 29205, Warsaw: World Bank.

Wprost (2007) 'Potega kapitalizmu' [The power of capitalism], 25. Available on: http://100najbogatszych.wprost.pl/?e=42&p=0 (last accessed November 2007).

Zalewska-Zemła, M. and Zielińska, E. (eds) (2003) *Równe Prawa i Szanse Zawodowe Kobiet i Mężczyzn: Sytuacja Prawna w Unii Europejskiej i w Polsce* [Equal occupational rights and opportunities for men and women: legal system in EU and in Poland], Gliwice, Opole: Dom Współpracy Polsko-Niemieckiej.

Zysman, J. (1996) 'The myth of the global economy: enduring national foundations and emerging regional realities', *New Political Economy*, Vo. 1, No. 2: 157–183.

INDEX

Compiled by Sue Carlton

Printed and bound by CPI Group (UK) Ltd, Croydon, CR0 4YY

09/06/2025

14685865-0002